Proof That You're God

A Dualistic Unity Book

Paperback Version:

Proof That You're God
Copyright © 2024, Dualistic Unity Media Inc.
All rights reserved.

Disclaimer
The information in this book is provided for educational and informational purposes only. The author and publisher make no representations or warranties with respect to the accuracy, applicability, or completeness of the contents of this book. The information contained herein is not intended as a substitute for professional advice. The reader assumes full responsibility for their use of the information contained in this book.

Trademark Notice
Any trademarks, service marks, product names, or named features are assumed to be the property of their respective owners, and are used only for reference. There is no implied endorsement if these terms are used.

ISBN: 979-8-9918186-1-2

First Edition: 2024

Contents

Preface

Hello and welcome! Enclosed within this book, you will find proof that you are God. Eternal, omnipresent, and unifying—you are the alpha and the omega, the beginning and the end.

A bold claim, right? Maybe you're thinking, "That's impossible," or perhaps even, "Bullshit." But if you've picked up this book and decided to find out for yourself, we ask only that you approach it with an open mind and a sense of adventure. There's nothing you have to do or believe. In fact, staying skeptical will help. Think of this book as a friendly conversation about life, how we see ourselves, and how we interact with the world. Together, we'll reflect on both personal and collective challenges and explore the truth beneath it all.

But let's be honest: proving that you're God is no simple task. Not because it isn't obvious, but because—right now—you don't really want to see it. You're deeply invested in being who you think you are, and it's going to take time and effort to shift your perspective enough to remember your divinity.

Throughout this book, you'll find exercises and sections entitled *"Something to Reflect On"*. These are opportunities to sit with your thoughts and insights before moving forward. We highly recommend taking advantage of these breaks, as they'll make the later chapters easier to digest in a meaningful and impactful way.

So, take your time. Be patient with yourself. After all, this is no small undertaking—and it's certainly not for the faint of heart.

Chapter 1 - The Power to Rewrite Yourself

Who are you when you stop telling yourself who you are? Pause for a moment, close your eyes, and envision your life as a blank page, free from the endless narrative you've been repeating. Without the stories imposed by others or yourself, what remains?

It's a deceptively simple question, but one that most people never stop to consider. We move through life, carrying the weight of our past, our roles, our expectations, and the stories we've been told since childhood.

Over time, countless self-help strategies have emerged to address this perceived problem of identity, treating it as though it's something fundamentally broken that needs fixing. Popular methods often focus on reshaping habits, rewiring thought patterns, or setting goals based on who we think we should be. The underlying assumption is that we are the sum of our behaviors, thoughts, and past experiences—that our identity is a fixed construct made up of parts that can be rearranged or optimized. Modern interpretations of the word *ego*—originally a term rooted in psychological theory—have become shorthand for everything from self-importance to insecurity, with many self-help systems offering ways to "tame" or "overcome" the ego. These approaches treat the ego as the problem to be solved, like an organism of its own living within us, rather than simply the tendency to think of ourselves as a fixed self.

But what if this fixation on the self and self-improvement is missing the point entirely? Instead of recognizing that we are ever-changing, fluid beings, many strategies reinforce the illusion that we are defined by the stories we've inherited and told ourselves. What if, rather than trying to fix who we are, the real freedom lies in questioning whether those stories are based on any truth at all?

Throughout history, many have questioned the idea of a fixed, unchanging self. From ancient traditions to modern thinkers, people have long recognized that who we are is not set in stone, but shaped by our experiences. This idea suggests that your identity is not something you are born with or something you inherit from society—it's a living, evolving narrative. Nietzsche, for example, argued that the self is not stable but is constantly in flux, reshaped by every moment. The belief that you are a fixed entity may feel comforting, but it often becomes a psychological and cultural trap, holding you to roles and expectations that no longer fit or serve you.

As you navigate life, you will continue to find that you are not defined by your past, your roles, or the stories others have told about you. While these factors may have shaped how you see yourself, they do not capture the entirety of who you are. Whether you realize it or not, much of your sense of 'self' is shaped by external forces—family, society, and circumstance. It's time to consider whether these labels truly reflect who you are in this moment. The notion of a fixed, unchanging self may feel reassuring because it offers certainty in an unpredictable world. But this certainty can also become a trap—limiting you to outdated, superficial definitions that do not reflect your potential.

It's time to embrace the limitless potential of your ever-changing story, knowing you can rewrite it with each experience. The tales that once defined you were simply chapters—now, you hold the pen to craft something new.

"Fame, money, and everything else are just part of the simulation, part of the game. They are tools, but I'm not my name, I'm not my nickname, I'm not my skin, I'm not even my thoughts—I am the listener of my thoughts. Authenticity for me is just that—being you."

Javier "Chicharito" Hernández, a world-renowned footballer and guest on Dualistic Unity, reflects on the illusion of identity. His words highlight the importance of letting go of societal labels to embrace a deeper sense of self.

The self you think you are is much like a rough draft—pieced together from the stories you've been telling yourself, or been told, all your life. These narratives often sound familiar: "I'm a good person," "I'm not good enough," or "I always fail." These beliefs shape your sense of identity and dictate how you approach your life, influencing your decisions, your reactions, and even your sense of success or failure. But what if these stories aren't reality? What if they're just early drafts, full of revisions waiting to be made? When you step back and ask yourself whether these stories are serving you, you create space to rewrite them.

If you think about it, many of the stories you cling to are not even your own. Much of the identity you hold onto—whether tied to your career, relationships, or personal traits—has been shaped by external forces: family, society, and circumstance. While it may seem comforting to hold onto a fixed sense of who you are, this often becomes a trap—a limiting narrative that keeps you stuck. Rather than seeing yourself as confined by these definitions, recognize that you are a blank page, capable of being rewritten with each new experience.

Take the story of Viktor Frankl, a Holocaust survivor who faced circumstances that wiped his previous identity clean, leaving him with nothing but a blank page. In the depths of unimaginable suffering, he discovered that his true freedom didn't depend on his external situation—it was rooted in his ability to rewrite his story. Frankl chose to see himself not as a victim of circumstance, but as someone capable of finding meaning, even in the darkest times.

Frankl's experience demonstrates that the stories we tell ourselves are never permanent, despite how immutable they might seem. They are rough drafts, waiting for us to rewrite them. The power lies in recognizing that these narratives are only as strong as we allow them to be. When we shift our attitude towards them, we can reshape the way we see ourselves, regardless of external challenges.

For years, Jim Carrey was known as a funny man—a persona the world adored. But as he once revealed, the person behind that role felt trapped. While Frankl was stripped of his identity by external circumstances, Carrey found himself imprisoned by a character he had helped create.

He was always performing, not just on stage, but in life. The comedian, the celebrity, the man the world admired—it was all a carefully crafted identity. But beneath it, he felt empty.

> "You were born with wings, why prefer to crawl through life?"
>
> —Rumi

"I think everybody should get rich and famous and do everything they ever dreamed of, so they can see that it's not the answer," Carrey once said. After years of playing a role, he came to a realization: the "self" he thought he was—famous, adored, validated by others—was only as real as his commitment to it. It was just a story. And stories can be rewritten.

As Carrey and Frankl's experiences illustrate, our identity is not something we are born with or something that is set in stone. It's a narrative, a construct built over time. If these individuals could reshape their stories in such different and challenging circumstances, what might be possible if you questioned the story you've been telling yourself

When people begin to question who they are, it often doesn't happen in some dramatic moment. There's rarely a flash of enlightenment; instead, it happens slowly, like cells multiplying and evolving into something new, one small shift at a time. Even moments of sudden realization will fade without the willingness to continue questioning. Realizing that much of what we believe about ourselves—how we define success, worth, and failure—has more to do with external influences than with anything authentic. Like the transition from one season to another, it's a gradual realization: We are not the static identities we've been conditioned to believe we are. And this realization can be disorienting.

Most people, if they stop and think about it, realize their identity has been shaped by factors beyond their control: family expectations, societal norms, personal experiences, and the assumptions they've made about themselves from limited experience and incomplete information. The identity you hold dear—whether tied to your profession, relationships, or personal traits—isn't really you. It's a character you've written, helped and shaped by those around you, and decided to play. Complete with armor and a mask, this character is designed to protect you and help you fit into the world. But after playing this role for long enough, the armor starts to feel real and heavy, and the mask begins to obscure your vision. It becomes so familiar that it feels like you've become the character itself, when in reality, it's still just a story.

Let's ask a simple but revealing question: When was the last time you questioned the story you tell yourself? The story about who you think you are, where you fit into the world, what you're capable of, and what you deserve. For many, the answer might be "never."

And that's understandable. From a young age, we're taught to define ourselves by labels: "You're smart." "You're shy." "You're a troublemaker." These labels follow us into adulthood, hardening into a fixed narrative. We take on a character—daughter, father, worker, artist, failure—constructed by the labels we've internalized and mistake this character for who we really are. Over time, this character becomes so deeply ingrained in our story that we forget we're even playing a role.

Consider Bruce Lee, the martial artist, actor, and philosopher. Known globally for his physical prowess, Lee didn't allow himself to be confined by a single identity. He believed in the power of fluidity—adapting not just in movement but in life, embracing change as a constant. He refused to be trapped by a fixed character. Lee's philosophy was simple: Be like water. Water takes the shape of whatever container it fills, yet it is always water—flowing, adapting, never rigid. This adaptability is key when it comes to questioning the stories we habitually identify with. Just like writing a new chapter, who you are today may not be who you need to be tomorrow.

The challenge arises when we cling to a static sense of self, trapping ourselves in the character we've been playing. This fixation limits our ability to explore new possibilities, making it easy to believe that our past defines our future and that change is out of reach. We lose sight of our capacity to grow, seeing our identity as set in stone rather than a work in progress.

History and everyday life offer countless examples of individuals who refused to be defined by their circumstances, showing us that change is not only possible but inevitable when we recognize the blank page beneath, giving ourselves the space to rewrite the character we've been playing.

"All that we are is the result of what we have thought: it is founded on our thoughts, it is made up of our thoughts."

— Dhammapada

Take Nelson Mandela for example. After spending 27 years in prison, Mandela could have allowed his identity to be shaped by his suffering, becoming a victim or a prisoner. Instead, he saw himself as someone capable of creating change—not defined by his circumstances but by his vision of freedom. When he emerged, he led South Africa into a new era of reconciliation, showing that our story is fluid—shaped not by what happens to us but by how we choose to rewrite the character we've been playing in any given moment.

The truth is, you're always changing, even when you don't realize it. Every experience, relationship, and failure shapes you into someone new. And if you stop clinging to the idea that you are one static 'self,' you can begin to see that you're actually much more than you give yourself credit for—a blank page with endless potential, where anything can be written or rewritten.

Take J.K. Rowling's story as another example. Before her success with *Harry Potter*, she struggled with poverty, divorce, and depression. At one point, she described herself as a "failure" by all conventional metrics. But instead of letting those circumstances define her, she reinvented herself. Rowling's journey shows that who we are is not fixed—that the labels and stories we attach to are assumptions, not facts.

You are not the story you've been telling yourself. The self is not static; it's dynamic, ever-changing, and far more expansive than any label or role. It's uncomfortable to admit that we've been playing a role, especially when we've invested so much in it. But recognizing this is the first step toward understanding that the role is a fiction—

one crafted to make sense of our place in the world. With that recognition, we can see that a blank page has always existed beneath the character and story, facilitating the freedom to create something new.

The idea of a 'fixed self' is something we cling to because it offers a sense of security in a world that feels uncertain. Who wouldn't want that sense of stability? But these scripts—the narratives that shape our daily lives—are rarely as self-created as we think. In reality, they are often borrowed, passed down, or imposed upon us, shaped by forces outside of our awareness. The character we think we are is often one written and conditioned by others, drawn from their pages, rather than from our own blank page of potential.

Many philosophical thinkers have recognized this challenge of the conditioned self, often emphasizing the freedom that comes from abandoning inherited stories and scripts.

Jiddu Krishnamurti speaks directly to this. He emphasized that much of our suffering comes from the deeply ingrained but false belief that we are our thoughts, our labels, and our experiences. In a talk he gave in Bombay in 1948, he said, "As long as we rely on the mind to give us a sense of who we are, we are trapped in the conditioning of the past."

This gets to the core of what we're exploring here: much of what we believe about ourselves isn't even ours. It's a product of our conditioning—our upbringing, our society, and our experiences. Until we begin to question these borrowed narratives and characters, we remain stuck in a version of ourselves that may no longer—or may never have—served us.

From the moment we're born, we're shaped by external forces beyond our understanding. Family, for example, plays a crucial role in how we see ourselves early in life. Whether it's the values we were raised with, the expectations placed upon us, or the subtle (and not-so-subtle) cues we picked up from our parents or guardians, family often writes the first draft on our page. These early influences teach us how to behave, what's right and wrong, and in many cases, shape what we come to see as normal or expected.

Think back to your childhood and how you were labeled. Maybe you were referred to as "the smart one" or "the shy one." These labels often become deeply embedded in us because they're reinforced over time. A child who's called "troublemaker" repeatedly is likely to internalize that label, even when they're just acting out in response to an environment they can't control. On the other hand, a child praised as "gifted" might grow up with a fear of failure, avoiding any challenge that could shatter that label. In both cases, these early influences become part of the character we're playing, shaping the story written on our page and forming the core of who we think we are.

Then comes society as a whole: school, friends, media, and culture— all of it pours more layers onto the page. We learn early on that fitting in is often the key to survival, so we adapt our character accordingly. Maybe we were taught that success meant good grades and a stable career, or that we needed to be tough and unemotional to survive. Maybe we learned that the opinions of others mattered more than our own. Without even realizing it, these influences reshape the draft being written, introducing new narratives that shape the character we gradually begin to accept as who we are, often at the expense of our own authentic voice.

Consider how societal expectations of success or failure impact the way we perceive ourselves. From a young age, we're exposed to stories that shape our idea of what a "good life" looks like. Success becomes a list of achievements—education, a career, a family. Failure becomes any deviation from that path. We're taught to measure our worth by these external metrics, and when life doesn't follow the script, we often internalize a new narrative, one of inadequacy or failure, reinforcing the character we think we're supposed to be.

The weight of these societal pressures often pushes us into roles we didn't choose. Think about how many of us pursue jobs, relationships, or lifestyles because we feel they're what we 'should' do rather than what truly resonates with us. Over time, this leads to a deep sense of dissatisfaction that we can't always explain. It's because the character we're playing isn't truly our own; our page is filled with the drawings and stories of others, validating the pages and characters they've written into their own lives. The expectations of family, society, and culture may have shaped us so profoundly that we struggle to recognize where their influence ends and where our authentic self begins. But, as we've already seen, we can find a way to break free and redefine ourselves on our own terms.

Nina Simone, initially recognized as a brilliant musician, defied societal expectations by transforming her platform into one of political activism. Simone used her music and her voice to challenge the status quo, breaking free from the roles society tried to impose on her as an African American woman. She didn't allow herself to be confined by the labels of others. Her life demonstrates that we can reject the identities imposed on us and rewrite our narrative in alignment with our authentic self.

That our identity is constructed is more than just a philosophical idea—it's a practical realization that can transform how we live. So much of the discontent and limitation we face is rooted in the false idea that we are the stories we tell ourselves, as fear and insecurity shape narratives that we mistake for reality.

Think about how fear of failure often leads us to define ourselves as 'not good enough.' Over time, that fear gets written into the story of who we think we are: I am a failure. I can't do anything right. This script becomes a perception we unknowingly adopt, limiting the actions we take and the risks we're willing to embrace. We avoid taking chances, trying new things, or pursuing our passions because in our minds, a permanent story is already written: we're not capable of succeeding.

Whenever we question where a narrative came from, we again realize it's not the truth—just a story shaped by past experiences and external judgments, rather than an accurate reflection of who we are or what we're capable of.

Let's pause for a moment and reflect on how the narratives we tell ourselves create a sense of certainty, even when that certainty feels limiting. There's a kind of safety and comfort in knowing who you are, even if that definition is false. When we forget that we can write a new story or change our current one, we often feel the only alternative is to cling to the current draft, even if it's no longer serving us. Telling ourselves, 'I'm not good at this,' 'I'll never change,' or 'This is just who I am' can give us an odd sense of security, even as it ruins our lives.

> "We do not see things as they are, we see them as we are "
>
> — Anaïs Nin

Krishnamurti urged us to live without certainty, to live in a state of constant questioning. In a talk he gave in San Diego in 1970, he said, "It is only when we live without the security of definitions that we begin to understand who we truly are." It's only in this state of uncertainty that real freedom is possible. And this doesn't mean chaos—it means openness. It means no longer being confined by the labels and identities that once defined us. When we stop clinging to fixed identities, we open ourselves to the infinite possibilities of growth and transformation.

Imagine what life might look like if we stopped committing to the false certainty of our self-imposed limitations. What if we stopped saying, "I'm just not that kind of person" or "I've never been good at this," and instead approached life with curiosity rather than judgment? We might discover that the identity we've been clinging to is just a small part of who we could become, with so much more potential waiting to be explored.

To live with energy, enthusiasm, and creativity is to embrace the fact that we don't need to be defined by any character we've been writing. Every moment, every interaction, every experience reshapes us. When we release the need for certainty, we open ourselves up to growth in ways we never thought possible. In doing so, we return to the blank page, ready to write a story filled with boldness and possibility. This is where real freedom begins.

Up to this point, we've started to shine a light on the character we've been writing—those deeply ingrained narratives we've accepted as truths. But awareness of your character is only the first step. Real transformation begins when we actively erase and rewrite the stories that have kept us stuck, powerless, or small. This is where the process gets uncomfortable because it asks us to confront the character we've been playing for years, sometimes even decades.

These stories—the ones that tell us who we are and what we're capable of—don't dissolve easily. They've been reinforced over and over by our experiences, by the people in our lives, by the culture we live in, and by our ongoing commitment to them. But that doesn't make them true.

Think about the narrative of "I'm not good enough." It often shows up in subtle ways, like hesitating to speak up in a meeting or avoiding a new challenge because of fear. Where did this belief come from? Maybe it's from early experiences where you were made to feel inadequate, or maybe it's a story that's been reinforced by your own internalized fear of failure.

It's tempting to think of identity as something permanent—solid and unchangeable—but having the courage to keep questioning each label and narrative is the only way to truly discover that identity is not fixed, it's just a penciled-in character that can be rewritten.

What matters most is recognizing the stories that no longer serve us and understanding how to let them go.

David Goggins, a man once trapped by self-imposed limitations, completely rewrote his identity by mastering his mind. After enduring an abusive childhood and battling obesity, Goggins decided to transform his life through mental resilience. He lost over 100 pounds, became a Navy SEAL, and set numerous endurance records. His story reminds us that the narratives we create for ourselves—often rooted in fear or failure—can be rewritten. Goggins' life is proof that the power to transform lies within our mindset.

While Goggins' transformation was extreme, your journey doesn't have to mirror his. Change happens and unfolds in your own way and at your own pace—the important thing is recognizing your potential to grow.

So how do we move forward? While awareness is the first step, the next is challenging the narratives that have been holding you back. These stories can be so woven into the fabric of our daily lives that they feel like facts. But they're not—they're just scripts we've internalized, often without even realizing it. It's not enough to recognize the character you've been playing; you must also question its validity and start rewriting the story in a way that aligns with your true potential.

Start by asking yourself some key questions:

- What beliefs do I hold about myself that feel limiting?
- Where do these beliefs come from? Are they from my own lived experiences, or have they been passed down to me by others—family, friends, society?
- How do these beliefs affect my life? In what ways do they stop me from acting, trying, or pursuing something new?

Take a few moments to consider these questions. Write down any limiting beliefs that come to mind. It could be something like, *"I'm not good enough," "I don't deserve success,"* or *"I'm not the kind of person who takes risks."* For each belief, try to trace its origin. Did someone once tell you that you weren't good at something? Was there a moment when you failed, and since then, have you labeled yourself a failure? Or is it simply that you've absorbed messages from society that make you feel like you don't belong?

This exercise might seem simple, but it can be incredibly revealing. The more we dig into the origins of our limiting beliefs, the more we begin to see how fragile they really are. They aren't facts—they're assumptions.

These assumptions show up as self-imposed limitations—things we tell ourselves we can't do or don't deserve. These limitations can be subtle, manifesting in ways that seem small at first but grow over time until they start to control major aspects of our behavior.

Take, for example, the belief that "I'm not good enough." This is one of the most common limiting narratives, and almost all of us have carried it at some point in our lives. It often shows up when we're faced with a new challenge or opportunity. Instead of embracing the possibility of growth, we hesitate. We tell ourselves that we're not skilled enough, smart enough, or worthy enough to succeed. So we don't even try.

This narrative might stem from a single failure or a string of disappointments. Maybe it was reinforced by someone in our lives—whether a parent, a teacher, or a partner—who made us feel inadequate. Over time, this one belief grows into a larger narrative that impacts everything we do. It stops us from taking risks, pursuing our passions, and embracing change.

Another common narrative is "I'll always fail." This often arises from past failures or setbacks that have been internalized as evidence of our inadequacy. It convinces us that trying again isn't worth the effort because failure is inevitable. The fear of repeating past mistakes becomes so overwhelming that we avoid stepping outside our comfort zone altogether.

What we often overlook is that failure is a part of growth, not the end of the story. Every failure is feedback—an opportunity to learn and improve. But when we cling to the narrative that failure defines us, we miss out on the lessons that could help us grow.

Malala Yousafzai's journey serves as a powerful example of breaking through societal limitations. Shot by the Taliban for advocating girls' education, Malala did not let that traumatic event define her. Instead, she reshaped her narrative, turning her suffering into a global movement for education and empowerment. Her story reminds us that we always have the power to rewrite our narrative, no matter how limiting the world around us may seem.

As we explained earlier, we often hold on to limiting narratives because they offer a sense of certainty. While Malala chose to challenge the role the world tried to assign her, many of us find it difficult to let go of the familiar, even if it confines us. These narratives give us something to cling to—a way to understand the world and our place in it. If I believe I'm not good enough, then I don't have to face the fear of stepping into the unknown. I don't have to risk failure, rejection, or uncertainty.

Limiting narratives are like limits we place on our own page to stay safe. They protect us from the unknown and the discomfort of growth. But they also imprison us. They keep us stuck in the same patterns, the same cycles, and prevent us from exploring what lies beyond.

Think about it: What would happen if you let go of the belief that you're not good enough? What if you stopped telling yourself that you'll always fail or that you don't deserve success? What might open up for you? What possibilities could become available?

Releasing these narratives can be terrifying because it means willingly stepping into a space of uncertainty. It means facing the unknown without the familiarity of your old character. But this is also where freedom lives, because uncertainty and potential are synonymous.

So how do we break down these narratives? How do we challenge the stories that have held us back for so long?

Recognizing that these stories are just that—stories—is essential. They aren't objective truths about who you are; they're interpretations, often shaped by past experiences that don't define your true potential.

For each limiting belief you wrote down earlier, ask yourself these questions:

- Is this belief objectively true? Can I prove it beyond any doubt?
- Has there ever been a time when this belief didn't hold true? Can I think of moments when I succeeded, took a risk, or proved myself wrong?
- What might be possible if I let go of this belief? How would my life change if I stopped identifying with this story?

Take your time with these questions. Really dig into the belief and see it for what it is: a mental construct, not an inherent truth about who you are. The more you question it, the weaker it becomes.

Once you've begun challenging these limiting beliefs, the next step is to start rewriting them—not with blind optimism, but with a realistic, open-minded approach. This isn't about convincing yourself that everything will always be perfect. It's about embracing a new, more empowering narrative that reflects the possibility of growth rather than assuming limitations.

Let's revisit the belief, "I'm not good enough." Instead of accepting this as truth, you might replace it with a more open-ended perspective: "I don't know what I'm capable of, but I'm willing to find out." Notice how this shifts the focus from a fixed identity to an attitude of attentive curiosity. You're not defining yourself by past failures or limitations; instead, you're open to growth, possibility, and change.

The key to dismantling old narratives and adopting new ones is repetition. Just as your limiting beliefs were reinforced throughout your entire life, your new, empowering beliefs need to be reinforced through consistent practice.

Start by regularly questioning the narratives you find yourself holding onto. Write down your thoughts, say them out loud, or reflect on them in meditation. Whenever you notice an old, limiting belief surfacing, pause and explore it. This is where awareness becomes your most powerful tool. Rather than operating on autopilot, you're staying curious and attentive, allowing yourself to see beyond the usual stories and remain open to different possibilities.

Another powerful practice is to take small, deliberate actions that challenge your existing beliefs. If you find yourself questioning an old narrative, such as 'I'm not capable,' experiment by trying something new or engaging in an activity that stretches your comfort zone. These actions aren't about proving a new and improved permanent story but about exploring what might be possible. Each step you take helps loosen the grip of limiting beliefs and opens up space for discovery.

This is a process, not a one-time event. Breaking down limiting narratives and moving into the recognition that our impermanent identity has limitless potential takes time and patience. But the more you practice, the more natural it becomes. Over time, you'll find that the stories that once held you back lose their power, and you become more open to the possibilities that emerge with each new experience

Now think about what your life might look like if you let go of that belief. What would change? How would you act differently? What opportunities would you pursue?

Instead of holding onto a limiting belief, try exploring an alternative perspective—one that reflects the possibility of growth rather than reinforcing your limitations. In the coming days, practice staying open to different ways of seeing yourself and notice how that feels.

Make it a habit to catch yourself when old beliefs start to surface. Notice the thoughts, notice the feelings, and instead of letting them dictate your actions, pause and reflect. Ask yourself whether these beliefs still serve you, and remain open to seeing things differently. The more you engage in this process, the more natural it becomes to question the stories that limit you and explore new possibilities.

Think of this approach as nurturing your untapped potential. With care, attention, and patience, you'll find that new opportunities emerge, new ways of understanding yourself arise, and new ways of engaging with the world become possible.

This is the power of questioning your narrative. It's not about changing who you are at your core; it's about peeling away the layers of false identity that have been imposed on you and discovering the freedom to grow beyond any single story.

As we begin to question the stories that have shaped us, something powerful starts to happen. Without the weight of those limiting narratives, we find ourselves standing in a new space of potential— no longer defined by the past or constrained by others' expectations.

But this space, as freeing as it is, can also feel unsettling. It's in this discomfort that we confront one of the most important questions we'll ever face: Who am I really?

And when we ask this question, our mind quickly responds with another concept or label, tempting us to believe that our "authentic self" is just another role to play.

For many of us, authenticity has felt like a distant ideal—something we strive for but can't quite define. We long to live more authentically, but how can we be our "authentic selves" when we've spent so much of our lives tied to labels, roles, and identities that never truly belonged to us? And if we are never a single, fixed character, what then is authenticity?

Think of yourself as an ever-changing form, constantly adapting to new experiences, reshaping as you grow. Yet you remain fundamentally you. Authenticity lies in embracing this fluidity — allowing yourself to change and grow without clinging to a fixed identity. The misconception that a 'real' self exists beneath the surface, waiting to be uncovered, only limits you. Instead, authenticity is about showing up as you are, evolving moment to moment, perfectly suited to the experience of living in a world of uncertain potential.

But letting go of a fixed identity brings us face-to-face with vulnerability. At the heart of authenticity is the willingness to show up as you are, even if you see yourself as imperfect. This can feel unsettling because it asks us to release the judgments we've carried—judgments that have shaped our identities in an attempt to shield us from, ironically, vulnerability itself.

We often build these personas as a way of controlling how others see us, compensating for our own fears and desires. We play a part in an effort to connect, even when deep down we know it's not who we truly are. In doing so, we project our own insecurities onto the very people we're trying to connect with, assuming they're judging us by the standards we've set for ourselves. This is the rising cost of relying on roles or fixed characters as a strategy for dealing with life. The more we depend on them, the more disconnected we become from our reality, ourselves, and everyone else. We end up living in a constant state of performance, always worrying about living up to the judgments of others, never realizing those judgments are, in fact, our own.

Vulnerability is the antidote to this. When we allow ourselves to be vulnerable, we open the door to real connection—with ourselves and with others. We no longer need to perform or pretend. Instead, we give ourselves permission to show up as we are, with all our imperfections.

Think about the people you feel most connected to in your life. Chances are those connections were built not on well acted performances, but on moments of vulnerability—when someone allowed you to see them fully, as the blank page beneath the character. When we allow ourselves to be seen this way, we create space for authenticity to thrive.

Vulnerability isn't just about being open with others. It's also about being open with yourself. It's about admitting when you don't have all the answers, allowing yourself to make mistakes, and embracing the fact that growth is messy. Authenticity requires a willingness to be honest with yourself, even when it's uncomfortable.

If we're committed to living authentically, we have to accept that growth and change are constant and inevitable. But growth isn't always easy. It often requires us to let go of old identities, relationships, or habits that no longer serve us. And that process can feel like loss.

Think about a time when you experienced a significant change in your life. Maybe it was a job transition, a move to a new city, or the end of a relationship. As exciting as growth can be, it's also often accompanied by grief. We grieve the version of ourselves we're leaving behind, even when we know that change is necessary.

This is normal. As with all stages of maturity, letting go is a natural part of the growth process. It doesn't mean we're doing something wrong; it means we're evolving. Just as cells adapt and renew themselves, we must let go of old beliefs to unlock what's next. But renewal isn't always comfortable. The key is to recognize that growth and authenticity aren't about "arriving" at some final version of ourselves. There is no final version. Growth is an ongoing process, and authenticity is about showing up honestly in that process, wherever you are.

As you grow, you will change. Your priorities will shift. The things that once felt important might no longer resonate with you. Relationships will evolve, and so will your sense of self.

Authenticity isn't about resisting this change or trying to hold on to who you once were—it's about embracing it. It's about trusting that the version of yourself emerging on the other side of this change will be you—not because you've discovered some final perfect self, but because you've allowed yourself to be change itself.

As we continue to question the stories that have shaped us, we begin to see that our transformation is not a singular event—it's an ongoing process, much like the way cells in our bodies constantly adapt, renew, and grow. Each experience, like every new cell, adds a new layer to who we are, and yet, the fundamental essence of life— our potential—remains unchanged.

Living authentically is an ongoing practice. It requires us to stay present, to let go of the need for certainty, and to remain open to the unknown. Here are some practical ways to start embracing growth and authenticity in your daily life:

Practice Self-Reflection: Take time each day to check in with yourself. How are you feeling? What are you learning? Are there areas of your life where you're holding onto old stories or identities? Reflection helps you stay connected to your growth process and recognize where change is needed.

Let Go of Perfectionism: Authenticity isn't about being perfect; it's about being real. Let go of the pressure to "get it right" all the time and give yourself permission to be a work in progress. The more you let go of the need to be perfect, the more space you create for genuine growth.

Surround Yourself with Support: Find people who support your growth—those who encourage you to be your authentic self and aren't invested in keeping you the same. Authentic relationships thrive in mutual respect and vulnerability. Surrounding yourself with others committed to their own growth makes the process less daunting.

Embrace Discomfort: Growth feels uncomfortable because it pushes us beyond what we know. But discomfort is a sign that you're expanding. Instead of avoiding it, lean into it as a signal you're on the right path. Authenticity requires us to be present with discomfort and trust it's leading us toward something meaningful.

Allow Yourself to Change: Don't be afraid to outgrow old versions of yourself. As you grow, you'll find that the things that once defined you no longer fit. Let go of old identities and trust that as you change, you're becoming more aligned with who you truly are.

Something to Reflect On:

Take a moment to reflect on how authenticity shows up in your life. Are there areas where you feel like you're holding back or playing a part? What would it look like to show up more authentically in your relationships, work, or daily life?

Now think about growth. Where are you being called to grow right now? What old identities, beliefs, or habits might you need to release in order to step into the next version of yourself?

Remember, growth isn't about arriving at a final destination. It's about embracing the journey, wherever it takes you. So take a deep breath and trust that every step toward authenticity brings you closer to the freedom of being fully, unapologetically yourself.

Up to this point, we've explored the significance of breaking down limiting stories, embracing change, and stepping into authenticity. But, as mentioned earlier, knowing these concepts isn't enough — and this cannot be stressed enough. The real shift happens through practice, by actively applying these ideas in the choices you make every day. Growth unfolds gradually, not in an instant, but through small, consistent actions that accumulate over time.

This section offers practical exercises and opportunities for self-reflection that are designed to help you integrate these ideas into your life. They aren't meant to be done all at once or in any particular order. Instead, approach them as tools you can return to again and again as you navigate your own journey of self-discovery, growth, and authenticity.

Exercise 1: Identifying Your Limiting Beliefs

Before we can break down limiting beliefs, we need to become aware of them. Often, these beliefs operate beneath our consciousness, shaping behavior without us even realizing it. The goal of this exercise is to bring those beliefs into the light so you can begin questioning them.

Step 1: Reflect on areas of your life where you feel stuck or limited.

- o Is there a goal you've been putting off because you don't believe you can achieve it?
- o Are there situations where you feel inadequate, unworthy, or incapable?
- o Do you avoid risks or challenges out of fear of failure?

Step 2: Once you've identified a limiting area, ask yourself:

- o What belief underlies this feeling? (*e.g., "I'm not smart enough," "I always fail," "I don't deserve success"*)
- o Where did this belief come from? Was it something someone told you? Based on past experience? Or something you internalized over time?

Step 3: Write down the belief and its origin. For example, if you believe you're not good enough, reflect on where this story began. Did a specific event trigger that feeling, or did it build over years of comparison?

Step 4: Challenge the belief. After writing it down, ask yourself: Is this belief really true? Can you find evidence beyond past experience to support it? Has there been a time when you succeeded or overcame a challenge? Reflect on those moments.

Exercise 2: Exploring Your Narrative

Now that you've identified some of your limiting beliefs, it's time to question and explore them. This exercise will help you shift from a disempowering narrative to a more open-minded approach that supports your potential for growth.

Step 1: For each limiting belief you've identified, write down an alternative perspective. Instead of creating a new fixed story, explore a different way of seeing the situation. For example, if your belief is "I'm not good enough," consider: "I don't know what I'm capable of yet, but I'm willing to find out." If your belief is "I always fail," reframe it as: "Failure is a natural part of growth, and I can learn something valuable from each setback."

Step 2: Reflect on these alternative perspectives regularly. Write them down somewhere you'll see them often—on your phone, a sticky note, or in a journal. Use them as reminders to stay curious and open rather than latching onto any one narrative.

Step 3: Take actions that encourage exploration rather than reinforcing a fixed story. Instead of trying to prove a new belief, focus on experimenting and being curious. Try something you've been avoiding, take on a challenge, or engage in an activity that allows you to discover new possibilities without being attached to a specific outcome.

Exercise 3: Embracing Vulnerability and Authenticity

Living authentically requires vulnerability — to show up as we are without hiding behind personas. This exercise helps you practice vulnerability both with yourself and others, so you can step more fully into your authentic self.

Step 1: Reflect on where you feel most vulnerable in your life. Where do you feel the need to hide parts of yourself? Are there situations where you hide behind old narratives or avoid expressing your true feelings? Write down examples where you've felt disconnected from your authentic self due to the need to perform or protect yourself.

Step 2: Identify one area where you can practice vulnerability. Choose a specific situation where you typically avoid being vulnerable. It might be in a conversation with a friend, at work, or in a relationship. Think about how you can bring more authenticity to that situation. For example, if you tend to avoid showing your emotions in conversations, challenge yourself to be more open next time. If you hold back from sharing ideas at work due to fear of judgment, contribute your thoughts in the next meeting.

Step 3: Reflect on the experience. After practicing vulnerability, take time to reflect on how it felt. Was it uncomfortable? Did it bring up fear or resistance? Or did it create a sense of relief, connection, or authenticity? Journal about the experience and consider how vulnerability deepens your relationships and your connection with yourself.

Exercise 4: Letting Go of Old Identities

Growth often requires us to let go of old identities, roles, or beliefs that no longer serve us. But letting go isn't always easy. This exercise will guide you through identifying what you're ready to release and making space for new growth.

Step 1: Reflect on the parts of yourself you feel ready to release. Is there an identity you've been holding onto because it feels familiar, even if it no longer resonates with who you are? It could be a role you've outgrown (such as always being the "caretaker" in your relationships) or a belief that no longer serves you (such as "I avoid risks").

Step 2: Write down what you're ready to release. For each identity or role you're ready to let go of, write down why it no longer serves you. What was its purpose? How did it help you in the past? Why is it time to release it now?

Step 3: Focus on how you'll move forward. Instead of holding on to these old identities, think about the space you're creating for your growth. How can you shift your actions or mindset to align with the new version of yourself that's emerging? Write down a few specific steps you can take to embrace this change, whether it's trying something new, approaching a relationship differently, or adopting a new perspective.

Exercise 5: Cultivating a Growth Mindset

Authenticity and growth are deeply connected. When we embrace the idea that we're always evolving, we let go of the need for perfection and allow ourselves to grow. This exercise is designed to help you cultivate a growth mindset—a way of thinking that promotes learning, curiosity, and resilience.

Step 1: Identify areas in your life where you hold a fixed mindset. A fixed mindset is the belief that your abilities, intelligence, or personality are unchangeable. It might show up in thoughts like *"I'm just not good at this"* or *"This is who I am and it can't change."* Reflect on the areas where you've been holding onto this mindset.

Step 2: Reframe your thinking with a growth mindset. For each area where you've identified a fixed mindset, reframe it as a growth mindset. A growth mindset believes that abilities can be developed through effort. Instead of saying *"I'm not good at this,"* say "I'm still learning and I can improve with practice."

Step 3: Challenge yourself to learn something new. One of the best ways to strengthen a growth mindset is to take on something new — whether it's a skill, a hobby, or a project that challenges you. Approach it with curiosity rather than judgment and allow yourself the freedom to be a beginner. As you practice, be mindful of the moments when your fixed mindset starts to reappear. Notice the frustration, resistance, or fear of failure that may arise. Then gently remind yourself that growth takes time, and mistakes are a natural part of the process.

Exercise 6: Daily Self-Check-In

A daily self-check-in is a simple yet powerful way to stay connected to your growth and authenticity. This practice helps you reflect on your day, notice where you aligned with your true self, and identify areas where you may have held back.

Step 1: Set aside five minutes at the end of each day for reflection. Find a quiet space where you can relax and take a few deep breaths to center yourself.

Step 2: Reflect on your day by asking yourself these questions:

- Did I show up as my authentic self today?
- Were there moments when I felt disconnected from my true self? What was happening, and what triggered that feeling?
- Did I challenge any limiting beliefs today? If so, what belief, and how did I challenge it?
- Did I embrace opportunities for growth by stepping out of my comfort zone?
- How did I practice vulnerability? Did I allow myself to be seen by others, or did I hide behind a facade?

Step 3: Write down your reflections. Keeping a journal allows you to track patterns over time and provides insight into where you're growing and where you might still feel stuck.

Step 4: Set an intention for tomorrow. Before closing your journal, set a small, focused intention for the next day. It could be a step toward authenticity, a way to challenge a limiting belief, or a moment where you want to practice vulnerability. The goal is to take manageable, consistent steps toward living more authentically each day.

These exercises are tools to help you engage with the process of growth and authenticity. They are not about achieving perfection or reaching a final destination; rather they are about staying connected to your ongoing journey of self-discovery. Some days will be easier than others. There will be moments when you feel fully aligned with your true self, and there will be times when old patterns and limiting beliefs resurface, attempting to pull you back.

The key is to be patient with yourself. Growth isn't linear, and authenticity isn't something you "achieve" once and for all. It's a practice—a daily commitment to showing up as you are, embracing vulnerability, and allowing yourself to grow. Each time you engage with any of these exercises, you're taking another step toward breaking free from the stories that have held you back and embracing the fullness of who you're becoming.

Something to Reflect On:

After you've completed all six exercises, take a moment to reflect on which practices resonate with you most. Which exercise feels like it will help you the most on your journey toward growth and authenticity?

Write down your thoughts and choose one practice to start incorporating into your daily life.

Remember: You are not defined by the stories of your past. Every day is a chance to rewrite your narrative, embrace your true self, and grow in unexpected ways. Let this serve as your guide as you continue forward on your journey of self-discovery.

You've already begun the process of rewriting your story. It continues now. Take the insights you've gathered in this chapter and keep applying them—one belief, one story, one role at a time. The process may feel uncomfortable at first, but it's in this discomfort that you'll find your greatest potential for growth. You are dynamic, evolving, and capable of becoming something far beyond the assumptions you've attached to. The journey is already underway, and each step forward deepens your transformation.

Throughout this chapter, you have been uncovering the beliefs you've internalized about who you thought you were. You've been questioning the stories you've carried with you for so long and challenging the limiting beliefs that have shaped your identity. You've explored the power of vulnerability and taken steps toward living more authentically. This is the heart of growth—learning to see yourself not as a fixed entity, but as a work in progress, always changing, always evolving.

But where does this journey lead? As we move forward, the path becomes less about "fixing" yourself and more about realizing that you were never broken to begin with, just weighed down by a story that felt heavy because you believed it was real. The more we question the old stories and identities that have held us back, the more we see the blank page that has always been there. Beneath all the labels, roles, and expectations, you are not a character set in ink—you are the writer, with the freedom to shape and reshape your story endlessly.

The exercises you've worked through in this chapter are just the beginning. By questioning your stories and exploring the fluidity of identity, you are laying the groundwork for even deeper transformation.

The next phase of this journey is an invitation to go even further. It's about looking beyond the beliefs and roles you've questioned so far and diving deeper into what keeps you tethered to them. The path ahead isn't about finding answers, but about embracing the questions.

As you reflect on the journey so far, what parts of your identity feel most difficult to release? In taking the next step toward loosening these attachments, what potential might you unlock within yourself?

Your story is waiting to be rewritten—one sentence, one choice, one change at a time.

Chapter 2 - Loosening the Grip

Imagine trying to hold onto the bank of a fast-moving river. The water rushes by, threatening your grip on the rock you believe will save you. It beats against you, pulling at you, yet still, you cling to the rock, fearing what potentially lies further down the river. The unknown feels too risky, so the rock seems preferable, despite the relentless pressure and drag you experience. This is what we do with our attachments—grasping at relationships, careers, beliefs, or outcomes as if they could guarantee a life of peace, fulfillment, value, and certainty, because we don't know what life might be without these goals to ensure our success.

As we explored in Chapter 1, just as it's not the character on the page that limits us, but our hesitation to question it and let it go, the problem is not the river itself, but our fear of the river. Is the stone we cling to truly helping us navigate the river, or is it merely keeping us in place, overwhelmed by the current because we resist its flow?

Something to Reflect On:

Reflect on an attachment that feels particularly strong in your life—something you fear losing or feel anxious about. Instead of simply identifying the stress it creates, ask yourself: What deeper need does this attachment fulfill, and is there another way to meet that need? Consider how loosening your grip, even slightly, could open up new possibilities for meeting this need in healthier, more flexible ways.

Attachments are pervasive, often unnoticed until they begin to limit us. We hold onto things that make us feel safe, secure, or worthy: a career that defines our value, a relationship that validates our identity, or a belief system that offers control in a chaotic world.

Attachments are like heavy stones we carry for safety while attempting to float down a river. They weigh us down, giving us a sense of control but making it harder to move with the current. Over time, the weight of these attachments leads to exhaustion and anxiety, as we constantly struggle to hold onto the very things that leave us feeling tired, overwhelmed, and unable to adapt to the river's changing currents. This state of chronic stress and dissatisfaction can even bring a persistent sense of emptiness, as if something vital is always just out of reach.

Suffering often arises not from what we lack, but from what we cling to. It's not the absence of something that causes pain, but our refusal to release it when the time comes. We become so focused on maintaining our grip that we miss out on the freedom and joy that may come from learning to live with the river instead of against it.

Consider attachment to outcomes. How many times have you set a goal and felt like you were swimming against the current when things didn't go as planned? Perhaps you didn't get the promotion, a relationship ended, or a personal project fell short of expectations. In those moments, it's easy to feel like you're being pulled under by the current of failure, as though your worth is tied to that outcome. But is that really true? Or is it just a story you've been telling yourself?

In questioning the story, we're presented with a new option: non-attachment. Unlike detachment, which involves withdrawing from experiences or emotions to avoid being affected by them, non-attachment is about fully engaging with life while letting go of the need to control or cling to specific outcomes. It means embracing the story, but not as a measure of reality—recognizing it as a part of your experience without letting it define your worth. This allows us to appreciate relationships without fearing their loss, to pursue careers and goals without equating them with our identity, and to hold beliefs lightly without rigidly clinging to them. We remain open to life's unfolding, less burdened by the need for things to be a certain way, and more able to find alignment with the present moment, regardless of our opinions or circumstances.

Mahatma Gandhi embodied non-attachment while leading India's independence movement. He famously said, 'The reward is in the action, not the result.' For Gandhi, the focus was always on doing what was right, regardless of the outcome. His ability to remain unattached to success or failure allowed him to persevere through setbacks and opposition. Gandhi's example shows that letting go of the need to control outcomes frees us to focus on our actions and intentions—where true power lies.

"If you realize that all things change, there is
nothing you will try to hold on to."

— Tao Te Ching

Something to Reflect On:

Reflect on something you're clinging to in your life—whether it's a job, relationship, or a specific self-image. Rather than simply imagining relaxing your grip on it, ask yourself: What fears arise at the thought of letting it go? What stories have you told yourself about why this attachment is essential? Now, consider what it would mean to release those fears, even briefly, and trust that life could carry you in a new direction.

As explored in Chapter 1, we often cling to the stories we tell ourselves about who we are, but this tendency extends beyond identity to the attachments we rely on for security. Whether it's a career, a relationship, or a belief, these things seem to offer stability in an unpredictable world. Yet, the mind's resistance to letting go is strong, rooted in the illusion that holding on provides safety. But what if that security was only a story itself? What if real freedom comes from releasing, not clinging? From flowing with life, not fighting against it?

In the pages that follow, we're going to explore these questions more deeply. We'll look at the nature of attachment, not as something to be avoided or judged, but as something to be understood. We'll see how our attachments shape our identity and how loosening them can create space for a more authentic, free-flowing experience of life. This isn't about giving up on the things you care about—it's about caring in a way that doesn't shackle you, in a way that allows for growth, change, and freedom.

Let's begin by reflecting on a recent experience where you felt frustrated or disappointed. Was that frustration tied to how things 'should' have gone? Was it linked to an expectation that didn't align with reality? Sit with that thought for a moment. As we continue, we'll explore how attachments, like expectations, create suffering—and how loosening your grip can lead to greater peace.

Attachments often go unnoticed until they create enough conflict or consequence. They appear as familiar comforts—harmless habits, reassuring roles, and patterns we believe guide us through the flow of our lives. Yet, as subtle as they seem, these attachments shape how we navigate decisions, relationships, and our understanding of ourselves. The need to achieve specific outcomes or maintain certain beliefs becomes so ubiquitous that we rarely pause to ask: Is this adding to my life or limiting its potential?

To explore this further, let's break down some common types of attachments in daily life—the things we feel we need to feel complete, in control, or secure. Understanding these habits is a necessary step in recognizing their hold on us.

Material Attachments

Material attachments are often the most obvious. These are the things we attach ourselves to: money, possessions, and external status symbols. They represent security, success, or even love. It's easy to see how someone might tie their self-worth to the car they drive, the house they own, or the clothes they wear. These external markers can seem like proof of accomplishment or stability.

The danger with material attachments is their impermanence. The shiny new car loses its appeal, the trendy clothes go out of fashion, and the big house demands constant upkeep. Yet the attachment to these things persists because they've become symbols of success. If you lose the car or the house, does your worth diminish? Logically, we know the answer is no. But emotionally, the attachment tells a different story.

Emotional Attachments

Emotional attachments are more subtle but just as powerful. These are attachments to relationships, validation, and others' approval. They appear in our deep need to be liked, accepted, or validated by those around us. This can surface in romantic relationships, friendships, or even at work, where we strive to be seen as competent or worthy of respect.

Imagine the emotional attachment to being perceived as reliable. Someone might say yes to every favor, every project, every request—even at the expense of their own well-being. Their identity becomes tied to being dependable, and the idea of letting someone down feels like a failure of livelihood.

Emotional attachments also extend to personal relationships—being a good partner, friend, or parent. We often measure our worth by how well we fulfill these roles, which can lead to self-sacrifice or codependency. When the attachment to a relationship becomes too strong, we lose sight of ourselves. The problem with emotional attachments is that they create an illusion of control over others' feelings. We may believe that if we love someone enough, they'll never leave us. But the truth is, we can't control how others feel, nor can we make them stay.

Conceptual Attachments

Conceptual attachments tie us to our beliefs, ideas, and identity. These are the stories we tell ourselves about who we are and how the world should work. For instance, we might cling to the belief that life should be fair, that hard work guarantees success, or that we must always appear strong and confident to others.

These attachments often run the deepest, as they are closely tied to our sense of self. When someone challenges a core belief, it can feel like a personal attack. You've likely witnessed—or experienced—the defensiveness that arises when your worldview is questioned. This is a natural response, as our attachments to beliefs form the foundation of who we think we are.

Conceptual attachments can be especially hard to release because they feel like truths. The more rigidly we hold onto our beliefs, the more resistance we create when life doesn't align with those beliefs. This rigidity makes it difficult to adapt to change or embrace new perspectives. For example, someone who believes success comes only through hard work may struggle to accept moments of serendipity with grace. They might even sabotage opportunities that come easily because it doesn't fit their attachment to the idea that success must be earned through effort.

Attachments—whether material, emotional, or conceptual—shape the decisions we make every day. They influence how we interact with others, face challenges, and perceive success and failure.

Consider a student who is deeply attached to the goal of academic success. This attachment informs almost every decision, from how they spend their time to the pressure they place on themselves. It drives them to study long hours, sometimes sacrificing social activities or sleep, because they feel their future depends on maintaining high grades. Every achievement brings relief, but any setback causes anxiety and self-doubt, making it difficult to cope when things don't go as planned.

Similarly, think about someone attached to keeping a relationship intact at all costs. This attachment may lead them to prioritize their partner's needs over their own, constantly sacrificing their time and energy. While this dedication can seem admirable, it often results in stress or burnout when they feel unappreciated or the relationship encounters difficulties. The attachment to a specific outcome—the idea of being in a 'perfect' relationship—can create unrealistic expectations, setting the stage for disappointment.

In both cases, the attachment drives behavior in ways that can go unnoticed, as these desires often feel justified or necessary. But what happens when those attachments are challenged? When the grades slip or the relationship ends, the emotional impact can be profound, revealing just how much we've allowed external circumstances to determine our sense of security.

Something to Reflect On:

Reflect on how these roles were formed. Were they self-imposed, or did they come from external expectations? How does recognizing their origin change your relationship to them?

Something to Reflect On:

Reflect on how these roles were formed. Were they self-imposed, or did they come from external expectations? How does recognizing their origin change your relationship to them?

The devastation that follows unmet expectations isn't just about the grade or the relationship—it's about losing the identity built around it. This is why attachments feel so powerful. They provide not only a sense of security but also reinforce our sense of self.

Eckhart Tolle's life changed dramatically after a profound spiritual awakening following years of depression and anxiety. He realized much of his suffering came from attachment to his own mind—his thoughts and stories were like obstacles, disrupting the natural flow of his life. By letting go of these attachments, he found peace and presence, learning to flow with life rather than clinging to an identity rooted in fear or limitation. His transformation shows that true freedom comes when we release mental attachments and embrace the present moment.

Attachment often arises as a solution to fear—fear of the unknown, fear of change, and fear of losing control. We cling to people, possessions, and ideas, believing they can shield us from uncertainty. The more unpredictable life feels, the more desperately we hold onto these attachments, mistaking them for stability. Yet this sense of security is fleeting. No attachment can change the fact that life is always in flux, and trying to resist that reality only adds to our suffering.

The more we cling to attachments, the more anxious and fearful we become because, deep down, we know nothing is permanent. The job, the relationship, the belief—they are all subject to change. The tighter we hold on, the more we suffer when the inevitable happens.

Like stones carried into the river, attachments become a burden—weights that slow us down and prevent us from experiencing life's full potential. When we let go, we become lighter, freer, and more adaptable. We stop trying to control the uncontrollable and deepen our trust in the process of life.

Something to Reflect On:

Take a moment to reflect on the attachments in your own life. Are there areas where you feel the need to control outcomes or maintain a certain image? How does this attachment affect your decisions, your relationships, and your sense of self-worth? What might happen if you let go of the need to control these aspects of your life?

Attachments are often subtle, ingrained so deeply in our lives that we barely notice them until they're challenged. But attachments shape how we see the world, how we make decisions, and how we relate to others. To loosen their grip, we must first recognize where they exist. This section will guide you through the process of uncovering attachments that may be holding you back—whether material, emotional, or conceptual.

Start by asking yourself: What feels most essential in your life? These aren't necessarily survival needs like food, water, or shelter. Instead, they're things you feel emotionally or mentally tied to— things you believe you couldn't live without. They might be possessions, relationships, beliefs, or outcomes you're striving for. The key is to uncover what would leave you feeling incomplete or insecure if it were taken away.

Here's a list of categories to consider:

- **Possessions**: What material objects do you feel most attached to? Maybe it's your home, car, or favorite piece of technology. How do these items make you feel? Do they bring security, status, or comfort?
- **Relationships**: Who in your life do you feel strongly connected to? This might include your partner, family, friends, or coworkers. What role do these relationships play in your sense of self-worth? Are you attached to being seen as a good partner, reliable friend, or supportive parent?
- **Success and Achievement**: Are you attached to specific goals or outcomes? Perhaps it's a promotion, a financial milestone, or recognition in your field. How does pursuing these achievements shape your daily life? How would you feel if you didn't reach these goals?
- **Beliefs and Ideals**: What beliefs do you hold most strongly about yourself or the world? This could include political or religious beliefs, your moral compass, or your idea of how life should be. Are you attached to being "right" or to others seeing the world your way?
- **Roles and Identity**: What roles do you play, and how attached are you to them? Are you the caretaker, the achiever, the intellectual, or the peacemaker? How do these roles define your sense of self? What would happen if you could no longer fulfill these roles?

Spend some time reflecting on these questions. Write down the attachments that come to mind. Don't judge them—just observe. The goal isn't to label these attachments as 'bad' or to shame yourself for having them, but simply to bring them into your awareness.

Once you've identified some of your attachments, consider the emotional weight they carry. How do these attachments make you feel daily? Do they bring comfort, or do they bring stress and anxiety? For many of us, attachments create a constant pressure— which stems from either the fear of losing what we hold dear or failing to achieve what we've set our sights on.

Let's take the example of being attached to a particular relationship. You might feel that your relationship defines who you are as a person. Perhaps you've spent years cultivating the image of a devoted partner, always there for your significant other, always putting their needs ahead of your own. But what happens when the relationship hits a rough patch? What happens if your partner changes or grows distant?

Attachment to the relationship might bring feelings of insecurity or fear. You may overcompensate—trying to control the situation, fix the problems, or hold onto the relationship even when it causes you pain. This isn't just about the relationship; it's about the identity tied to it. The fear of losing the relationship becomes the fear of losing yourself. Over time, this dynamic can create tension and resentment, as the pressure to maintain the relationship at all costs may cause both partners to feel suffocated or disconnected.

The more attached we are, the more we're dragged by the current, vulnerable to losing what we're clinging to. This creates a cycle of anxiety, where we constantly try to maintain control over things that are, by nature, impermanent.

"In a way, everything absolutely is meaningless, and that was a thought that was sad to me at first. But then it became, 'Wait, this is kind of awesome because I get to assign meaning to everything.'"

Felecia Freely, entrepreneur and creative, shared this insight on Dualistic Unity. Her reflection captures the freedom in realizing that we are not bound by external definitions of meaning. Instead, we have the power to assign our own meaning to our experiences, loosening our grip on the attachments that cause anxiety.

Consider the attachment to success and achievement. Perhaps you've worked tirelessly to build a career, aiming for a specific title or level of recognition. You tell yourself that once you achieve it, you'll feel complete, secure, and validated. But what happens in the meantime? The attachment to future success creates pressure to constantly perform, to never let your guard down. It might even lead you to sacrifice other areas of your life—relationships, health, or peace of mind—all in pursuit of that goal.

The irony is that even when you achieve success, it rarely feels like enough. As soon as one goal is reached, another appears.

Reflection Exercise: Examining Your Attachments

1. Let's go deeper with a reflective exercise. Think about one attachment in your life—something that feels deeply important to you. It could be a relationship, possession, goal, or belief. Now ask yourself:
2. How does this attachment make me feel? Does it bring peace and contentment, or does it create stress, anxiety, or fear?

3. What do I fear would happen if I lost this attachment? How would I feel if this relationship ended, if I didn't achieve this goal, or if my belief was proven wrong? Would I feel like I lost a part of myself?
4. How does this attachment influence my decisions and actions? Does it cause me to behave in ways that aren't true to myself? Do I prioritize this attachment over other important areas of my life?
5. What might happen if I loosened my grip on this attachment? Imagine letting go of the need to control this outcome or maintain this identity. How might that change how I experience life?

This exercise isn't about forcing yourself to let go of something you care about. It's about becoming aware of how your attachment to that thing might be shaping your emotions, your decisions, and your overall sense of well-being. By bringing these attachments into your conscious awareness, you give yourself the opportunity to choose how tightly or gently you want to hold onto them.

We often fear that releasing something—whether a relationship, belief, or goal—will mean losing a part of ourselves. This fear is understandable, as attachments have provided us with a sense of identity and security for so long that letting them go can feel like giving up on who we are.

> "To be fully alive, fully human, and completely awake is to be continually thrown out of the nest."
>
> — Pema Chödrön

But consider this: What if letting go didn't mean losing yourself? What if it meant gaining a deeper, truer version of who you are— one that isn't defined by external factors or outcomes? Letting go can be seen as an act of trust. Life is like a river, and instead of fighting the current, we can learn to flow with it. When we cling to attachments, we're essentially swimming upstream, inadvertently exhausting ourselves. But when we let go, we allow the river to carry us, trusting it will take us where we need to go. Just as rewriting the character didn't erase the blank page beneath, letting go of your attachments doesn't mean losing anything—it simply reveals the openness and potential that was always there.

Krishnamurti often emphasized that freedom comes from loosening attachments. He suggested that most of our suffering arises from the tension between what we desire and what reality presents. When we're attached to a specific outcome or idea, we resist anything that contradicts it, creating conflict and pain. But when we release that attachment, we open ourselves to the possibility of experiencing life as it is—without judgment, without resistance.

In letting go, you're not abandoning the things that matter to you. You're simply releasing the need for them to define you. And in that space, you may find that the things you were so afraid of losing were never the source of your happiness to begin with.

As we end this section, choose one attachment from your list— something small and manageable. It could be a minor goal, a possession, or a role you've been playing. For the next week, experiment with loosening your grip on this attachment. How does it feel to let go of the need for this outcome or object to define your happiness? What shifts do you notice in your mindset, emotions, and actions?

Remember, loosening attachments isn't about drastic, overnight changes. It's about small, conscious steps toward greater freedom. As you recognize your attachments and gently release their hold, you'll begin to experience life with a new sense of openness. That's where real growth happens—not in controlling life, but in flowing with it.

Now that you've reflected on your attachments and their emotional weight, it's time to look into the practical steps for loosening them, the specific challenges you may encounter along the way, and the unexpected freedom that can emerge as you gradually release your grip.

At first, letting go can feel uncomfortable, even frightening. After all, you're stepping into the unknown, releasing the things that have anchored your identity and sense of security. But as you continue to loosen attachments, you'll notice a sense of lightness and an expansion in how you engage with life.

Jane Goodall's journey is a powerful example of this. Despite having no formal education in primatology, Goodall let go of the traditional expectations placed on scientists and followed her own instincts. By embracing her unique observational style and immersing herself in the habitat of chimpanzees, she made groundbreaking discoveries that revolutionized both science and conservation. Her willingness to release rigid structures and trust her own path allowed her to create a legacy far beyond what any traditional approach could have achieved.

Let's imagine someone tightly attached to their role as a caretaker in their family. They've always been the one to solve problems, offer support, and put others' needs ahead of their own. While this role has given them purpose, it has also led to exhaustion and resentment. By loosening their attachment to this role—allowing others to take responsibility for their own lives—they begin to experience freedom. No longer defined solely by the caretaker role, they can explore other aspects of themselves that have been waiting for attention.

Give yourself permission to explore new possibilities. You don't need to control every outcome or maintain every role to be whole. Imagine your attachments like the connections between cells. While these bonds provide structure, overly rigid connections prevent flexibility and adaptation. Similarly, clinging too tightly to roles or outcomes restricts your growth. Life has a flow. When we release the need to grasp tightly, we allow ourselves to be carried by the current, just as cells that release their rigidity can adjust and thrive in response to their environment, trusting that wherever it takes us, we'll find value and meaning.

Of course, changing a habit is easier said than done. You may find yourself reverting to old patterns, feeling the pull to cling to familiar roles, relationships, or outcomes. This is normal. Non-attachment is a practice, not a one-time event. It requires patience and self-compassion, especially when fear or resistance arises.

For example, if you're attached to the belief that you must always be "right" in your conversations with others, practice loosening that grip by allowing space for other perspectives. This doesn't mean abandoning your values or opinions—it simply means releasing the need for others to validate them. Over time, you'll notice that this release creates more peace and flexibility in your interactions.

Similarly, if you're attached to a specific outcome, like achieving a certain level of success in your career, practice letting go by focusing on the process rather than the result. Instead of measuring your worth by the title or promotion you receive, pay attention to the day-to-day experiences that bring you joy and fulfillment. What are the moments that make you feel alive, creative, or inspired? These are the true markers of success, not the external achievements we often fixate on.

Reflection Exercise: Non-Attachment

Choose one small attachment from your earlier reflection. It could be something as simple as the need for your partner to always agree with you or the attachment to finishing a project by a specific deadline. For the next week, intentionally practice loosening your grip on this attachment.

Here's how you can do it:

1. **Notice when the attachment arises**: Pay attention to the moments when you feel the need to control or cling to this attachment. What emotions surface? Do you feel anxious, fearful, or frustrated? Simply observe these feelings without judgment.
2. **Challenge the belief behind the attachment**: Ask yourself, "What am I afraid will happen if I let go of this?" Often, we discover that the fear behind our attachment is based on an illusion—the fear that we'll lose control, that we won't be loved, or that we'll fail. But when we look deeper, we see that these fears are not grounded in reality.
3. **Experiment with letting go**: In those moments, practice loosening your grip. If you're attached to being right in a conversation, try listening instead of arguing. If you're attached to finishing a project by a certain date, give yourself permission to take breaks or adjust the timeline. Notice how it feels to release the need for control. Do you feel more relaxed? More open? Less burdened?

After a week of this practice, reflect on the experience. Did loosening your attachment create more space for peace or joy in your life? Were there moments when you still felt the need to hold on? This reflection is an opportunity to deepen your awareness of your attachments and how they shape your daily experience.

As you continue this practice, you'll start to notice something powerful: letting go of attachments doesn't diminish your life—it expands it. When you stop defining yourself by external outcomes, relationships, or roles, you create space for new possibilities to emerge.

In the next section, we'll explore more practical ways to release attachments and cultivate a sense of ease and flow in your daily life. For now, remember that loosening the grip is not about abandoning what matters—it's about freeing yourself from the illusion that these attachments define you.

The more you loosen your grip, the more space you create for joy, peace, and unexpected growth. Take the insights from this chapter and practice letting go—just a little. Trust that, as Alan Watts said, "The more a thing tends to be permanent, the more it tends to be lifeless." Loosen your hold, and allow life to flow naturally, trusting that the river will carry you to where you need to be.

Practical Application

So how do we work to loosen the grip on our attachments? It's a gradual practice that starts with awareness and moves toward action. Let's explore a few practical steps that can help you along the way.

Step 1: Start with Awareness

The first step to loosening your grip is becoming aware of when and why you're holding on so tightly. Ask yourself:

- **What triggers my attachment?** Is it fear of losing something? Is it the need for approval, validation, or control?
- **What am I afraid would happen if I let go?** Am I worried that I won't be loved, respected, or successful if I loosen my grip?
- **How does holding on affect me?** Do I feel more relaxed and at ease, or do I feel anxious, stressed, or exhausted?

Bringing awareness to these questions is key because it helps you understand the emotional underpinnings of your attachment. Often, we cling to things because they feel familiar and safe, even if they create stress in the long run. By observing when you hold on too tightly, you can start to gently question whether that tightness is necessary.

For example, let's say you're attached to always being seen as competent and reliable at work. You might notice that you feel anxious whenever a project isn't going perfectly or if you don't receive praise for your efforts. By becoming aware of these feelings, you can start to ask: *Is my value really tied to this one project? Is it possible that I am worthy even if things don't go as planned?*

Awareness is the first, and perhaps most important, step in the process. It's like recognizing the branch you've been stuck to in the river's current. Once you see the branch, you can begin to free yourself from it and allow yourself to flow freely.

Step 2: Challenge Your Need for Control

The second step is to challenge the need for control that underpins many of our attachments. At the heart of most attachments is the belief that if we can just hold on tightly enough, we can control the outcome. But this belief often leads to frustration and disappointment because life is inherently unpredictable.

While we can influence outcomes to a degree, we cannot fully control them. This is especially true in relationships, where our attachment to how others should behave can cause unnecessary suffering. We believe that if we say the right things, do the right things, or love someone enough, they'll act in the way we want them to. But, the more we try to control others, the more we push them away and create tension.

Let's take an example of someone who is deeply attached to their partner's happiness. They believe it's their job to ensure that their partner is always happy and content. But over time, this need to control their partner's emotions can lead to burnout, frustration, and even resentment. The partner, feeling the pressure of someone else's expectations, might feel suffocated or pushed away.

In this case, loosening the grip means recognizing that you cannot control how someone else feels or behaves. You can offer love, support, and kindness, but their happiness is ultimately not in your hands. By letting go of the need to control their emotions, you create more space for a healthier, more balanced relationship.

A practical exercise to challenge your need for control is this: The next time you find yourself trying to control a situation or person, pause and ask yourself, *What would happen if I let go of my need to control this outcome? How might things unfold if I trusted the process instead of forcing it?*

Step 3: Shift Your Focus to the Process, Not the Outcome

A common source of attachment is the fixation on specific outcomes. We often believe that our happiness depends on achieving a particular result—whether it's getting a promotion, securing a relationship, or reaching a personal goal. But when we become too attached to the outcome, we lose sight of the process, and life becomes a series of expectations and disappointments.

For instance, imagine you're training for a marathon, and your goal is to finish the race in a certain time. If you become overly attached to this outcome, the joy of training can disappear. You may start to push yourself too hard, ignore the progress you're making, or feel discouraged if you don't hit every benchmark. But if you loosen your grip on the outcome and shift your focus to the experience of running—the feeling of your body moving, the fresh air, the daily improvements—you'll find more fulfillment in the process itself.

Something to Reflect On:

Choose one goal or area of your life where you're focused on the outcome, and consciously shift your attention to the process. How does this change the way you approach your goal? Do you feel more present, more at ease? What new joys or insights emerge when you stop fixating on the result and embrace the moment-to-moment experience?

Step 4: Practice Letting Go, One Step at a Time

"Loosening up" is a practice that happens gradually. It's not about flipping a switch and suddenly being free of all attachments—it's about taking small, consistent steps toward being aware of your habitual grip.

You might find that letting go brings a sense of relief, a lightness that you hadn't expected. Or you might feel resistance, a desire to cling even tighter. Either way, be gentle with yourself. This process isn't about perfection; it's about progress.

Step 5: Trust the Flow of Life

At the heart of loosening attachments is learning to trust the flow of life. When we're tightly attached, it's because we don't trust that things will unfold as they do. It's not about believing that everything happens for a reason, but rather recognizing that whatever happens is simply what is. It's easy to know what was meant to be—if it happened, it was meant to be.

Trying to control life's natural flow is futile, like attempting to direct a river's current. The harder we try to force outcomes, the more we exhaust ourselves. True ease comes when we allow life to carry us, flowing without resistance with its natural course. Trusting the flow doesn't mean giving up on our goals or desires; it means trusting that we are part of something larger, something that is unfolding in ways we may not always understand but can learn to embrace.

One way to cultivate this trust is through mindfulness. Spend a few minutes each day practicing being fully present with whatever is happening in your life. Notice the sensations in your body, the thoughts in your mind, and the emotions that arise. Instead of trying to change or control these experiences, simply observe them. By practicing mindfulness, you develop the ability to sit with uncertainty and trust that whatever happens, you will be able to navigate it with grace.

Something to Reflect On:

As you reflect on these steps, consider this: *What would it feel like to trust the flow of life, rather than trying to control it?* How might your experience of daily life change if you loosened your grip on the things you've been clinging to? What new possibilities might open up when you stop fighting the current and start moving with it?

As you practice loosening your grip, you'll notice a shift in the way you experience life. The tightness, the tension, the need for things to go a certain way—it all begins to soften. This doesn't mean that you stop caring or that you no longer have goals, dreams, or desires. Rather, you start to engage with life with open hands, a way that feels more fluid, more flexible, and ultimately more fulfilling.

Living with open hands means approaching everything—
relationships, work, aspirations, even your sense of self—with a
sense of ease. You recognize that while you may want certain
outcomes, your happiness isn't dependent on them. You may invest
in a relationship, but you don't cling to it as if it defines you. You
may work toward a goal, but you don't measure your worth by
whether or not you achieve it. Open hands allow life to flow
naturally, rather than trying to control or possess it.

Something to Reflect On:

Take a moment to reflect on how your life
might change if you loosened your grip on
the things you've been attached to. What
would happen if you released the need for
control, validation, or specific outcomes?
How might your relationships, your work,
or your sense of self evolve if you allowed
yourself to live with open hands?

One of the most profound lessons in life is the contradiction of
letting go: the more you release, the more you gain. This may seem
counterintuitive at first. After all, we're often taught that holding on
tightly to the things we want—whether it's success, relationships, or
personal goals—is the key to achievement and happiness. But what
we often fail to realize is that clinging too tightly creates tension,
anxiety, and a sense of lack. We become fixated on controlling
outcomes, and in doing so, we limit our ability to experience life
fully.

Let's say you're attached to the idea of being successful in your
career. You've worked hard, and you've built your identity around
being a high-achiever. But this attachment creates stress, because
every setback or challenge feels like a threat to your sense of self.

Now imagine loosening your grip on that attachment. You still care about your work, and you still strive to do your best, but you no longer tie your sense of worth to the outcomes. If a project doesn't go as planned, or if someone else gets the promotion, it no longer feels like a personal failure. Instead, you see it as part of the process—an opportunity to learn, adapt, and grow.

Non-attachment, or non-resistance, allows you to move through life with a sense of ease, even in the face of challenges. You're no longer trapped by the fear of failure or the need for external validation. Instead, you become free to explore, experiment, and take risks— knowing that your value isn't tied to the outcomes. This freedom not only empowers you in the present but also informs future successes, as each experience becomes an opportunity for growth rather than a measure of your worth.

One of the most powerful aspects of this freedom is that it creates space—space for growth, new experiences, and deeper connections. When we loosen our attachment to specific outcomes, we open ourselves to the opportunities that arise along the way. Without the tunnel vision that comes from being fixated on a particular goal, we become more receptive to the other paths that are unfolding before us, paths we may not have noticed before.

Think of your attachments like cellular adhesion—where cells bond together to provide structure. When you focus too rigidly on a single attachment, like cells clumping together too tightly, it can restrict movement and limit flexibility. Meanwhile, other areas of your life, like cells waiting to move freely and adapt, remain underdeveloped. By loosening that adhesion—allowing cells to detach and reconnect—you create space for new growth and possibilities to emerge, just as allowing space in life opens you up to new opportunities and relationships.

When we let go of the need for things to go a certain way, we begin to discover new passions, build new relationships, and find joy in unexpected places. Letting go creates the space for growth—both internally and externally.

A key component of the freedom in letting go is trust. Trust in yourself, trust in the process, and trust in life itself. When we're tightly attached, it's because we don't trust that life will flow as it should unless we control it. But the reality is, life is full of currents—both calm and turbulent—and much of it is beyond our control. The more we trust in the river's flow, the less we feel the need to direct every current or manage every detail, and the more capable we become in navigating the river with sensitivity.

Trusting the flow of life is much like kayaking. You can't control the river, but you can learn to work with its currents. Some stretches will be calm, while others will be rough, but when you trust your ability, you'll experience a sense of joy and freedom, moving with life's natural rhythms instead of fighting against them. It's when you try to fight the currents or control the river that you exhaust yourself.

Something to Reflect On:

As you continue to practice non-attachment, take a moment to reflect on what freedom feels like for you. How does it feel to release the need for things to go a certain way? What emotions arise when you allow yourself to trust the flow of life, rather than trying to control it?

"I had to let go of being attached to the outcome. Every time I got attached to what I wanted, it flipped to 'what if it doesn't happen?' So I just started letting that go—letting go, letting God."

Don Joseph Goewey, brain tumor survivor and author of The End of Stress, shared this insight in his episode on Dualistic Unity, where he discussed his journey through fear and uncertainty before his surgery. His story highlights how detaching from specific outcomes brought him peace, aligning with the message of releasing control.

As you reach the end of this chapter, take a moment to recognize how far you've come. You've explored the nature of attachments and how they shape your life, learned to identify the things that weigh you down, and practiced loosening your grip to create space for growth. You've taken important steps toward understanding that true freedom doesn't come from controlling life, but from trusting its flow. By reflecting on your attachments and experimenting with letting go, you're beginning to see and experience life with new openness and resilience. Celebrate this progress—each step, no matter how small, is a meaningful part of your journey toward greater peace and self-awareness.

Now we're ready to explore one of the most transformative tools for growth: facing fear and failure. Letting go of attachments is like stepping into the river—you must be willing to feel the current's force, to be afraid, and to occasionally feel overwhelmed or ill-equipped. In the next chapter, we'll dive deeper into how embracing fear and failure, rather than avoiding them, can help you navigate the river of life with greater resilience and wisdom. It's in these moments, when the water feels rough and the flow unpredictable, that the most profound transformation occurs.

As a final exercise, think about one specific area in your life where you feel particularly attached to an outcome—whether it's in your career, relationships, or personal goals. For the next week, practice releasing control over the outcome. Focus not on what you want to happen, but on how you engage with the process. Notice your thoughts, emotions, and actions as you let go, and at the end of the week, reflect on any changes in your mindset or experiences.

This exercise will help prepare you for our discussion in Chapter 3.

"By letting it go, it all gets done. The world is won by those who let it go. But when you try and try, the world is beyond the winning."

— Tao Te Ching

Chapter 3 - Fear and Failure as Allies

Fear and failure are pivotal forces in shaping human experience. From an early age, we're conditioned to believe that life's purpose is to steer clear of fear and evade failure at all costs, as though these experiences mark the boundaries of who we are and what we're capable of. But what if everything we've been taught about fear and failure is incomplete? What if, instead of barriers, they are gateways? What if they're not signs of weakness but invitations to grow? What if, just as with our belief in a fixed identity and attachments to specific outcomes, we've missed something important?

Imagine how different life would be if we stopped viewing fear and failure as the enemy. What if, instead of retreating from fear, we embraced it as the refining heat of the forge, a process that shapes us? Rather than trying to avoid failure, we could see it as the hammer striking the metal, offering life's feedback to strengthen us. These experiences aren't barriers but forces that transform raw material into resilience, tempering us with each challenge.

This shift in perspective is at the heart of this chapter. Fear and failure, when understood and embraced, are not obstacles but powerful forces that mold us into something more adaptable and resilient, guiding us toward deeper self-awareness, growth, and transformation.

The goal of this chapter is not simply to help you cope with fear and failure but to help you embrace them as key elements of your growth. Together, we will explore how fear and failure, when fully integrated into our lives, can become the very forces that propel us forward, helping us unlock our potential and discover new depths of resilience, courage, and authenticity.

Fear and failure often hold more power over us than we realize. Society conditions us to see them as enemies—barriers to success and self-confidence. But what if we've misunderstood their role?

At its core, fear is a survival mechanism, a biological response meant to keep us safe from danger. While early humans needed fear to survive physical threats like predators, today's fears are less tangible: fear of rejection, uncertainty, or failure. These fears aren't life-threatening, but we often react as if they are.

Fear arises as we step into uncharted territory—where growth is possible. It signals not only potential danger, but also opportunity. It shows us where we are still attached to old identities or beliefs that no longer serve us.

Fear is not the enemy; it's a path to change. It's telling us to look closely at the areas in our lives where we've become rigid and unchangeable, where we've avoided discomfort to maintain illusions that limit us. Fear is like the heat of the forge, softening us so that what's rigid can be reshaped into something stronger. The next time fear arises, instead of retreating, what if you leaned into it? What would you discover about yourself in the process?

"Let go of the past, let go of the future, let go of the present. With a heart that is free, cross over the river of life to the shore beyond."

— Dhammapada

Something to Reflect On:

Identify a recurring fear in your life. What underlying beliefs might be fueling it, and how does this fear show up in your daily actions? Rather than retreating, consider one small step you could take to engage with this fear and use it as a catalyst for growth.

While fear shows us where we need to grow, failure often follows as the natural hammer strike that shapes us when we step into the unknown. The two are deeply intertwined—fear ignites the forge, and failure provides the blows that refine and strengthen us.

Society has trained us to see failure as something to be avoided at all costs, as a sign of weakness or inadequacy. This mindset is rooted in the belief that success is the opposite of failure, that failure marks the end of an effort, the final defeat. But this belief is flawed.

A compelling example is Sara Blakely, the founder of Spanx, who attributes much of her success to her early relationship with failure. Her father would regularly ask her and her brother, "What did you fail at this week?" By encouraging them to embrace failure rather than fear it, he reframed failure as a sign of effort and growth. This mindset allowed Blakely to take risks without the paralyzing fear of judgment, a fortified resilience that became crucial as she built her company.

When she started Spanx, Blakely faced numerous rejections from potential investors who didn't understand her vision. Instead of being discouraged, she viewed these setbacks as part of the process, learning from each one and continuing to move forward. Today, Spanx is a billion-dollar brand, and Blakely credits her success to her willingness to stay curious in the face of failure.

Her story serves as a reminder that failure is not the opposite of success but a necessary part of the journey. It's a tool for refining our approach and building resilience.

"We can show kids that they can achieve anything they want in any part of their life, but sometimes that takes work. The goal is to foster excellence without fostering comparison and ego."

Trish Horrocks, founder of the award-winning youth fiddle group Fiddelium, emphasizes the value of personal excellence over comparison on a Dualistic Unity podcast, highlighting that growth comes from embracing challenges and learning from failure.

Recall some of the most transformative moments in life. They were likely preceded by failure. That project that didn't go as planned, that relationship that ended in heartbreak, that goal that seemed out of reach—each of these failures taught you something. They may have been painful, but they also forced you to re-evaluate, to grow, and to try again with an expanded understanding of yourself and the world around you.

Failure is life's way of providing feedback, showing us where we need to adjust and grow. Every great achievement is built on a foundation of missteps and lessons learned.

"The wound is the place where the Light enters you."

— Rumi

Michael Jordan's journey provides a perfect example of how failure leads to success. Known as one of the greatest basketball players of all time, Jordan once remarked, "I've missed more than 9,000 shots in my career. I've lost almost 300 games. I've failed over and over again. And that is why I succeed." His story shows another example that failure is not the opposite of success but an essential part of achieving it.

Likewise, James Dyson, inventor of the Dyson vacuum cleaner, spent 15 years creating 5,126 failed prototypes before he finally succeeded with the 5,127th model. His persistence through thousands of failed attempts illustrates how vital it is to embrace failure as a necessary part of the journey toward success.

It's time to reclaim fear and failure as part of your journey, not as things to be feared or avoided. Fear shows us where we need to grow. Failure teaches us how to improve. Together, they form a powerful dynamic that pushes us forward in life, challenging us to expand our understanding of ourselves and the world.

When you face a fear or experience failure, instead of asking, "What did I do wrong?" ask, "How is this experience refining me?" This simple shift in perspective can open up a world of possibilities. Instead of seeing failure as a personal shortcoming, see it as part of the natural process of becoming. Instead of viewing fear as a barrier, see it as a process of refinement.

Fear and failure are not enemies but allies, guiding us through life's rhythm. The more we engage with them, the more we realize that life isn't about getting every step right—it's about learning to move with its ups and downs.

Something to Reflect On:

Think about a recent situation where fear held you back. What did this fear reveal about your perceived limitations? How might reframing failure as feedback allow you to approach similar situations differently in the future?

We've been taught to view failure through a narrow lens—as something to avoid, something to be ashamed of. It's drilled into us from a young age: failure equals inadequacy. This narrow lens is shaped by the attachments we discussed in Chapter 2 and the idealized character society encourages us to embody, as we explored in Chapter 1. But what if we could see failure differently? What if failure were not a sign of weakness or defeat, but simply feedback—an opportunity to learn and grow beyond the limitations of our attachments and self-concepts?

Failure is one of life's most valuable teachers, offering us insights we wouldn't gain otherwise. When we stop viewing failure as an endpoint and instead as part of an ongoing process, it becomes a tool for refinement. Each misstep provides feedback on what worked, what didn't, and what needs adjustment. By approaching failure with curiosity, we gain wisdom and clarity, turning setbacks into growth opportunities.

Every time we stumble, every time something doesn't go as planned, life is providing us with critical information. What worked? What didn't? How can we adjust? When we approach failure with curiosity rather than judgment, we begin to understand that it's not about whether we succeed or fail, but about what we learn in the process.

Failure reflects reality. It shows us where our assumptions, strategies, or beliefs didn't align with the world around us. This doesn't mean we are flawed or inadequate; it simply means there's something we need to adjust. Failure tests the strength of our actions, behaviors, and beliefs, revealing where change is needed.

When a plan doesn't go as expected, it's easy to feel bent or broken. But failure is rarely the end. More often, it's a blow that reveals where we need to be reshaped, where we need to refine our approach. It's not a setback but part of the process of forging us into something stronger, opening us to new possibilities.

Consider how many of history's greatest achievements were born from failure. The process of scientific discovery, for example, is built on the foundation of repeated failures. Every hypothesis that's proven wrong is a step toward uncovering the truth. Thomas Edison famously remarked, "I have not failed. I've just found 10,000 ways that won't work," reflecting the idea that failure is simply feedback—necessary steps along the path to success.

In our own lives, failure shows up in various forms—whether in a career, a relationship, or a personal endeavor that didn't unfold as expected. In those moments, it's tempting to view failure as a reflection of personal inadequacy. But when you step back and look at the situation objectively, failure often becomes the greatest source of clarity. It highlights where adjustments are needed, prompts you to question your approach, reconsider your values, and realign with your true purpose.

Life doesn't punish us with failure; it forges us through it. When something doesn't go as planned, we are given an opportunity to grow. But growth requires that we be willing to step back into the forge, to confront failure head-on and see it not as a flaw, but as the fire that tempers us into something stronger and more resilient.

Think about the times in your life when you experienced the greatest growth. Were those moments born out of ease and success? Or were they forged in the fire of challenge and failure? Often, the most profound transformations come when we are forced to face our limits, to confront our fears, and to rise above setbacks. It's the blow of the hammer that tempers us, pushing us to step outside our comfort zones, to question our assumptions, and to evolve.

We tend to avoid failure because it makes us uncomfortable. It challenges our sense of identity, our belief in our own competence. But discomfort is where growth happens. If we remain in our comfort zones, avoiding failure at all costs, we also avoid growth. To grow, we must be willing to fail, to take risks, and to learn from the process. In this sense, failure becomes a powerful tool—a way for life to help us change, learn, and expand.

When we stop judging ourselves for failing, we open up space for curiosity. Instead of asking, "What's wrong with me?" we can ask, "What can I learn from this?" This shift from judgment to curiosity transforms failure from something to fear into something to explore. Each failure becomes an opportunity to gain new insights, to refine our approach, and to grow as individuals.

Imagine a child learning to walk. They fall over and over again, but each time they get back up and try again. The child doesn't judge themselves for falling—they simply keep moving forward, adjusting their balance and learning with each step. We could learn a lot from this approach.

Think of failure like a cellular stress response. Just as cells adapt under stress to survive and thrive, failure pushes us to adjust and grow. The intention remains the same, but the path to get there might need to change. Failure isn't telling you to stop pursuing your goals—it's prompting you to reconsider how you're approaching them and whether they still align with your growth. Sometimes, failure reveals that we're holding too tightly to a particular outcome or strategy, and it's only by letting go of those attachments that we can evolve and move forward.

In moments of failure, it's important to pause and ask: What is this stress trying to teach me? Just like cells adapting to stress to survive, we need to adjust to thrive. When we approach failure with this kind of openness, it becomes a catalyst for growth, guiding us toward a deeper understanding of ourselves and our lives.

Part of the reason failure feels so daunting is because we've internalized the illusion of perfection—a belief shaped by the attachments discussed in Chapter 2 and the character ideals we explored in Chapter 1. Our attachments reinforce the fixed roles and identities we cling to, creating a rigid self-image that we feel compelled to live up to. When these attachments are threatened, the character we've constructed feels at risk, making failure seem like a blow to our very sense of self. But perfection is a myth—an unattainable standard that keeps us trapped in cycles of self-doubt and frustration. Instead of striving for an ideal that doesn't exist, we can learn to see failure as feedback—an invitation to reassess our attachments, adjust our approach, and embrace the growth that comes from imperfection.

The pursuit of perfection is not only unrealistic—it's counterproductive. It stops us from taking risks, experimenting, and refining ourselves through trial and observation. Perfectionism keeps us trapped in that all-too-familiar fear that drives our overcommitment to the character on the page or the stones along the river—the fear of the unknown. Without the idea of 'perfect,' we can feel lost and directionless, unsure of what to do next. But unlike a piece of metal that is eventually finished after forging, we are never truly done. We are continuously shaped and reshaped by life's challenges. If adaptation is constant, then perhaps perfection is already unfolding in the process.

When we let go of the need for "perfection", we begin to see growth as an ongoing process. We allow ourselves to experiment, take risks, and learn from our experiences. True development doesn't come from chasing an ideal, but from engaging with each challenge as an opportunity to adapt and evolve. By accepting setbacks and difficulties as essential parts of this journey, we free ourselves from rigid expectations and discover the potential that unfolds in every moment.

Life isn't a smooth, linear process from success to success. Like forging steel, it requires repeated heating, shaping, and tempering. Failure isn't a disruption—it's an essential part of this process. Each time we face challenges and rise again, we become more aware of our strengths and refine the direction we're moving in.

Each failure provides us with invaluable information about what's working and what's not. It's a signpost on the journey, guiding us toward a deeper understanding of ourselves and our path and the journey we're on. Each time we fail, we receive feedback—on our strategies, our assumptions, and even on our priorities. This feedback is invaluable because it helps us refine our approach. With each failure, we gain clarity. We become better equipped to adjust, adapt, and move forward with more wisdom than before.

So, how do we put this new understanding of failure into practice?

It's one thing to talk about facing fear and failure, but it's another to confront the emotional weight that comes with it. The experience is real and often uncomfortable, filled with vulnerability, doubt, and even pain. Yet, remember that these emotions are not beyond your capacity to handle. The belief that you can't deal with them, or that you shouldn't have to, is just another narrative—much like the ones we've discussed in previous chapters. Facing the discomfort of failure isn't just about enduring the emotions that arise; it's about recognizing that they do not define you. By challenging the narrative that you can't handle these feelings, you cultivate an unshakeable resilience and discover the strength to engage with life more fully.

This is where courage comes in. It takes immense bravery to risk failure, especially when the stakes feel high. But this is the kind of courage that leads to growth. To fail is to be brave, to step outside of the comfort zone, and to push the boundaries of what we believe is possible. Failure, in this sense, is a sign that we're living fully, that we're taking risks and allowing ourselves to be vulnerable.

Courage is not the absence of fear—it's the willingness to move forward with it. When we embrace failure as part of the process, we develop resilience, a deeper trust in ourselves, and a greater capacity to handle whatever life throws our way. Each failure builds this courage muscle, making us more willing to take future risks and less likely to be deterred by setbacks.

Think about the people in your life who seem the most resilient. Chances are, they're the ones who have faced the most failure. They've experienced hardship, loss, and setbacks, but instead of being broken by these experiences, they've used them to learn and grow stronger. Resilience is built not by avoiding failure but by embracing it, by allowing each failure to strengthen our resolve and deepen our understanding.

This doesn't mean we won't feel the blow of failure—it's natural to feel disappointed, frustrated, or even heartbroken when things don't go as planned. But resilience means we don't stay in that place of despair. We acknowledge the feelings, learn from the experience, and move forward with greater clarity and strength. In this way, failure becomes a tool not only for learning but for building inner strength.

To cultivate this resilience, we need to shift our perspective on failure. Instead of seeing it as something to avoid, start viewing it as a natural and necessary part of the process. When you experience a setback, rather than sinking into self-judgment, ask yourself, *What is this trying to teach me?* This simple question can shift your entire perspective, moving you from a place of frustration to a place of curiosity and learning.

Let's take a practical example. Imagine you've just failed a major project at work. The instinctive reaction might be to feel defeated, to believe you're not cut out for the task, or that you're simply not good enough. But what if, instead of diving into that narrative, you paused and asked yourself what the failure is revealing? Perhaps the failure highlights a miscommunication, or maybe it reflects that you need more skills in a certain area. In this light, failure becomes an opportunity to identify areas of improvement or adjustment.

It's natural to feel frustrated and impatient when faced with failure because it implies that the journey to success, certainty, and value isn't going to end as soon as we'd hoped. But the truth is, it wouldn't have ended there anyway. As we know from our earlier discussions, these self-defining stories are fleeting and constantly threatened by new experiences. Investing in them creates a vicious cycle, and the impatience to achieve them only makes us run in circles faster. Often, this impatience stems from our misunderstanding of the forge and our potential within it. The more we focus on trying to escape the discomfort, the more intense it becomes. There will always be more projects, more goals, and more life unfolding. By recognizing that growth is a continuous process, we can ease the urgency we feel and allow ourselves to be shaped by the journey, rather than rushing through it.

Once you've identified what the failure is teaching you, it's time for action. Failure without reflection is wasted, but failure followed by intentional adjustment is powerful. Take what you've learned and use it to refine your approach. If a relationship has failed, use that feedback to learn how to communicate better or set clearer boundaries in the future. If a personal goal hasn't been met, reevaluate your methods—maybe the goal wasn't aligned with your values, current skills, or areas of strength, or perhaps your strategy needs tweaking.

Failure is only truly failure if we refuse to act on the lessons it offers. By turning failure into action, we transform it from something painful into something productive.

Ultimately, failure is the only path to mastery. Whether we're talking about personal growth, career success, or even relationships, mastery comes not from getting everything right the first time but from continually learning, adjusting, and improving.

Mastery doesn't happen overnight. It's the result of years of consistent effort, repeated failures, and ongoing learning. Think about any skill you've mastered in your life. Whether it's learning to drive a car, play an instrument, or communicate effectively, you didn't achieve mastery the first time you tried. You stumbled, you made mistakes, and you learned from them. Each failure was a step toward greater proficiency.

The same is true for life itself. Mastery in life doesn't come from avoiding failure; it comes from embracing it as part of the journey. Each failure is an opportunity to refine our approach, to deepen our understanding, and to move closer to our goals. In this way, failure is not an obstacle—it's the very thing that propels us forward.

Something to Reflect On:

Reflect on a past failure and reframe it as valuable feedback. What assumptions did it challenge about yourself or your approach? How has it reshaped the way you view your abilities or your goals? Use this new perspective to identify one specific way you can apply the lessons learned to face future challenges with a mindset of growth rather than defeat.

As Joseph Campbell wisely said, *'The cave you fear to enter holds the treasure you seek.'* Fear signals that you're standing at the threshold of something significant, urging you to step beyond your comfort zone and discover the strength and potential that lie hidden within.

Consider how fear has played a role in your own life. Think about the moments of greatest change—perhaps a new job, a move to a different city, the beginning or end of a relationship. Fear was likely present in all of those moments, not because you were in danger, but because you were stepping into the unknown. Fear is always present in moments of change, not because it wants to hold us back, but because it is showing us that we are growing.

There's a saying: "Growth begins at the end of your comfort zone." But the end of the comfort zone is exactly where fear resides. It's the place where we start to feel vulnerable, uncertain, and exposed. This is where fear becomes a powerful teacher.

"Fail fast. People get scared, but you have no idea how many things I've tried just to learn what doesn't work."

Rama Mayo, entrepreneur and founder of Green Street Agency and Hall of Flowers, shared his insights on failure and creativity on *Dualistic Unity*. He emphasizes the importance of embracing failure quickly, using each experience as a lesson for growth rather than something to fear.

When we lean into discomfort, we begin to realize that fear is not the enemy—it's the experience of change. It's where we learn the most about ourselves and what we're capable of. In moments of fear, we are confronted with our limitations, our insecurities, and our vulnerabilities. But it's through confronting these things that we grow.

What if, instead of trying to banish fear, we could use it as fuel? Fear, when embraced, can become a source of energy, motivation, and inspiration. It has the power to propel us forward, to push us toward action, and to ignite the changes we need to make.

When we allow fear to inform us, it can help us break through barriers we didn't even know we had. It can show us the areas of our lives where we've been holding back, playing small, or staying safe. And it can give us the courage to step into those spaces with confidence.

I remember a time when I was faced with a fear that almost kept me from pursuing something important. I had been toying with the idea of offering one-on-one coaching sessions, but the thought of actually doing it filled me with doubt and uncertainty. I kept asking myself, 'Do I have anything of value to offer these people? What if I make things worse?' The fear was real and persistent, and for a while, it held me back.

But then I realized that the fear wasn't there to stop me—it was there to show me where I had been playing small and holding back. Instead of trying to banish the fear, I decided to step into it. I began offering coaching sessions despite the uncertainty, allowing myself to move forward even if I wasn't completely confident. As I embraced the discomfort and took action, I found that the fear actually became a source of energy, pushing me to grow and learn. It didn't just drive me to overcome self-doubt; it also informed a greater degree of sensitivity in my coaching. The fear revealed areas where I might have rushed to give potentially harmful advice just to feel like a 'good coach' and soothe my own anxiety. By staying mindful of my vulnerability, I became more attuned to the needs of those I was helping, connecting more deeply and offering guidance that was both empathetic and effective. What I had initially seen as a barrier turned out to be an opportunity to break through self-imposed limitations and discover a new level of capability.

Fear is a form of energy, and like all energy, it can be harnessed and directed. When we stop resisting fear and start working with it, we can use that energy to fuel our transformation. Fear becomes a source of power, not something that holds us back, but something that propels us forward.

Think of the fear you feel before taking a big step—a new job, a major life decision, or even a creative project. That fear is not a signal to stop; it's a signal to move forward. It's the energy that will push you through the discomfort and into the next phase of your growth. When we embrace fear as fuel, we stop letting it control us and start using it to our advantage.

Something to Reflect On:

Identify one fear you've been avoiding. How does this fear show up in your daily life, and what specific actions have you taken (or not taken) because of it? Rather than resisting it, imagine using this fear as a guide—what small step could you take today to move toward growth and confront this fear directly?

Practical Techniques

Understanding that fear and failure are tools for growth is a powerful realization, but how do we begin applying that knowledge in our everyday lives? It's one thing to acknowledge that fear and failure are part of the journey, but it's another to face them head-on. In this section, we'll explore practical techniques that will help you engage with fear and failure, not as enemies to overcome, but as allies to work with.

The key to facing fear and failure is to meet them with openness, curiosity, and intention. It's about creating space for these experiences and learning how to use them to your advantage. With the following techniques, you'll have tangible tools to help you not only cope with fear and failure but also harness them for your growth.

Reframing Fear Through Journaling

One of the most effective ways to begin facing fear is to bring it into the open. Often, we keep our fears buried, unknowingly allowing them to influence us from the shadows. By writing about your fears, you can bring them into the light, where they can be examined, understood, and reframed.

Exercise: Start by identifying a fear that has been holding you back. This could be something small, like a fear of public speaking, or something larger, like a fear of failure in a career or relationship. Once you've identified the fear, write about it in detail. Describe the fear, where it shows up in your life, and what you believe it is trying to protect you from.

Then, ask yourself these questions:

1. What is this fear trying to teach me?
2. What is the worst possible outcome if I face this fear, and how likely is that outcome?
3. Do I truly know that this is the worst outcome? How certain am I about its likelihood?
4. How could embracing this fear lead to personal growth?

By writing about your fears, you create distance between yourself and the emotion. Fear thrives on vagueness and avoidance, but when you bring it into the open, it begins to lose its power. This journaling process helps you see that fear is not something to avoid—it's something to engage with consciously.

Visualization: Reframing Failure as Feedback

Visualization is a powerful technique for shifting your perspective on failure. Instead of seeing failure as a defeat, you can train your mind to view it as feedback—a natural and essential part of growth.

Exercise: Visualize a recent or anticipated failure. Close your eyes and vividly imagine the event. Picture the moment when you realize you've failed. Instead of focusing on the feelings of defeat or frustration, shift your focus to what this failure is teaching you. What valuable information are you gaining? What lesson is hidden within this experience?

Now, visualize yourself using this new information to try again, with greater clarity and insight. See yourself taking the lesson from the failure and applying it to your next attempt. Imagine the sense of progress and growth that comes from using failure as feedback.

This technique helps retrain your mind to see failure as part of the process, not the end of it. Visualization can be a powerful tool for reshaping how you experience failure, allowing you to approach it with curiosity and openness rather than fear and resistance.

Cultivating Resilience Through Appreciation

Appreciation is a powerful tool for reframing fear and failure. When we practice appreciation, we shift our focus from what's going wrong or what's uncomfortable to recognizing the value in our challenges. This shift in perspective helps us build resilience, allowing us to see fear and failure not as threats but as opportunities for growth.

Exercise: The next time you experience fear or failure, take a moment to reflect on what you can appreciate about the situation. This might feel counterintuitive at first, but with practice, it becomes a powerful way to reframe challenges.

For example, if you fail at a project, pause and consider what you can appreciate about the process. Perhaps the failure taught you a new skill, introduced you to a different perspective, or helped you build relationships. If fear arises before taking a big step, practice appreciating the courage it takes to face the unknown and the opportunity for growth that comes with it.

Appreciation allows you to see the inherent value in every experience. It shifts your focus from avoidance to engagement, helping you recognize that even in moments of discomfort, there is something to learn, something to gain.

"Micro-Failures" for Building Tolerance

One way to build your resilience to failure is by intentionally creating small "micro-failures" in your life. These are low-stakes opportunities to practice failing and learning from it. Micro-failures help normalize the experience of failure, making it less overwhelming when bigger challenges arise.

Exercise: Set yourself a series of small, manageable challenges where failure is a possibility but not a catastrophe. These could include trying a new skill you're unfamiliar with, reaching out to someone you admire for advice (with the possibility of rejection), or taking on a task that stretches your abilities.

The goal is not to seek failure but to expose yourself to situations where you may fail and then learn from the experience. After each micro-failure, take time to reflect on what you learned and how you can adjust your approach in the future. This practice helps desensitize you to the fear of failure and teaches you how to extract valuable lessons from every misstep.

Mindfulness for Facing Fear in the Moment

Fear can feel overwhelming in the moment, especially when it shows up as anxiety, self-doubt, or physical sensations like a racing heart or shortness of breath. Mindfulness is an excellent tool for grounding yourself when fear arises, helping you stay present and reduce the emotional intensity of the fear.

Exercise: The next time you feel fear rising—whether it's before a big presentation, a difficult conversation, or trying something new—practice mindfulness. Start by focusing on your breath. Breathe deeply and slowly, bringing your attention to the physical sensation of the air entering and leaving your body.

As you breathe, acknowledge the fear without trying to push it away. Simply notice it. Where do you feel it in your body? What thoughts are accompanying the fear? Stay present with the fear, allowing it to be there without judgment or resistance.

This practice helps you become less reactive to fear. By staying present with it, you reduce its power over you. Mindfulness allows you to experience fear as a temporary sensation, not something that defines or controls you.

Setting Stretch Goals

A powerful way to engage with both fear and failure is by setting "stretch goals"—goals that push you beyond your comfort zone and make failure a real possibility. The purpose of a stretch goal is not necessarily to succeed but to challenge yourself to grow, knowing that failure is part of the process.

Exercise: Identify one area of your life where you feel stuck or afraid to take a risk. Set a stretch goal in that area—a goal that feels slightly out of reach, but achievable with effort. For example, if you're afraid of public speaking, your stretch goal might be to give a short presentation to a small group. If you're nervous about starting a new project, your stretch goal could be to launch the first step within a week.

By setting stretch goals, you create opportunities for growth through failure. Whether or not you succeed at the goal, the process of stretching yourself builds confidence and resilience. And if you do fail, the lessons you learn from that experience will propel you forward.

Embracing the "Fear Ladder"

A "fear ladder" is a technique used to systematically face fears by gradually exposing yourself to situations that provoke anxiety, starting with smaller, less intimidating steps and working your way up to larger challenges.

Exercise: Identify a fear that has been holding you back—perhaps a fear of confrontation, public speaking, or failure in a particular area. Create a "ladder" of small, manageable actions that lead up to facing the full fear. For example, if you fear public speaking, your ladder might look like this:

> Step 1: Practice speaking in front of a mirror.

> Step 2: Share a brief idea during a meeting.

> Step 3: Speak in front of a small, supportive group.

> Step 4: Give a short presentation to a larger audience.

By gradually working your way up the ladder, you build confidence and resilience with each step. Each rung on the ladder is a small win, helping you face fear in a controlled and intentional way.

 ### Something to Reflect On:

Write down one fear or failure you are facing today. Using the techniques discussed, what is one step you can take to begin embracing that fear or failure as part of your growth?

In this section, we've explored a range of practical techniques for engaging with fear and failure in daily life. Through journaling, visualizing, practicing mindfulness, setting stretch goals, and more, you begin to see fear and failure not as roadblocks but as the fires of the forge—tools for transformation. These practices heat and soften us, allowing life to reshape and strengthen us with each challenge. As you apply them, you'll build resilience, deepen your self-awareness, and unlock your potential to grow in ways you may have never imagined. Fear and failure are no longer forces to avoid, but the essential elements that temper and refine who you are becoming.

Knowing this, the way we relate to fear and failure begins to evolve as we move through life. In the early stages, they may feel like obstacles, external forces that stand in our way. But as we continue to engage with them, we start to recognize that fear and failure are not temporary challenges to be overcome. They are ongoing companions—integral parts of the human experience that guide us toward deeper growth and understanding. The sooner we accept this reality, the more we can use fear and failure as tools for long-term transformation. There is no point in life where we "arrive" and are free from the possibility of failure or the experience of fear. To think that we can eliminate fear or avoid failure is to misunderstand their role in our lives.

Every new challenge, every next step, brings with it the potential for both fear and failure. As we grow and take on more responsibility and venture into uncharted territory, fear will always be present, whispering doubts and uncertainties. But rather than seeing this as a problem, we can learn to expect it. Each new level of growth will naturally evoke new fears, just as each new goal may bring with it the possibility of failure.

This doesn't mean that we are doomed to live in fear or constant failure. It means that these experiences are simply part of the rhythm of the forge. Natural parts of life that we can begin to partner with rather than resist. Resistance is what creates suffering. When we resist fear or try to avoid failure, we create tension within ourselves. We hold back, we second-guess, and we shrink from opportunities for growth.

But when we lean into fear and failure, we open ourselves up to life as it is, not as we wish it would be. We become more adaptable, more willing to take risks, and more accepting of the outcomes, whatever they may be. We stop trying to control every aspect of life and start to trust that, even in moments of fear or failure, there is something to be gained. This is where true resilience is born.

Though it rarely feels like it, one of the greatest gifts of fear and failure is the way they reveal our limitless capacity to adapt. When things are going well, it's easy to feel confident and in control. But it's in the moments of fear and failure that we truly see who we are. These experiences strip away the layers of ego and pretense, leaving us face-to-face with our vulnerabilities, our strengths, and our deepest desires.

There is a certain freedom that comes with this understanding. When we no longer fear fear itself or view failure as something to be ashamed of, we unlock a deeper sense of liberation. We are free to take risks, to try new things, to step into the unknown. We are free to fail and to learn from those failures without attaching our self-worth to the outcome.

Something to Reflect On:

Reflect on a time when fear or failure revealed something unexpected about yourself. How has your understanding of these experiences changed over the years? Consider a current challenge or fear—how might you approach it differently now, using what you've learned to turn it into a tool for growth?

So far, we've explored how fear and failure are not just unavoidable parts of life but are essential to growth and self-discovery. Now, it's time to take the next step: reconciling the fear and failure we still identify with. This is where the transformation becomes real—where we stop seeing fear and failure as signs that we lack value and start recognizing them as necessary steps that have helped us become who we are today.

Think about your life story. Every meaningful experience of growth, every breakthrough, likely came on the heels of fear or failure. These moments didn't derail your journey—they were the journey. They are part of what makes your story powerful and inspiring. By accepting fear and failure as key players in your story, you reclaim your power. You acknowledge that these experiences have shaped you into the person you are today, and that without them, you wouldn't have the depth, resilience, or wisdom you now possess.

Without those moments that you've judged as failures, you wouldn't be on the path you're on now—a journey you could have never anticipated at the time. It's those 'failures' that have molded you into the kind of courageous, open-minded person willing to tackle a book that challenges the traditional narrative of God itself. Embracing these experiences for what they truly are—stepping stones, not setbacks—allows you to see how far you've come and recognize the strength it took to get here.

Something to Reflect On:

Reflect on a significant moment of fear or failure. How did this experience contribute to your personal growth, and what strengths did it reveal in you? Consider how this moment continues to shape your journey today.

By reframing these experiences as integral parts of your story, you change them from setbacks to key moments in your transformation.

And so, once again, we rewrite the story we've been telling ourselves about who we are. Instead of judging ourselves for past mistakes, we begin to see them as unavoidable steps on the path of growth and maturity. We shift from viewing ourselves as people who need to avoid mistakes or sidestep fear, to recognizing that we are resilient, courageous individuals who are constantly evolving. We start to value growth over unerring perfection and understand that our worth is not determined by our successes or failures, but by our willingness to show up and engage with life, no matter what happens.

Throughout this chapter, we've explored the often misunderstood roles of fear and failure in our lives. From the initial dread we feel when confronting these experiences, to their eventual integration into our sense of identity, one thing becomes clear: fear and failure are not enemies. They are allies—persistent, unrelenting forces that push us to grow, evolve, and become more than we ever thought possible.

This realization is transformative. Instead of spending our lives trying to avoid fear and failure, we can learn to embrace them, using them as powerful tools for our personal and collective growth. Fear and failure are not barriers on the path; they are part of the path itself. They are the forces that challenge us to question who we think we are, and in doing so, they open the door to who we could become.

Fear signals where we are on the edge of growth, where we are being asked to move beyond what feels comfortable and familiar. Failure, like stress on a cell, reveals the limits of our current approach, urging us to adapt and evolve. It shows us where adjustments are needed and encourages us to try again with newfound clarity and strength. Together, fear and failure act like a cellular stress response—triggering the pressure needed to catalyze our transformation and build resilience.

This long-term perspective on fear and failure helps us embrace the reality that there is no final destination, no point at which we have "made it" and can relax into a life free from challenges. Life will always ask more of us, and that's a beautiful thing. It means we are constantly evolving, constantly growing, and constantly becoming more aware, resilient, and alive

Something to Reflect On:

How can you begin to embrace fear and failure as lifelong allies in specific areas of your life? Think about a recent situation where you faced fear or experienced a setback. What did it reveal about the limits you've placed on yourself? How can you use that experience to challenge those limits and redefine what's possible for you moving forward?

Each time we choose courage over comfort, we strengthen our ability to face life's challenges with resilience and grace. We stop shrinking from fear and failure and instead move toward them, knowing that they hold the keys to our growth. Courage becomes a habit, something we cultivate daily as we take risks, embrace uncertainty, and step into the unknown.

As we begin to see fear and failure as allies, a new question emerges: What else might we be holding onto that limits our growth?

"Run from what's comfortable. Forget safety. Live where you fear to live. Destroy your reputation. Be notorious."

— Rumi

Chapter 4 - Letting Go

First of all, congratulations. Truly. You've made it this far, and that's something worth celebrating. Not because there's some reward at the end of this process but because the process itself—the willingness to question, to reflect, and to grow—is more courageous and fulfilling than we often realize. It's not easy to dig into the foundations of who you are and start asking questions that most avoid. But you're still here. Still willing to peel back the layers and see what lies beneath. That's no small thing.

So, as we move into this next chapter together, take a moment to recognize that. Honor the fact that you are here, reading these words, and that your curiosity, your willingness to explore yourself more deeply, is its own kind of victory.

Now, let's dive into something that touches all of us—control. As we've explored in earlier chapters, our desire for control is deeply rooted in the need for security. We cling to familiar roles, beliefs, and outcomes as though they can shield us from the unpredictability of life. We've used the metaphor of clinging to a rock in a fast-moving river—gripping it tightly because the current feels too overwhelming to navigate. Yet, just like the river's flow, life unfolds regardless of our attempts to hold on.

Control gives us the illusion of safety, like gripping the steering wheel in a storm, believing that if we just hold on tighter, we can steer our way to calm waters. But here's the thing—most of the time, that wheel isn't actually connected to the rudder. It's like trying to steer a ship without control, while the storm continues unabated. The chaos, the uncertainty, the change—they keep unfolding, no matter how hard we try to steer the ship.

Still, we cling to the idea of control. Why? Because the alternative—not having control—feels terrifying. The unknown feels like a threat. We've been trained to believe that we *must* know what's next, that we need a plan, a backup plan, and even a backup for the backup. That's how we've been taught to survive in life.

But what if I told you that the very act of gripping so tightly is the reason you feel so powerless? This is something we've touched on before—the idea that all this effort to control the uncontrollable might actually be holding you back. Like the attachments we've discussed and the desire for a fixed narrative, our need for control acts as a heavy weight, limiting our sensitivity and preventing us from moving with life's currents. Instead of flowing freely, we find ourselves exhausted, constantly struggling against the natural tide.

> "If you realize that all things change, there is nothing you will try to hold on to."
>
> — Tao Te Ching

In this chapter, we'll explore control in more detail—not just control over outcomes or situations, but also over ourselves: the stories we tell, the expectations we carry, and the constant need to have everything figured out.

As we move forward, remember: this isn't about having all the answers. It's about staying open to the questions.

Something to Reflect On:

Think of a recent situation where you tried to control the outcome. How did that effort make you feel? Did things unfold as you expected, or were you surprised by the result? Write down how your attachment to control shaped your experience.

The concept of control doesn't just appear out of nowhere. It's an assumption about life that we adopt very early, often without even realizing it. From our first steps, the belief that we can—or should— have control shapes how we respond to uncertainty. Everywhere we look, we see the idea reinforced: if we put in effort, we should see a result. Naturally, we come to believe that the right effort, done with precision, should yield a specific outcome. For example, we put effort into walking, and we learned to walk. But learning to walk didn't guarantee that we wouldn't stumble, fall, or end up somewhere different from where we thought we'd arrive.

The reality is that we don't truly have control—only influence. Yet, we struggle to recognize this consistently. To understand why we cling so tightly to the illusion of control, we need to examine where it originates and how it's reinforced throughout our lives. By taking a closer look, we can begin to see control for what it really is: a learned behavior based on assumption, not a fundamental truth.

At its core, the need for control is rooted in our relationship with the unknown. When the future feels uncertain, our minds instinctively seek ways to create a sense of safety. As we touched on in Chapter 2, this drive isn't just a modern psychological quirk; it's hardwired into us through evolution. Our ancestors didn't have the luxury of simply hoping for the best. They needed to understand their environment and how to influence it to survive. This meant recognizing patterns, making assumptions, and acting on those assumptions—whether it was predicting weather changes, gathering and storing food, or dealing with predators. In those days, exerting some influence over the world wasn't a matter of preference; it was a matter of survival. Over time, our brains adapted to anticipate, plan, and exert control as ways to navigate the inherent uncertainty of life.

And as we shaped the world with our will over thousands of years—building cities, roads, technology, and more—we found ourselves surrounded by the illusion of control. Despite the obvious reality that none of these things last forever, we have become so accustomed to the appearance that they do, that we now make the absurd assumption that control is no longer just a concept or assumption but a real possibility. The more we molded the world to our preferences, the deeper this illusion of control took root, making it harder to recognize that life remains as unpredictable as it has always been.

While we've evolved beyond almost all of the physical dangers our ancestors faced, our desire for control remains undiminished. The saber-toothed tiger has been replaced by looming deadlines, difficult conversations, and the fear of failing to meet societal expectations. The underlying mechanism—fear of the unknown—remains as strong as ever, despite how many unknowns we've seemingly conquered. In fact, it has evolved into something more abstract and pervasive. Today, our fears are not about immediate physical survival but rather about the survival of our identity and sense of self-worth.

From early childhood, we are exposed to a way of life largely free from primal dangers, where survival depends more on emotionally and psychologically adapting to a world that appears carefully managed and structured, in contrast to the unpredictable and threatening experience of our ancestors. Within this new, modern environment, without the heightened awareness that uncertainty and danger demand, our minds begin to prioritize a different kind of need shaped by society's growing fixation on the promise of internal control offered by our characters and attachments—such as the need to avoid losing value or certainty. This shift is evident in Maslow's hierarchy of needs, where love, belonging, self-worth, and recognition are treated as necessities rather than natural outcomes of self-acceptance, flowing with life as it unfolds, building relationships with open hands, and being willing to release attachments.

Think of the first time a child is separated from a parent, left at daycare, or with a new caregiver. That initial anxiety is rooted in a loss of control: "Did I do something to make them reject me?" "What if I don't fit in with my new environment or group?" These questions may not be conscious, but the emotional response is undeniable. Children learn, often in subtle ways, that when things feel unpredictable, they must do something to regain a sense of safety in their relationships with others—whether it's crying to attract attention or adapting their behavior to meet perceived expectations.

It's important to recognize that this behavior in children is completely normal. Our species has evolved into this new way of living, and it is through us that society continues to transform. However, rather than aspiring to mature beyond these needs in adulthood, our society often convinces us that the approval of others is an absolute necessity for our survival. But framing social contact as an innate need is misguided; a person does not die the moment they are alone, and loneliness does not have to be a debilitating fixation. When we treat social connection as an essential requirement, it can pressure individuals to conform to harmful social norms, remain in toxic relationships, or tolerate manipulative dynamics to avoid isolation at any cost. It may also leave us vulnerable to exploitation, where the fear of alienation is used as a control mechanism in authoritarian systems or unhealthy group settings.

By recognizing that social connection is not a rigid need but rather an important enhancer of life, we can reduce the anxiety surrounding loneliness and cultivate a healthier relationship with solitude. This perspective allows us to prioritize the quality of our relationships over the need to fit in, finding fulfillment in meaningful connections without compromising our authenticity. Understanding that solitude can be a source of growth and resilience enables us to navigate social interactions on our own terms, fostering a sense of autonomy that empowers us to walk away from unhealthy situations without fear.

As we grow, societal conditioning reinforces our attachment to control, which becomes a key factor in how we perceive our self-worth and confidence in achieving success. Throughout school, we're taught that doing things right equates to greater personal value, and the message is clear: those who meticulously plan, work hard, and stay disciplined are the ones who will thrive. Meanwhile, those who choose to "let go" or "go with the flow" are often labeled as irresponsible or naive. This conditioning extends beyond academics; success in school, work, and relationships is framed as a measure of how effectively we can control our circumstances. Society instills in us the belief that staying on top of it all is not just the path to achievement—it's seen as a direct reflection of our value as individuals.

Think about how we're rewarded for "staying in control" throughout our lives. In school, we're praised for following the rules, managing time efficiently, and keeping our emotions in check. Later, in our careers, we're valued for staying on top of tasks, meeting deadlines, and organizing resources effectively. Control isn't just encouraged—it's glorified. We're led to believe that the more we manage, the better we are. If we control our circumstances, we're told, success and happiness will follow.

Consider the language we use: "Take control of your destiny," "Be the master of your fate," "Control your emotions." These phrases suggest that control is not only necessary but noble. Losing control, on the other hand, is seen as a weakness, a mistake. We come to believe that without it, we might unravel or lose our place in the world.

But what happens when life throws something at us that we can't control? Illness, job loss, relationship breakdowns—these are the moments that reveal just how fragile our carefully built control systems really are. No matter how meticulously we plan, life often has its own agenda. It's in these moments—when control slips through our hands—that we realize it was never ours to begin with.

As we continue to notice and unravel these patterns, it becomes clear that control is often just a shield for fear—fear rooted in the needs of the character we've committed to playing and the stones it chooses to carry into the river of life. We tell ourselves that if we can control the outcomes, we can avoid the uncomfortable emotions. Our need for control often arises from the fear that if we let go, everything will fall apart, leaving us feeling naked, alone, and afraid. Yet, in reality, it's our clinging to these attachments and stories that creates the very confusion and isolation we're trying to escape.

One of the clearest ways control manifests is in our desire to manage how others perceive us. We carefully curate our image, making calculated decisions about how we present ourselves, while avoiding vulnerability because being real feels too risky. Yet, this control comes at a rising price: it creates a gap that continues to widen between who we truly are and the image we show the world. That gap becomes a source of conflict and discontent, trapping us in a cycle of maintaining appearances rather than embracing our true selves.

Just as we attempt to control how others perceive us, we also strive to control ourselves—our thoughts, emotions, and behaviors. We're taught to "control our temper," "manage our impulses," and "take control of our destiny." But this is not only an impossibility; it's a dangerous belief. The idea that we can fully dictate our inner world is misleading and sets us up for frustration and self-blame because thoughts and emotions often arise spontaneously, beyond our conscious control. While we can influence how we respond to them, even those responses are shaped by deeper conditioning and subconscious patterns. Our inner experiences happen naturally, and efforts to control them can create the same tension and disconnect that we feel when we try to manage our outward image.

Emotions naturally arise in response to situations, people, or memories, ebbing and flowing in their own time. While we can influence how we respond to them, the emotions themselves are not something we can control. They are as natural as waves in the ocean, rising and falling in response to the currents of life.

Reflect on a time when you tried to suppress or control your emotions. What was the emotional result of trying to maintain control? Did it lead to frustration, exhaustion, or a sense of failure? Now, imagine allowing your emotions to arise naturally without judgment or the need to control them. How do you think this would change your relationship with those emotions? What would it feel like to accept and observe your emotions instead of suppressing them?

This doesn't mean we're helpless in the face of our thoughts and emotions, but it does mean that the kind of control we seek — the ability to dictate and manage every internal experience — is an illusion. By trying to control these internal processes, we create unnecessary tension and resistance. The harder we try to suppress or manipulate our thoughts and emotions, the more they push back, demanding to be felt or acknowledged.

This constant tension is like walking through life while holding your breath, always anticipating the next thing that could go wrong. But living this way limits our ability to experience life fully, with all its unpredictability and messiness. Releasing control doesn't mean becoming passive or indifferent. Instead, it's about recognizing when the need for control is holding us back and finding the courage to embrace uncertainty.

Amelia Earhart exemplified what it means to trust the unknown. Her willingness to let go of the need to predict every outcome allowed her to navigate each flight with a sense of freedom, embracing life's inherent uncertainty and making history in the process. While her final journey ended in disappearance, it's undeniable that she truly lived before then, embodying the courage to follow her passions. As she once said, "The fears are paper tigers. You can do anything you decide to do... the process is its own reward." Her life reminds us that letting go is not about guaranteeing a safe outcome but about trusting the journey, embracing the risks, and living fully, even when the future remains uncertain.

But this isn't just about extraordinary figures from history. Consider Sarah, a member of the Dualistic Unity community and project manager at a tech firm, who always felt the need to control every aspect of her team's work. Every email had to be reviewed, every meeting micro-managed. But as the projects grew larger, Sarah realized she was burning out and losing the trust of her team. She decided to let go—allowing her team to take more ownership. To her surprise, not only did the quality of the work improve, but she found more time for creative thinking and long-term strategy. By loosening her grip, Sarah gained the freedom to focus on what truly mattered.

The more we let go of our need for control, the more we align ourselves with life's natural flow. And within that flow, we find a different kind of power—one that comes not from controlling outcomes, but from trusting the process itself.

 **Something to Reflect On:**

Reflect on a recent experience where you initially resisted letting go of control but eventually had no choice but to surrender. How did your perspective or emotional state change after accepting the situation? What did you learn about your relationship with uncertainty? Write down any insights that emerged during this process.

As we start to let go of control, the first thing we notice is often a shift in our mindset. For many, it feels like a weight being lifted off their shoulders—like all the tension, anxiety, and pressure that came with trying to control everything suddenly fades, leaving space for something lighter.

"Be like a tree and let the dead leaves drop."

— Rumi

This release comes from realizing that in letting go, we're not actually losing anything. In fact, we gain freedom from the constant stress of managing, predicting, and trying to control outcomes. It's a radical shift in perspective—moving us from a mindset of scarcity and fear to one of trust and openness.

Maya Angelou's life exemplifies the strength of surrender. Despite facing systemic racism, poverty, and abuse, she chose to rise above circumstances she couldn't control. Through her memoir *I Know Why the Caged Bird Sings*, Angelou reflected on how we may not control everything that happens to us, but we always have the choice in our response.

"You may not control all the events that happen to you, but you can decide not to be reduced by them."

— Maya Angelou

Her story serves as a reminder that letting go is not about giving up but about finding strength and dignity in how we respond to the uncontrollable.

Something to Reflect On:

Consider a time when letting go of control led to an unexpected positive outcome in your life. What fears did you have beforehand, and how did the actual experience compare to your expectations? Reflect on how this could influence your approach to situations where you still feel the need to tightly manage the outcome.

When we let go, we stop fighting against the current of life. Instead, we allow ourselves to move with it, letting life carry us in the direction it's already flowing. And here's the beautiful part: life's flow often takes us to places we never anticipated, places we might not have chosen if we were trying to control every step. In letting go, we find a sense of ease and relief that comes from no longer having to manage every outcome, freeing ourselves to experience life with greater spontaneity and openness.

But how do we trust the flow when everything in us screams for control? It starts with small acts of surrender. We begin by recognizing that life has been flowing all along, whether or not we were actively trying to control it. Think about the moments in your life when things worked out without your interference—maybe a conversation led to an unexpected opportunity, or a problem resolved itself in a way you never could have planned. These moments might feel miraculous, but they remind us that sometimes the best thing we can do is step back and let life unfold on its own.

Letting go isn't about passivity or losing direction—it's about changing how we relate to life as it unfolds. Rather than trying to control every detail, we learn to trust our ability to adapt as things fall into place. Instead of obsessing over the outcome, we focus on how we show up in each moment, trusting that we'll continue to adjust and respond as needed.

This shift from control to trust is gradual and requires patience. As we practice letting go in small ways, we gradually build confidence in our ability to navigate life's uncertainties. Unexpected outcomes can often bring surprising opportunities for growth and alignment, reminding us that surrendering control can lead to possibilities beyond our initial plans.

When we let go of the need to control outcomes, we open ourselves to new opportunities for growth. Suddenly, life has room to surprise us. Instead of rigidly sticking to our plan, we become flexible, adaptable, and open to the unexpected. And it's often in these unexpected moments that we experience the most profound growth.

Think about the process of personal transformation. Real change rarely happens in controlled environments. It happens when we're pushed into new experiences, challenged by uncertainty, and forced to adapt. Letting go creates space for these transformative moments. It allows us to move beyond the limits of our plans and step into the unknown, where real growth happens.

From an early age, we are conditioned to believe that self-control is not only possible but necessary for success and happiness. We're told to control our tempers, resist our impulses, and stay disciplined in our pursuit of goals. This conditioning creates a strong sense of identification with the idea that we *should* be able to control ourselves—that we are somehow failing if we cannot.

But this belief is based on a misunderstanding of how the mind and emotions work. As we've discussed, thoughts and emotions arise naturally, often without our conscious control. And yet, we judge ourselves harshly when we can't "get it together," when we feel anger bubbling up despite our best efforts to stay calm, or when our mind races with anxiety even though we know we *should* relax.

This conditioning runs deep. It teaches us to see self-control as a measure of worth, discipline, or strength. We praise those who seem "in control" of their emotions and behaviors, and we view those who struggle with self-control as weak or undisciplined. But this is a false dichotomy. It's not about strength or weakness—it's about understanding the nature of the mind and emotions.

What happens when we let go of the need to control ourselves? What happens when we stop fighting against our natural thoughts and emotions and instead allow them to arise and pass without judgment?

When we stop resisting a thought, it passes through like a cloud in the sky.

Observing our thoughts and emotions without judgment or attachment allows us to see the futility of trying to control them. By simply watching the mind and its movements, we free ourselves from the struggle to manage or suppress our inner world. In this state of pure observation, we begin to sense a deeper intelligence at play—the natural ebb and flow of the mind and emotions, which require no interference to function.

Letting go of self-control opens the door to authenticity. When we stop trying to shape ourselves into a fixed image or mold, we allow ourselves to be who we truly are in each moment. This authenticity is not something we need to work toward; it is our natural state when we stop trying to control how we are perceived or how we experience life.

By now, we've explored the struggles of control in various forms— over our circumstances, others, and even ourselves. Through this journey, we've seen how the constant effort to manage a "controllable" identity can create tension and discontent. But as we've discovered, letting go of this need for control allows us to free ourselves from the exhausting pursuit of being a certain way, thinking certain thoughts, or feeling certain emotions to be worthy or whole. In embracing this letting go, we realize that we are already whole, already enough, without the need to control or manage anything.

This realization brings about the same profound sense of freedom that embracing the forge does. We no longer feel the need to fight against our own nature or the nature of life. Instead, we can move through the world with a sense of ease, trusting that life—and the self—will continue to unfold in its own way. Yet, even with this understanding, we often resist going with the natural flow, fearing that letting go will lead to chaos. We worry that without control, we'll be exposed to random, unpredictable events.

Something to Reflect On:

 Reflect on a recent situation where you noticed your impulse to control your thoughts or emotions. How has your understanding of control shifted since beginning this chapter, and how might you approach similar situations differently now?

Think about how cells operate in the body. There isn't a single authority dictating each interaction; instead, cells adapt and respond fluidly to their surroundings, maintaining balance and health. In the same way, letting go allows us to find a natural rhythm, where we respond to life's changes without the constant need to manage every detail. The tension arises not from the flow of life itself, but from our resistance to it.

The struggle with control comes from deeply rooted assumptions and habits—patterns we've been unraveling as we've worked through each chapter. Embracing the flow isn't always easy because our minds are conditioned by our environment and primal instincts to seek certainty, create plans, predict outcomes, and avoid surprises in response to self-made stakes born out of confusion. So how do we reconcile this ingrained desire for safety with the fact that life is inherently unpredictable?

This shift from attachment to openness doesn't happen overnight. It requires frequent practice, patience, and a willingness to sit with discomfort. But as we gradually loosen our grip on specific outcomes, we begin to see life in a new way. We come to understand that while we can set intentions and take action, we are not in control of every detail or result—and that's not only okay, it's liberating.

As we embrace the flow of life, a remarkable transformation occurs: the feeling of freedom and creativity becomes a guiding light, leading us out of the illusion of control and its promises of temporary happiness. No longer confined by rigid plans or fixed outcomes, we open ourselves to inspiration, intuition, and fresh ways of thinking. Rather than forcing solutions, we allow ideas and possibilities to emerge naturally, finding joy in the unfolding process.

In many ways, the solution is counterintuitive, much like the lessons we've explored in previous chapters. Instead of seeking control as a means to fulfillment, we find that the more we allow ourselves to fully engage with life—embracing its unpredictability and immersing ourselves in the present moment—the less necessary control becomes. The experience itself becomes the teacher, showing us that a truly engaged and fulfilling life arises not from managing every detail, but from letting life unfold on its own terms. As we trust the process, the need for control gradually loses its grip, and we realize that a deeper sense of freedom and contentment is found not in trying to secure happiness, but in allowing it to emerge naturally.

Creativity thrives when we let go of the need to steer the ship through every wave and gust. When we stop clinging to control, we give ourselves permission to explore, adapt, and sail with the wind instead of against it. We stop worrying about charting a "flawless" course and start embracing the journey itself. This applies not only to artistic endeavors but to life as a whole.

In many ways, life is like navigating a ship through an open sea. Each day, we co-create our experience with the ever-changing waters and winds around us. When we embrace the uncertainty of the storm, we tap into a deeper level of creativity—one that isn't limited by fear, control, or attachment. We start seeing challenges as opportunities to adjust our sails, obstacles as chances to find new routes, and the unknown as an open horizon full of unexplored possibilities.

Living without fixating on the illusion of control not only enhances our creativity, it also deepens our connection to others. When we're no longer trying to manipulate outcomes—whether in relationships or social situations—we become more present, more authentic, and more open to genuine connection.

This openness also helps us connect more deeply with ourselves. By letting go of the need to manage every part of our inner world, we create space to explore who we truly are beyond the labels, expectations, and judgments we place on ourselves. We begin to realize that our worth isn't tied to how well we control our lives or meet external standards. Instead, we discover that our worth is inherent—something that doesn't need to be earned or proven.

Something to Reflect On:

Reflect on how your perspective on control and flow has shifted while working through this chapter. What insights have emerged, and how might they influence the way you approach challenges or unexpected changes moving forward?

As we come to the end of this chapter, it's time to reflect on everything we've explored so far: the illusion of control, the deep roots of our need to manage life, our assumptions of what fear and failure mean, the freedom that comes with surrendering our need for a specific outcome, and the natural flow that awaits us when we finally let go. There's a powerful insight at the heart of all of this: in letting go, we don't lose power—we gain something far greater. We gain the ability to move with life, to trust the process, and to experience the unknown with curiosity instead of fear. We discover that there's power hidden in powerlessness.

The counterintuitive nature of this truth is what makes it so difficult to grasp. How can strength emerge from surrender? How can letting go bring clarity? And yet, it's in the release of our need to dominate, predict, and force outcomes that we tap into a deeper, more aligned sense of power—one that doesn't rely on external validation or certainty. It's the strength of trusting in life itself, of recognizing that even when things don't go according to plan, we are still exactly where we need to be.

When we think of power, we often associate it with control—control over our circumstances, others, or even ourselves. But the kind of power we're exploring here goes beyond that. It's about aligning with life's rhythm and understanding that we don't need to control every outcome to be okay. True power emerges when we let go of the illusion that we must direct every detail, recognizing that we are part of something far greater than the small sense of self that tries to hold the reins.

The power of this partnership is rooted in trust—trust in the process, trust in our ability to adapt, and trust that whatever happens, we have the inner resources to handle it. We stop resisting the inevitable changes and challenges that life brings, and instead, we learn to navigate them with grace and ease. In this state, we're no longer fighting the storm but moving with it, finding power in our ability to respond rather than react.

There's also a profound sense of freedom that comes from embracing our powerlessness over certain aspects of life. By acknowledging that we can't control everything—whether it's other people's actions, the future, or even our own thoughts and emotions—we free ourselves from the exhausting effort of trying to manage the unmanageable. We stop wasting energy on what we cannot change, and instead focus on what we can influence: our presence, openness, and willingness to engage with life as it is—not as we wish it to be.

In this freedom, we find room for spontaneity, creativity, and joy. Life becomes less about following a rigid plan and more about showing up fully for whatever each moment brings. We learn to embrace uncertainty as an integral part of the adventure rather than something to be feared or avoided.

This freedom extends to our relationship with ourselves as well. When we stop trying to control every thought, emotion, or behavior, we allow ourselves to be more authentic, more human. We begin to accept that we don't need to be perfect and that our worth isn't tied to how well we manage or control our lives. We realize that our true strength lies in our capacity to be present, adaptable, and open to whatever comes our way.

This journey of letting go is not one we take in isolation. Even though the path to surrender may feel deeply personal, it's a shared experience—one that connects us to others in ways we might not expect. By embracing the flow of life, we begin to see that we are all navigating the same currents, each of us learning to let go of control in our own way and at our own pace.

As we surrender our need for control, we realize that we are not separate from the rest of life. While each of us may feel alone in our personal journey, we are all in that experience together. Yes, we are alone, but we're alone together.

When we embrace this sense of interconnectedness, we discover a deeper sense of belonging. We're not struggling in isolation; we're part of a collective process, moving with the same currents, facing challenges, and experiencing joys in our own unique ways. This shared flow reminds us that we're never truly alone, even as our experiences differ. Each moment offers a new opportunity to practice living in this flow with acceptance, attention, and sensitivity—whether it's letting go of a minor irritation, releasing the urge to control an outcome at work, or simply allowing an emotion to arise and pass.

As we close this chapter, I want to leave you with an invitation: to trust life, even in its uncertainty. Trust that you don't need to control every outcome or have all the answers in order to be okay. Trust that by letting go, you are not losing power, but stepping into a deeper, more authentic kind of strength.

Let go of the need to manage every detail, to predict every outcome, or to control every emotion. Instead, repeatedly invite yourself to be present with life as it unfolds. Trust that, like gripping a steering wheel in a storm, sometimes loosening your hold allows life to carry you more smoothly—even when you don't know exactly where it's taking you.

What remains when there is no need to hold on, no fixed identity to defend, and no outcomes to chase? Perhaps, in the space left behind, we find something far more enduring—a quiet presence, a deeper sense of being that doesn't require labels or validation. In the absence of the need to manage and define, we may begin to uncover a freedom that feels surprisingly familiar, as though it was there all along, just waiting to be noticed.

"Letting go gives us freedom, and freedom is
the only condition for happiness. If, in our
heart, we still cling to anything—anger,
anxiety, or possessions—we cannot be free."

— Thich Nhat Hanh

Chapter 5 - The Power of Authenticity

Merriam-Webster's 2023 Word of the Year was "authentic".

The definition is as follows:

1. not false or imitation
2. true to one's own personality, spirit, or character is sincere and authentic with no pretensions

Let's break this down, knowing what we do now, and see how these definitions hold up when examined in the context of our discussions.

"Not false or imitation: real, actual"

At first glance, this definition seems clear—something authentic is "real" or "actual." However, when we examine what it means to be "real," especially in the context of personal identity, the term becomes elusive. What does it mean for someone to be a "real" person? Is it a matter of fulfilling certain roles or expectations, or is it about expressing something deeper? In earlier chapters, we've explored how much of what we think is "real" about ourselves is shaped by societal influences and external labels. Without questioning these influences, the idea of being "real" can still be based on inherited roles or personas that may feel comfortable but aren't necessarily a true reflection of one's deeper nature. So, the definition lacks clarity unless we examine what it means to be "real" beyond social constructs.

"True to one's own personality, spirit, or character"

This definition introduces the idea of being true to oneself, but what exactly does it mean to be "true" to one's own personality, spirit, or character? If our personality has been shaped by cultural conditioning, societal expectations, or even past experiences, then adhering to that personality could simply mean reinforcing an identity that isn't freely chosen. Earlier chapters encouraged us to question whether these aspects of identity are genuinely ours or are constructs we've come to accept over time. The idea of being "true to oneself" can therefore be misleading if we haven't first questioned who or what that "self" actually is. It risks becoming another form of attachment to a fixed idea of identity, rather than allowing space for an evolving, fluid self.

Without the discussions we've had, these definitions can create confusion. They imply that being "authentic" is about matching some established criteria of "realness" or "truth," yet they don't address the deeper question of how we come to recognize or define those criteria in the first place. Our previous chapters have looked into how much of our identity is shaped by external influences, attachments, fears, and societal norms, making it clear that understanding authenticity requires peeling back these layers to discover what lies beneath them.

> "To be yourself in a world that is constantly trying to make you something else is the greatest accomplishment."
>
> — Ralph Waldo Emerson

Through our explorations, we've seen again and again that authenticity is not about meeting an objective standard or adhering to a fixed sense of self. In Taoism, the metaphor of the mirror is often used to represent clarity and the ability to reflect reality as it is, without distortion. A mirror, in its natural state, reflects everything clearly and impartially. However, over time, dust and grime accumulate on its surface, obscuring its ability to reflect with accuracy. In a similar way, we each begin life like a pristine mirror, capable of reflecting the world without the distortions of external conditioning. But as we move through life, society imposes labels and expectations that cloud our natural clarity. We become 'successful' or 'unsuccessful,' 'outgoing' or 'reserved,' 'driven' or 'lazy.' As time goes on, these roles restrict our perception, leaving us feeling incomplete and disconnected from our authentic selves.

The challenge, of course, is that society often doesn't make space for the kind of authenticity we've been discussing here. We are encouraged and convinced to 'fit in,' to align with the expectations of the collective. This creates an internal conflict—between the desire to be true to ourselves and the pressure to be accepted. However, authenticity isn't about rebelling for the sake of rebellion or rejecting societal norms out of spite. It involves living in alignment with your self-honesty while being mindful of your circumstances. It's about navigating the balance between expressing who you truly are and considering the realities of your environment. Authenticity requires awareness, not only of your inner experiences but also of the potential impact and consequences of your actions.

As Lao Tzu wrote in the *Tao Te Ching*: 'He who knows himself is enlightened.' This wisdom reminds us that the journey to authenticity isn't really a journey at all. It is in knowing and accepting ourselves as we are that we unlock authenticity.

Something to Reflect On:

Reflect on a time when you felt most in tune with your clear reflection, free from the need to perform for others or fit into societal roles. How did that moment feel? How did it change your interactions with others?

A large part of self-acceptance is self-awareness. Over time, we've adapted to meet the expectations of others—whether through the professional identity we present at work, the agreeable side we show to friends, or the persona we adopt with family. These roles were originally created and learned to help us fit in, but they can distance us from our authentic selves. It can help to remember that they don't disappear simply because we want them to. When we feel afraid, it's natural to revert to these lifelong strategies, falling back into old habits and conditioned responses because they have served us as defenses for so long.

We took on these responses, beliefs, and roles under the assumption that they would protect us from judgment, rejection, and suffering. Yet, as we're coming to realize, they often come at the cost of our true potential. It's through that recognition that the mirror becomes clearer.

The issue isn't just that we adopt these personas; it's that we rarely take the time to reflect on what drives them or explore who we are underneath. Often, we don't even realize we're doing it. Consider the different roles you play in life—partner, parent, employee, friend. In each situation, you may present a slightly different version of yourself to meet the expectations of that environment. This is common, but the more you shift between these roles, the harder it becomes to understand who you are at your core.

Something to Reflect On:

What roles or personas do you find yourself playing most often in different settings, such as work, family, and social situations? Which of these feels most disconnected from your authentic self?

These facades protect us from vulnerability. They act as camouflage, preventing others from seeing our imperfections, uncertainties, and fears. But in doing so, they also prevent us from being seen for who we truly are. Authenticity requires vulnerability. It means letting people see not just the polished, perfected performance but the messy, unflattering parts too. And while that can feel scary, it's also where the real magic of connection happens.

During a talk in New York in 1970, Jiddu Krishnamurti said, "To be is to be related." In this context, "to be" is not about performing a role or fitting into a predefined identity. It's about being open, transparent, and connected to the moment and the people around you. The roles we play, however, create distance. They keep us at arm's length from the people we interact with, preventing genuine connection. When we're constantly performing, we might feel admired, respected, or even loved, but the truth is that it's the act being loved, not us.

You can't change what you don't recognize. Start by noticing when and where you feel the need to adopt a persona. Is it around certain people? In specific situations? Do you wear it to feel in control, to avoid judgment, or to fit in? Awareness is key because, without it, the roles will continue to feel like part of you. But once you can see them for what they are, you can begin to loosen their hold.

It's also important to understand that doesn't mean you have to reject all the roles you play in life. You can still be a leader at work, a caretaker at home, or a peacekeeper among friends. But the difference is that you'll be approaching these roles from a place of awareness rather than performance. You'll no longer be acting out of fear or obligation but from a deeper sense of alignment with who you truly are.

Something to Reflect On:

Reflect on the personas you adopt in different areas of your life. Make a list of the roles you play and consider: Which ones feel authentic, and which feel like performances? Where do you feel most comfortable being your true self, and where do you feel the need to hide behind a persona? The aim is not to judge or criticize, but to increase awareness of how authentically you present yourself to the world.

Once you've identified these roles, consider how they shape your interactions. Do they help you connect more deeply with others, or do they keep you from being truly seen? Authenticity involves recognizing the roles you play and deciding whether they align with who you truly are or if it's time to let them go.

The process of shedding conditioned responses takes time. It's not about changing everything at once, but about gradually examining these roles with compassion and curiosity. As you do, you'll begin to rediscover a version of yourself that feels freer, more aware, and more in tune with your true nature. In this way, you'll continuously uncover authenticity—not as something to achieve, but as something that has always been within you, hidden beneath layers of societal conditioning.

Living authentically takes courage. It's not easy to stand apart from the stories we've told ourselves or the expectations others have placed on us. The world often encourages us to fit into predefined molds, to act in ways that are comfortable for others, and to follow paths that lead to predictable outcomes. Authenticity disrupts that.

It often requires us to go against the grain, to step into the unknown, and to reveal the parts of ourselves that may not align with societal expectations. But this courage—the courage to be—is at the heart of living a fulfilling, authentic life.

Be who the fuck you are at this very moment, because if you are that, you will literally thrive in the time that you are physically here."

Shaun T, renowned fitness expert, emphasized the power of living authentically during his appearance on Dualistic Unity. His story shows how embracing who you truly are, without conforming to external expectations, leads to personal freedom and success.

Courage here doesn't mean boldness or defiance. It's not about fighting the world or shouting your truth at every opportunity. Instead, it's a quiet, steady commitment to live with who you truly are, even when others meet that truth with judgment, resistance, or misunderstanding. The courage to live authentically means embracing the openness of being yourself—allowing yourself to be seen fully, raw and real, without hiding behind the personas society has carved for you.

You've already reflected on how conditioning shapes us to believe that certain versions of ourselves are more acceptable than others. It takes courage to break free from these subtle forms of conformity, to step beyond the comfort of familiar roles and expectations, and to fully embrace the unique expression of who you are.

Alan Watts often spoke about the concept of *wu wei*—a Taoist principle that refers to "effortless action" or the art of going with the natural flow of life rather than fighting against it. Authenticity, in many ways, is about embracing *wu wei*. It's not about striving to *be* anything; it's about allowing yourself to exist naturally, without forcing yourself into a box or trying to meet external expectations. When we live authentically, we're not fighting to prove ourselves. We're simply allowing ourselves to *be*, in the most effortless and natural way possible.

But that doesn't always feel easy to do. Fear often gets in the way. Fear of rejection, fear of failure, fear of being misunderstood. We worry that if we show our true selves, we'll be judged or excluded. We fear that our authentic selves aren't enough—that they won't measure up to the ideals that have been imposed on us. These fears are powerful, and they can keep us trapped in inauthentic, hollow roles for years, even decades.

But here's the thing: the fear of being authentic is absurd. It's based on the false belief that who you are isn't enough but a carefully curated version of you somehow is. There's no legitimate evidence to support this—it's just a story we tell ourselves. But that belief is the very thing keeping you from experiencing the freedom and fulfillment that comes with living authentically.

To embrace authenticity, you must first confront this fear. You must ask yourself: *What am I so afraid of?* What do you believe will happen if you stop pretending and start being honest? Often, the things we fear most—judgment, rejection, failure—will happen whether or not we live authentically. People will always have opinions, no matter what version of yourself you present to the world. But the difference is, when you live authentically, you're no longer trying to control those opinions. You're no longer trying to manipulate how others see you. And that's incredibly liberating.

Think of a stem cell in the body, full of potential yet undefined. Over time, it responds to signals from its environment and naturally transforms into a specialized cell—a neuron, a muscle cell, or a skin cell—each with its own unique role. It doesn't force itself to become something else or worry about how it compares to other cells. It simply follows its natural path of growth, becoming what it was always meant to be. In the same way, living authentically is about allowing yourself to unfold according to your own nature and circumstances. Instead of trying to conform to external expectations or fit into predefined molds, you embrace who you truly are, shaped by your unique journey, without worrying about how you measure up to others.

Authenticity doesn't mean you'll never make mistakes or face challenges. In fact, living authentically often involves stumbling, falling, and learning along the way. But the difference is that when you're authentic, these experiences don't diminish you. They simply become part of your journey. You stop seeing failure as something to avoid at all costs and start seeing it as feedback—a necessary part of growth.

As discussed earlier, it takes courage to reframe failure in this way. We live in a world that often equates failure with losing value, but when you look closely, you'll notice that the most authentic people—those who live in alignment with their true selves—are often the ones who have faced the most failure. Why? Because authenticity requires stepping into the unknown, taking risks without the guarantee of success or approval. Yet, the reward for embracing that risk is far greater than anything you can gain by playing it safe.

Something to Reflect On:

In what areas of your life are you holding back your true self to gain approval or acceptance? Consider your relationships, career, and personal goals. Where are your choices driven by what you think others want, rather than by your own true desires? What would it look like to let go of that need for approval and live in alignment with your authentic self?

As you reflect on these questions, you might notice that fear shows up in surprising ways. It might disguise itself as practicality, telling you that it's too risky to pursue what you really want. It might show up as modern perfectionism, convincing you that you can't be authentic until you have everything figured out. These are just defense mechanisms. They're the mind's way of keeping you safe, even if that safety comes at the expense of your happiness and freedom.

Remember, authenticity isn't about having all the answers. It's not about always knowing the right thing to do. It's about being willing to show up as you are, flaws and all, and trusting that who you are is enough. It's about giving yourself permission to be human, to be flawed, and to be real.

Each time you choose to show up authentically, you build the muscle of courage. And with time, it becomes easier. You start to realize that the things you feared—rejection, judgment, failure— aren't as scary as they once seemed. You start to trust that you can handle whatever comes your way, because you're no longer living for the approval of others. You're living for yourself.

Living authentically is also a radical act of self-love. It's a way of telling yourself, "I am enough as I am." And that's the most courageous thing you can do. Because in a world that constantly tells us we need to be more, do more, and have more, choosing to accept that you are enough just as you are is nothing short of revolutionary.

So, take a deep breath. Let go of the need to be perfect, to be liked, to be understood. Instead, embrace the courage to be—to be real, to be vulnerable, and to be you. The world doesn't need more "perfect" people. It needs more people who are willing to show up authentically, in all their messy, beautiful humanity.

We've talked about vulnerability before, and it bears repeating because it's crucial to remember. In a world that values control, force, and certainty, vulnerability is often seen as weakness. From a young age, we're taught that showing our emotions, admitting we don't know the answer, or exposing our insecurities is dangerous. We learn to guard ourselves, hide our deeper feelings, and present only the parts of ourselves that feel safe. But the truth is, vulnerability is not a weakness. In fact, it's one of our greatest strengths because it serves as the gateway to authenticity.

To live authentically, you must embrace vulnerability. There is no way around it. Vulnerability is the courage to show up, to be seen, and to be who you are, even when there are no guarantees of how you'll be received. It's the willingness to reveal your unscripted self, knowing that you might be judged or misunderstood, but doing it anyway because the alternative—hiding your unfiltered reflection— is far more limiting and painful. In this way, vulnerability is true strength.

A beautiful example of this is Fred Rogers, the beloved host of *Mister Rogers' Neighborhood*. In an era when children's television was becoming more commercialized and fast-paced, Fred Rogers stayed true to his gentle and sincere nature. Rather than conforming to the industry's demands for quick entertainment, he used his platform to address difficult emotional topics like fear, sadness, and self-worth. Rogers believed that children needed a space where they could feel safe and understood—a place where vulnerability was embraced, not avoided.

Despite pressures to change, Rogers never wavered in his authenticity. He invited his audience to be emotionally open, and in doing so, created deep, lasting connections. By emphasizing self-acceptance with his famous phrase, 'I like you just the way you are,' Rogers made his show a sanctuary for children and adults alike, where being vulnerable was seen not as a weakness, but as a path to real understanding and growth. Through his quiet strength, Fred Rogers taught us that by embracing our authentic selves, we make room for true connection and empathy.

> "The greatest gift you ever give is your honest self."
>
> — Fred Rogers

Fred Rogers taught us that when we embrace our true selves, we allow for meaningful connections with others. His life reminds us that vulnerability is not about weakness but strength in being genuine.

Like Rogers, we have the power to build relationships that reflect our true selves, not our fears. Authenticity is the foundation for meaningful connection.

Something to Reflect On:

Take a moment to reflect on where you may be holding back in your own life. Are there situations where you're still hiding your true self to meet others' expectations? What might happen if, like Rogers, you embraced your authentic self fully?

Consider the people you admire most—the ones who seem genuinely authentic. What often makes them stand out is their willingness to let their guard down, embracing vulnerability as a strength rather than a weakness. They openly share their imperfections and struggles, not to seek sympathy, but because they understand that authenticity invites deeper connection. When you show your true self, you create a space where others feel safe to do the same, transforming not only your relationships but the way authenticity is experienced together.

Brene Brown, a research professor known for her work on vulnerability, authenticity, and shame, provides an inspiring real-life example of the power of embracing one's true self. In her famous TED Talk, Brown shared how her own journey toward vulnerability transformed her professional and personal life. Initially resistant to vulnerability, she recognized that only by embracing her imperfections, rather than hiding behind the facade of professionalism, could she connect more deeply with others and foster authentic relationships. Brown's vulnerability was the key to her connection with millions, and her story serves as a reminder that embracing authenticity allows us to live more courageously.

"Authenticity is the daily practice of letting go
of who we think we're supposed to be and
embracing who we are."

— Brené Brown

And yes, this kind of openness can feel terrifying. But the alternative—guarding yourself, staying closed off, and keeping your true self hidden—well, you know where that leads you.

It's important to understand that vulnerability doesn't mean exposing every part of yourself to everyone you meet. It's not about oversharing or seeking validation. Vulnerability is about discernment—knowing when and with whom to open up. It's about trusting yourself enough to decide when it's safe to let down your guard and when it's better to hold your boundaries. The key is that the choice comes from a place of self-trust, not from fear.

Embracing vulnerability in everyday life can be incredibly useful. You don't need to make grand gestures; small, manageable acts can have a significant impact. It might mean admitting you don't have all the answers during a conversation, allowing yourself to cry in front of someone you trust, or letting a friend know you're struggling instead of pretending everything is fine. These everyday acts of vulnerability help clear away the layers that obscure your true self, gradually revealing a more authentic reflection. Each step towards openness brings you closer to living as your true self, imperfections and all.

 **Something to Reflect On:**

Reflect on a time when you allowed yourself to be vulnerable. What happened, and how did it feel to let go of control and be seen, imperfections and all? Did it lead to deeper connections, or did it bring up fears that held you back? Consider how vulnerability has influenced your relationships and how you might embrace it more fully.

Another key aspect of vulnerability is learning to be vulnerable with yourself. This might sound strange at first, but many of us spend so much time avoiding our own feelings, denying our emotions, or pushing away uncomfortable truths about ourselves. We keep ourselves busy, distracted, or numb to avoid facing the parts of ourselves that feel raw or unresolved. But self-awareness requires vulnerability. You can't be truly authentic if you're not willing to be honest with yourself about your fears, your flaws, and your deepest desires.

Take a moment to sit with yourself. How do you feel right now? What emotions are coming up for you? Maybe there's anxiety, fear, or doubt. Maybe there's a part of you that's struggling with something you've been avoiding. Whatever it is, let yourself feel it. Allow yourself to be vulnerable with yourself, without judgment. This act of self-compassion is just as important as being vulnerable with others. When you learn to embrace your own vulnerability, you'll find it much easier to be authentic in your interactions with others.

When we contemplate vulnerability, we often encounter the fear of rejection. It's natural to worry that showing your true self might lead to being judged or misunderstood. But not everyone will accept you, and that's okay. Authenticity isn't about pleasing everyone; it's about being honest with yourself, regardless of others' opinions. The more you embrace vulnerability, the more you realize that rejection reflects someone else's perspective, not your worth.

Ultimately, embracing vulnerability means letting go of the idea of perfection. It's about accepting that your flaws don't make you any less worthy of love or connection. The people most likely to build meaningful connections with you are the ones who appreciate you not in spite of your imperfections, but because of them. Vulnerability is what makes you relatable and real, and in a world where so many people are hiding, being genuine is the bravest act you can choose.

So, the next time you find yourself hesitating to show your true self, ask yourself: What am I protecting? What am I afraid of losing? And then consider this: What might others gain from your openness, and what experience are you keeping from yourself by holding back? The answer might surprise you.

The more you practice vulnerability, the more you'll find that it doesn't weaken you; it strengthens you. It deepens your relationships, enhances your self-awareness, and allows you to live a life fully aligned with your authentic self. This is where the real power lies—not in being invulnerable, but in embracing the courage to be vulnerable.

Think of a developing organism, where cells constantly evolve and find their specialized roles. If we try to force a cell to become something it's not, it struggles and fails to function properly. But when we allow it to follow its natural course, it integrates seamlessly into the larger system, performing its role effortlessly. Similarly, vulnerability invites us to release the need to control every aspect of who we are or how we are perceived. It allows us to grow and evolve naturally, aligning with our true nature and flourishing as we find our place in the greater flow of life.

Authenticity thrives in the space created by vulnerability. It is in that space—where we are no longer consumed by managing outcomes or perceptions—that we find the true power to be ourselves. And in doing so, we discover that the greatest freedom comes not from controlling life, but from surrendering to it.

Now that you've reflected on the power of authenticity, choose one area of your life this week where you feel the pressure to perform or conform. Practice letting go of the need to control how you're perceived and allow yourself to be vulnerable, even if it feels uncomfortable. Reflect on how this changes your interactions and consider how you can gradually bring this practice into other areas of your life.

Think of a situation where you tried to control how others saw you or an outcome in your life. What was the result? What might happen if you allowed things to unfold naturally without trying to control every aspect?

Just like a mirror reflects everything as it is—dust, cracks, and all—your authentic self shines through when you release the pressure to appear perfect. True liberation comes from allowing yourself to be seen, imperfections included.

It's important to reiterate that this liberation isn't a one-time event. It's a process—a moment to moment practice of choosing authenticity over fear, trust over control. There will be moments when it feels easier to slip back into old habits, to pick up the roles and narratives, and to try to control how things unfold. But each time you choose to let go, you're strengthening your ability to live authentically.

In the next chapter we will explore how authenticity not only transforms your internal world but also impacts the collective. The ripple effect of living authentically is profound. It not only changes the way you experience life but also influences the people around you, inviting them to do the same. Authenticity can be contagious. When you live from a place of truth, you inspire others to question their own narratives and to step into their own power.

This journey of authenticity doesn't end here. It's a constant unfolding, a continual practice of returning to yourself. But with each step, you'll find that the liberation that comes from living authentically is worth the discomfort, the vulnerability, and the unknown. Because in the end, the greatest freedom you can experience is the freedom to be who you truly are—without apology, without fear, and without the need to control.

"The privilege of a lifetime is to become who you truly are."

— Carl Gustav Jung

Chapter 6 - Stepping Into the Unknown

Everything we've explored so far—the characters you've written on your blank page, the attachments you've nurtured, and the fears and ambitions that have driven you—have been necessary steps toward a single recognition. Through moments of reflection, we've contemplated how we identify with the character we've created, what we thought the benefit of doing so was, and where that character's narratives might have come from, and the habitual attachments that we willingly used to defend and reinforce that character. Likewise, we've dissected the fears stemming from those attachments and have come to terms with how "failure" just meant any outcome outside our carefully orchestrated, character-centric plan.

In short, we've taken the time to skeptically examine the beliefs and ideas we've lived by for our entire lives—often without knowing it consciously or realizing how we played along—because it's in recognizing that **we can and do fool ourselves**, that we are now able to move deeper into understanding how else we've done so.

In Chapter 1, we discussed the limitless potential of your ever-changing story. Since then, we've been deconstructing that story, its details, and your belief in it in order to help free you from the restrictions those beliefs come with. We've shifted from seeing identity as fixed and immovable to recognizing it as something that changes naturally. The ice, as it were, is starting to melt, allowing us to experience a fluid, evolving sense of identity. This fluidity has always been available; it's our commitment to a rigid character that blinds us to it. The more committed we are to being a fixed idea, the more we unconsciously defend that idea when we feel it's being threatened.

This behavior is called **cognitive dissonance**—the mental

discomfort that arises when we're confronted with information that conflicts with our deeply held beliefs or sense of self. In response to this discomfort, the brain engages in dissonance reduction, employing various strategies to restore internal consistency.

Psychologist Leon Festinger, who first introduced the theory of cognitive dissonance in 1957, explained that this process is akin to how hunger prompts actions aimed at reducing hunger—our brains actively work to alleviate the discomfort.

To reduce dissonance, we often unconsciously employ one of four primary strategies: **denial**, where we refuse to accept the conflicting information; **avoidance**, where we steer clear of situations or people that might increase the discomfort; **vilification**, where we discredit or attack the source of the dissonance; and **justification**, where we rationalize the conflicting information to align it with our existing beliefs.

While these strategies may offer short-term relief, they can reinforce false narratives and habitual ways of thinking, trapping us in a cycle of defensiveness and limiting our potential for growth. Awareness of these mechanisms is crucial for transcending dissonance and moving toward a more open, flexible mindset where our identity is not so rigidly defended.

Here's the key takeaway: the dissonance or discomfort comes from our attachment to a fixed identity, not from identity itself. When we loosen our grip on a single, rigid idea of who we are, we allow that idea to change and flow with our life. By surrendering the need to cling to one stable character, we open ourselves to the limitless potential of who we can become.

Trevor Noah offers a compelling real-world example of this fluidity. He grew up in apartheid-era South Africa as a child of mixed race. Born to a black mother and a white father at a time when interracial relationships were illegal, his very existence was a political act. In his memoir *Born a Crime*, Noah reflects on how his identity was shaped not only by the color of his skin but also by the societal labels imposed on him. In some settings, he was seen as not black enough; in others, not white enough. These shifting identities, forced upon him from the outside, led to a constant negotiation of self.

Yet, rather than being confined by these identities, Noah used his fluidity to navigate different worlds—from the impoverished townships of Johannesburg to his rise as a global comedian and host of *The Daily Show*. He moved beyond the roles that were thrust upon him, embracing his identity as a storyteller capable of transcending cultural and racial boundaries. In doing so, Noah exemplifies how letting go of rigid labels opens the door to a more expansive, adaptable sense of self. His journey shows us that identity is not something fixed—it is something we continuously create, adapt, and redefine in response to our circumstances.

"I became a chameleon. My color didn't change, but I could change your perception of my color."

— Trevor Noah in *Born a Crime*

In many ways, our identities are like waves rising and falling in the ocean of life. If we allow, our identity forms and reforms, shaped by experience and choice. If we resist, the wave that forms freezes in place, becoming familiar and comfortable, though brittle and immovable, and we begin to mistake the frozen wave for the whole of who we are and defend it accordingly. But what happens when we stop identifying with the waves? What happens when we begin to see ourselves as the vastness of the ocean beneath? That's where the journey beyond identity begins.

Likewise, just as waves rise and fall in the vast ocean, reflecting the ebb and flow of life, our bodies experience a similar internal rhythm. Beneath the surface, cells are in constant motion, migrating and adapting to meet our body's needs. While these cellular shifts are subtle, they echo the same truth: our identity, like our biology, must remain flexible, continually adapting to life's ever-changing circumstances.

A concept like identity is far more powerful than we understand. It gives us a sense of place in the world, a way to navigate life's unknowable complexity. But the security it provides is the security of a prison cell; while it makes us feel safe, it also confines us. Identity can create a simplified, controllable version of life—a way to reduce the complexity of the world so it feels less overwhelming. By holding tightly to fixed roles, beliefs, or labels, we make life smaller, narrowing our experience to "the known". This might feel safer, but in doing so, we limit our capacity to grow and adapt. Life, by its nature, is vast and ever-changing, and when we cling to a fixed identity, we miss out on the broader possibilities that come with embracing change.

As *Krishnamurti* observed, "The constant assertion of belief is an indication of fear." Clinging to a fixed identity is rooted in fear—the fear of the unknown, and the fear of not knowing who we'll be if we let go of the stories we've constructed. When we assert our identity too rigidly, we're often simply shielding ourselves from the discomfort of uncertainty, not realizing that true freedom lies within that place of vulnerability.

There's comfort in believing we are a certain kind of wave—it offers a sense of control, something identifiable amidst the unpredictability of life. In identifying ourselves with a fixed form, whether it's a particular role, belief, or label, we create the illusion of stability. This wave becomes something familiar we can rely on when the ocean of life feels vast and uncertain. Holding onto this wave gives us a sense of who we are, a clear identity in a world where nothing else seems certain. It allows us to navigate relationships, society, and our own sense of purpose without questioning too much of the unknown. After all, a wave has a set direction.

The wave offers boundaries, structure, and predictability in a world that can often feel chaotic. The idea of letting go and surrendering to the ocean beneath—the vast, fluid, ever-changing reality of who we are—can feel terrifying.

The unknown is daunting, but it's also where possibility thrives. It's where the boundaries of self dissolve, revealing that we are far more than the forms we've been clinging to.

> "In the process of letting go, you lose many things from the past, but you find yourself."
>
> — Deepak Chopra

When we let go of the need for identity to be something solid, we allow ourselves to flow with life, to adapt to the moment, and to become whatever the moment calls for. This doesn't mean you lose yourself or become disconnected from who you are. It means you stop clinging to a single version of yourself and begin to embrace the truth that you are ever-changing and ever-evolving.

A powerful example of this is the life of Frida Kahlo. After a tragic accident left her in constant physical pain, Kahlo could have allowed her suffering to define her identity. Instead, she transformed her experience through her art, exploring themes of identity, gender, culture, and body image. Refusing to be confined by traditional roles, she painted her evolving sense of self, often portraying herself in raw, vulnerable ways. Her work challenged societal expectations and reflected her ability to embrace fluidity in her identity, never settling into one version of who she was. Kahlo reminds us that even in the face of adversity, we can choose to redefine ourselves, adapting and growing through each chapter of life.

Something to Reflect On:

Think about a time when your identity felt like it was being reshaped—perhaps during a transition or a moment of uncertainty. How did you respond to that change? Did you cling to familiar roles, or did you find yourself opening to new aspects of who you could be? Reflect on what you discovered about yourself in that process, and consider: What if you allowed your identity to flow more freely, without the need to anchor yourself to any one version of who you are?

As we continue to unravel the concept of identity, it becomes clear that letting go of a fixed sense of self doesn't mean we stop having a character altogether. Instead, it's about recognizing that the character we identify with is always being reshaped—adapted to whatever purpose or experience we're navigating now. You don't need to hold onto any one version of yourself, because a new version will always emerge. It's in surrendering the need to cling to a specific identity that you free yourself to continually remake and redefine who you are, based on the ever-changing circumstances of your life.

We've already explored at length how the roles we play in life— parent, partner, professional, or friend—become intertwined with our sense of self. These roles, while necessary, are also temporary. Over time, they shape how we perceive ourselves and how others perceive us, and we begin to say, "I am a mother," or "I am an entrepreneur," believing these roles are fixed parts of our identity.

But roles, by their very nature, are temporary. Life is fluid, and the circumstances that once gave meaning to those roles will inevitably shift. Perhaps your child grows up, your career takes an unexpected turn, or a business venture comes to an end. When these changes occur, if you've tied your sense of self too tightly to that role, it can leave you feeling lost and unmoored.

This is where the opportunity for reinvention comes in. While the role may change or even end, it doesn't have to define the entirety of who you are. By clinging too tightly to a single role, we may spend our lives avoiding the very changes that are essential for our growth—at the cost of our happiness. The role isn't the problem; it's our attachment to it that creates conflict. When we allow ourselves to step beyond the roles we once held so firmly, we give ourselves the freedom to adapt and evolve with life's changing tides.

Reinvention is not only possible but necessary. The key is to recognize that roles will always shift, and rather than resisting that change, we can embrace it, knowing that each new chapter offers an opportunity to create a new version of ourselves. The role doesn't define you; it's simply a part you play for a time. When it no longer serves you or begins to feel restrictive, it's time to let go, trust in your ability to recreate, and step into the next iteration of who you can become.

Something to Reflect On:

Think of a role or label that has defined you, one that feels central to how you've seen yourself. Now, consider how this role has evolved and how life may be inviting you to step into something new. Instead of loosening your attachment to it, reflect on how you might allow this role to transform or dissolve entirely. What new roles or opportunities are beginning to emerge? How might your sense of self evolve if you welcomed these changes and embraced the uncertainty of reinvention?

A real-life example of embracing identity fluidity is David Bowie, who continually reinvented himself throughout his career. From Ziggy Stardust to the Thin White Duke, Bowie embodied different personas, each like a wave rising from the depths of his creativity and vision. His ability to shift and reshape his identity over time shows that we are not bound by a single form, but can continuously evolve in response to new phases of life. Bowie didn't lose himself in these transformations; instead, each new wave expressed a different aspect of his ever-changing self, always connected to the limitless ocean of potential within him. His journey is a powerful reminder that clinging to a fixed identity limits growth. By embracing reinvention, we remain open to the endless possibilities that life offers.

You are not any single wave or role. You are the ocean—the source from which all waves arise. When one dissolves, the ocean remains whole and complete.

Beneath the surface waves of identity lies a deeper ocean of limitless potential, filled with infinite perspectives and possibilities. The roles and identities we've taken on—the waves we've identified with—are just one way our potential has been shaped by circumstances, experiences, and the other waves around us. But these waves are not fixed; they could have risen in entirely different forms, molded by different circumstances, and yet the core potential beneath them would remain exactly the same.

Consider this: the person you are today, shaped by your upbringing, culture, and society, could have been an entirely different person in a different context. Your environment and experiences have formed this particular version of "you," but if those influences had been different, a completely new wave would have arisen. Yet, beneath it all, you would still be the same limitless potential—just shaped differently.

Something to Reflect On:

How have family, cultural, or societal expectations shaped your current decisions and sense of self? Consider one decision or belief you hold today—how might it change if you let go of these external influences?

For example, if you grew up in a family that valued academic achievement above all else, you might have internalized the belief that your worth is tied to your intellectual abilities or career success. Alternatively, if you were raised in a culture that emphasized traditional gender roles, you might have internalized specific beliefs about what it means to be a "good" man or woman. These beliefs, shaped by external circumstances, become woven into the fabric of our identity, often without us even realizing it. But here's the key: had you been born into a completely different set of circumstances, your identity could have been shaped in an entirely different way.

Something to Reflect On:

Reflect on the beliefs and expectations that shaped your sense of identity—messages you received about success, gender, or roles. How did these influence your self-perception? Now, imagine how different circumstances might have shaped you into a completely different person. What aspects of you would remain unchanged, and what might be behaviors tied to your identity? Write down these beliefs and consider if they still feel true or if they were just one possible expression in a vast sea of potential.

As we continue to peel back these layers of identity, it's natural to feel resistance. Questioning who we are—realizing that the roles and beliefs we've taken on could have been entirely different—can be unsettling. It often brings up a common fear: the fear of not knowing who we'll be if we let go of these identities.

This fear is understandable. We've spent a lifetime building and reinforcing these layers, and they've provided a sense of security and stability. But the truth is, this security is an illusion. When we cling too tightly to these identities, we limit our ability to grow, evolve, and explore other versions of ourselves. We become trapped in a fixed idea of who we think we are, afraid to step into the unknown.

As you let go of the layers of identity, you're not losing yourself. You're simply uncovering the truth of who you are beneath all those layers. The process of maturity isn't about destruction; it's about revelation.

> "The individual has always had to struggle to keep from being overwhelmed by the tribe. If you try it, you will be lonely often, and sometimes frightened. But no price is too high to pay for the privilege of owning yourself."

— Maynard James Keenan

One of the biggest misconceptions we hold about identity is that it's something we need to discover or define once and for all. But what if identity were more like the lines we mentally draw between waves—arbitrary distinctions that only exist because we're looking for them? In the same way that waves appear separate only when we focus on the peaks and valleys, our identities are created when we choose to see them.

We often think certain things about ourselves without recognizing where those thoughts came from, the context or assumptions they're based on, or how they affect others. We fail to see that the line we've drawn between "our" thoughts and beliefs and those of others isn't real. The distinction between what we claim as ours—our ideas, opinions, or beliefs—and those influenced by the people around us, or the culture we live in, is often blurred, yet we treat it as solid and definitive. Take, for example, the phenomenon of non-theists or agnostics who, despite not believing in a god or afterlife, still express beliefs like "everything happens for a reason" or casually reference concepts like heaven. These ideas are so deeply ingrained in broader cultural narratives that they persist even among those who consciously reject religious frameworks. Their beliefs are shaped by the culture around them, and in turn, by repeating these ideas, they contribute to reinforcing and shaping those same cultural beliefs for others.

Similarly, modern conversations around gender roles reveal how this process works. Many people may consciously believe in gender equality, yet unconsciously adhere to traditional gender expectations. For example, someone might endorse progressive views but still expect men to be primary earners or women to handle most domestic responsibilities. These expectations are not only shaped by cultural norms but also reinforced by the individual's behavior, subtly influencing those around them, even when their stated beliefs seem to contradict those actions.

Political identity offers another powerful example. Someone might believe they hold an independent stance, but their views on specific issues are heavily influenced by the media they consume or the political groups they follow. At the same time, their opinions, expressed in conversations or on social media, shape the beliefs of others, feeding into the larger cycle of collective influence.

As discussed in Chapter 1, although we like to believe that our thoughts are entirely our own, formed independently, they are actually shaped by countless external influences—family, society, education, relationships, and even unconscious assumptions we've absorbed over time. When we identify with a belief or opinion, it feels like a personal truth, something unique to us. But, more often than not, these ideas are a mixture of inherited patterns, cultural conditioning, and shared experiences. The "line" we draw between what we think of as our individual beliefs and the collective thoughts and ideas of others is arbitrary. It's a way for us to simplify our sense of self, to create the illusion of a stable, coherent identity. In doing so, we ignore how interconnected our thinking is with the broader context we exist in.

For example, you might strongly identify with certain values or opinions, thinking they reflect who you are at your core, without ever questioning where those values came from. Are they truly yours? Or have they been passed down from your family, absorbed from your social group, or shaped by the cultural narratives you grew up in? If you surrendered them, would you stop being you?

Or are they just a convenient way to settle on an oversimplified character you can scrutinize, define, or even obsess over?

By letting go of the need to draw these lines, we open ourselves to the realization that who we are is not something fixed or separate. Like waves, the way we express ourselves is constantly shifting, interconnected, and shaped by both our environment, the waves that influence us and are influenced in kind, and by a deeper ocean of potential beneath and within. To hold on to a single identity despite all this change is enough to drive one mad.

This doesn't mean we have to abandon everything we know about ourselves. Rather, it means we stop clinging to the idea that we are defined by any one identity. Instead, we can embrace the reality that we are always in flux, capable of expressing countless possibilities, depending on the moment and context.

Something to Reflect On:

Think about a time in your life when you realized that the roles or beliefs you held about yourself weren't as fixed as you once thought. Perhaps it was a new job, a shift in a relationship, or a moment of personal insight. How did that experience reveal the fluid nature of your identity? Did you notice how certain beliefs or labels you once clung to no longer seemed relevant? Reflect on what this revealed about the arbitrary lines you've drawn between "who you are" and "who you can be."

When you reflect on your life, it's clear that the person you are today is not the same as the person you were ten years ago. Your thoughts, desires, and even personality traits have shifted over time. But here's what's more important: this change was inevitable. Rather than resisting or fearing it, what if we saw this ongoing transformation as an opportunity? What if the shifts in who you are could be embraced not just as something that happens, but as something that opens new doors to your potential?

Recognizing the fluidity of identity doesn't mean we have to let go of all sense of self. While some interpretations of radical non-duality suggest that the sense of a separate "I" is an illusion, in everyday experience, there is always an awareness of a self—a conscious "I" through which we navigate life.

Proponents of radical non-duality, like Tony Parsons, claim that *"There is no one. There is no separate individual... There is no one experiencing it."* This view, however, can be dangerous. It lacks empathy and serves as an escape from the pain and complexity of being an individual without ever truly understanding or growing from it. It avoids the reality of living as a person, relating to others, and finding meaning in shared experiences. Rupert Spira, another prominent voice in non-duality, echoes this view, saying, *"There is no individual self; there is only consciousness, pure awareness, and all experience arises within that."*

Yet, by dismissing the reality of individual experience, these philosophies can disconnect us from the very essence of what it means to be human. Of course, there's always an "I" at the root of every experience. The sense of self, while fluid and ever-changing, is fundamental to how we grow, evolve, and connect with others. Life happens through that "I," and it's what allows us to relate to others who are going through their own individual experiences.

This doesn't mean we need to cling to a rigid, fixed idea of who we are. Instead, we can recognize that while the "I" remains, the roles we play and the stories we tell about ourselves are constantly evolving. By letting go of a static identity, we open ourselves to growth, allowing new ways of being to emerge—ones that we may never have considered before. Embracing this fluidity not only helps us grow, but it also deepens our ability to relate to others and to face the human experience with compassion and openness.

Something to Reflect On:

Reflect on how your sense of self has shifted over the years—not just as a reaction to external events, but as part of your natural evolution. How has your identity changed while the core awareness of "I" has remained?

The single biggest reinforcement of our fixed identity is our will—our willingness to believe the stories we tell ourselves, to defend them, and to cling to them as if they define us. It's not just the stories themselves that hold us back, but our active commitment to maintaining and protecting them, even when they no longer serve us.

From an early age, we are shaped by societal conditioning—family expectations, cultural norms, and the beliefs we absorb from the world around us. In response, we begin crafting a personal narrative—a mythology that explains our experiences, our choices, and how we've become the person we are today. These stories give us a sense of coherence and certainty, helping us navigate life's complexities.

Take, for example, the story of someone who sees themselves as the "responsible one" in their family. This story may have originated from childhood, where they were often praised for their maturity and dependability. Over time, this narrative solidifies into a core aspect of their identity. But as they grow older, this responsibility may become a burden, trapping them in a role that no longer feels authentic. Yet, because the story has been reinforced for so long, it's difficult to let go of.

When we cling to a specific identity narrative, we often unconsciously act in ways that reinforce it. This is the trap of the self-fulfilling prophecy. If you believe, for example, that you are always 'the outsider,' you may begin to behave in ways that keep you on the periphery of social situations. You might avoid getting too close to people, withdraw when others try to engage with you, or interpret neutral actions as exclusionary. In doing so, you reinforce the very identity you feel trapped by.

On the other hand, assuming that everyone loves you can create its own limitations. You might become less attuned to how your actions affect others, unintentionally acting in ways that are inconsiderate. This belief in universal approval can also prevent you from acknowledging fears or doubts, as the desire to maintain the image of being universally loved takes precedence over honest self-reflection. Both extremes—whether grounded in self-doubt or self-assurance—can become narratives that cloud your perception of reality, limiting growth and authentic connection.

Now, imagine yourself as an actor in a play. Every day, you step onto the stage and perform the same role, following the same script, knowing it was the best way to be a valuable part of the show. You've learned your lines by heart, and you've become so good at the performance that the audience believes you are the character. To deliver this performance so masterfully, like any dedicated method actor, you've willingly convinced yourself that you *are* the character, rather than the actor playing it.

But today, something shifts. For the first time, you question the show itself. Letting go of your obsession with delivering a perfect performance, you notice something unsettling: your fellow actors seem tired, anxious, and unhappy, despite the facade they maintain alongside you. When you shift your gaze to the audience, you find that they too seem discontent, confused, or distracted—not watching out of genuine interest or fulfillment, but because it's all they know. The play continues, not because it holds meaning, but because it always has.

At this moment, you have a choice: You can continue playing the role because it's comfortable and familiar, or you can step back and question the entire play itself. Stepping away from the performance may feel disorienting—you don't know what lies beyond the stage or who you'll be without the script to guide you. But in that uncertainty lies freedom. And as you step back, you realize that the stage you were performing on wasn't real at all—it was imaginary, just like the roles you've been playing. This realization doesn't just free you; it opens up new possibilities for everyone, as they, too, are performing on their own imaginary stages, caught in roles they may not have questioned until now.

Just as cells migrate through the body, adapting to new environments and roles, you don't have to follow the same pathways every day. Most of the time, these cells move in familiar patterns, repeating what they know based on past conditions, reinforcing the same functions. But cells also have the ability to adapt, to change course when necessary, responding to the immediate needs of the body. What if, like those cells, you allowed yourself to move beyond the patterns of yesterday? What if you responded to who you are in this moment, without the constraints of past roles or definitions?

The potential for cellular migration is limitless. Cells move freely, forming new connections, responding to fresh conditions, and evolving into what the body requires. In the same way, you can release the idea of a fixed identity and let yourself evolve, making new connections and opening up new possibilities. Instead of continuing to perform, you can step off the stage altogether, leaving behind the need to play a role. By doing so, you realize that just as the stage isn't real, the audience you once performed for isn't an audience at all—they are cells, just like you, moving through their own transformations and navigating their own environments. Rather than being defined by roles of the past, you can now interact with them authentically, recognizing that you are all part of the same dynamic system, constantly shifting and adapting. In this space, beyond the stage and the roles, there is freedom to connect with others as they truly are, without the need for performance or validation.

There's tremendous power in seeing identity for what it is. When you stop trying to define yourself, you open up to the full spectrum of who you can become.

Letting go of the idea of a fixed identity—and the societal conditioning that reinforces it—you might notice that the boundaries between you and everyone else are beginning to blur. While you've always known that everything is connected, a deeper recognition of this simple truth has been obscured by the safe walls and rigid limits of a fixed, separate self. It's crucial not to overlook this insight, as it will naturally create some degree of cognitive dissonance. The belief in a solid identity has provided a sense of certainty, direction, and value throughout your life, so transitioning away from it will inevitably lead to a growing awareness of the unknown.

Marie Curie's life serves as a striking example of embracing the unknown and refusing to be confined by societal expectations. As a woman in science during a time when the field was dominated by men, Curie continually stepped beyond the boundaries set for her. She pursued her research in radioactivity despite the challenges, becoming the first person to win Nobel Prizes in two different scientific fields. Curie's willingness to enter uncharted territories, both intellectually and socially, reminds us that when we shed rigid self-definitions, we can open ourselves to groundbreaking discoveries—about both the world and ourselves.

The unknown can still feel daunting, and it's natural to want to cling to the familiar, even if it no longer serves us. After all, the certainty of a fixed identity has been a familiar source of control. But as you step into this new awareness, the key is not to resist the unknown, but to meet it with curiosity rather than fear. Instead of asking, "Who am I?"—a question rooted in the need for a fixed answer—try asking, "What becomes possible when I release the need to define myself?"

Something to Reflect On:

Reflect on a time when you faced the unknown, not just in your circumstances but in who you were becoming. As you stepped into that uncertainty, what aspects of your identity surprised you? Now, imagine letting your sense of self flow with the changes in your life, without clinging to a fixed idea of who you are. What might you discover about yourself if you embraced this ongoing state of becoming, rather than trying to hold onto a single identity?

And with this, I'd like you to ask yourself a question: Is the false certainty and divisive emotional consequences of a fictitious, superficial identity worth the conflict and suffering it creates within us and between us? Is it truly worthwhile to hold onto a concept that continues to harm both ourselves and humanity?

Among the many divisive concepts society reinforces, perhaps none are more deeply ingrained than those related to gender. From the moment we are born, we aren't just assigned a gender—we're handed a superfluous set of expectations about how that gender should behave, what should be valued, and what is appropriate to believe. These gender roles can be incredibly limiting, confining us to narrow definitions of 'masculine' or 'feminine' rather than allowing us to simply be what we are and let reality speak for itself.

For men, societal expectations often emphasize physical and mental strength, independence, and emotional stoicism. From a young age, boys are taught to suppress their emotions, to be competitive, and to define their worth through success and achievement. Vulnerability, softness, or reliance on others is often seen as weakness, something to be avoided at all costs.

For women, the expectations are often centered around caregiving, nurturing, and emotional expressiveness. Women are frequently expected to prioritize the needs of others over their own, to be empathetic and supportive, and to derive their sense of worth from their relationships and appearance. Ambition and assertiveness may be seen as undesirable, or even threatening, depending on the cultural context.

These gender norms, though slowly shifting, still exert a powerful influence on our identities. Many of us, regardless of gender, find ourselves struggling to fit into the molds society has created for us. We may feel pressure to conform to these roles even when they don't align with our true selves, leading to feelings of disconnection or dissatisfaction.

Something to Reflect On:

Take a moment to reflect on the role that gender has played in shaping your identity. What expectations were placed on you because of your gender, and how have those expectations influenced the way you see yourself? Consider whether any aspects of your identity feel inauthentic—perhaps shaped more by societal norms than by your true nature. How might your sense of self shift if you let go of these externally imposed labels and allowed yourself to exist beyond the confines of gender roles?

Gender is just one example of a divisive concept that has shaped our social conditioning, but it's far from the only one. Concepts like race, class, nationality, and even political identity can serve as boundaries that separate us from one another, reinforcing the illusion of a fixed identity and deepening the divide between "self" and "other." These labels are often used to define, categorize, and control, creating conflict both within us and between us. While these constructs may feel like secure parts of our identity, they are often limiting, preventing us from seeing ourselves and others beyond the surface labels imposed by society.

Freeing yourself from the constraints of social conditioning involves recognizing where it exists. This requires a level of self-awareness and honesty that can be uncomfortable at times. It means asking yourself hard questions about the beliefs you hold and where they come from. Are they truly yours, or were they handed to you by others? Are they assumptions you've accepted without question? Do these beliefs serve to validate your sense of a fixed identity? Are you biased in ways you haven't yet recognized?

Once you've recognized the influence of social conditioning, the next step is to release it. This doesn't mean holding onto only a few beliefs or expectations, but rather questioning them all. It's not about picking and choosing which ones to keep; it's about letting go of the need for certainty or validation through these beliefs. Imagine your mind as a filter that has become clogged by layers of sediment over time—the accumulation of societal norms, expectations, and assumptions that obscure your true nature.

As you begin to examine your beliefs and question their origins, you start to clear away the sediment. With each layer you release, you allow the flow of your authentic self to become clearer. This process isn't immediate, nor is it always comfortable. It's a gradual unraveling of the conditioning that has shaped your sense of self, one that requires patience and a willingness to face the discomfort of uncertainty.

As you continue to let go, you'll find that your sense of self becomes lighter, freer, and less confined by the roles and narratives that once defined you. The more you clear away, the more space there is for the unknown—the limitless potential that exists beyond the constraints of conditioned identity.

Something to Reflect On:

Consider an aspect of your identity that has been shaped by external expectations—whether it's your career, relationships, or gender roles. How has social conditioning influenced this part of your identity? What beliefs have you internalized that no longer serve you? Now, imagine what it would feel like to completely release those beliefs and expectations. How would your sense of self evolve if you no longer felt the need to conform to those external pressures? What possibilities might open up if you allowed yourself to exist beyond those limits?

By now, we've explored the fluid nature of identity, how social conditioning and expectations shape our sense of self, and the layers of stories we tell ourselves. But understanding the fluidity of identity on an intellectual level is only part of the process. **The real transformation happens when we put this knowledge into action—when we begin to experiment with our identity in real-world scenarios and see how it shifts and adapts.**

In this section, we'll explore practical ways to engage with identity fluidity, to push the boundaries of who we think we are, and to challenge the limits we've set for ourselves. This process of experimenting with identity doesn't require a complete overhaul of your life. It starts with small, intentional steps that invite you to step into different roles, explore new behaviors, and see how they feel.

One of the easiest ways to begin experimenting with identity fluidity is by making small, deliberate changes in how you present yourself in everyday life. This could be as simple as trying on a new style of clothing, changing how you speak, or adopting a new routine. These minor shifts may seem superficial, but they can have a powerful effect on how you see yourself and how others perceive you.

For example, let's say you've always seen yourself as the quiet, reserved type—the person who avoids drawing attention to themselves in social settings. What happens if, for one evening, you decide to be the life of the party? You might start a conversation with a stranger, tell a story in a group setting, or volunteer for an activity you'd normally shy away from. At first, it might feel uncomfortable, but in that discomfort, something important happens: You begin to see that you're not as fixed in your identity as you thought. You have the capacity to shift and change, even if just for a moment.

These small shifts don't have to be permanent. The goal isn't to replace one rigid identity with another. Instead, it's to explore the flexibility of who you are and to recognize that you can embody different aspects of yourself depending on the situation. Each time you try something new, you expand the boundaries of what you believe is possible for yourself.

Exercise: Trying on New Roles

Choose a situation or interaction where you typically respond in a predictable way. This could be at work, in a social setting, or with family. Now, challenge yourself to respond differently—whether it's through your tone, your body language, or the role you take on. If you're usually the one who listens quietly, try leading the conversation. If you tend to be assertive, practice stepping back and letting others take the lead. Notice how this shift affects your sense of self and how others respond to you.

Another way to engage with the fluidity of identity is by stepping into roles that feel unfamiliar or even uncomfortable. We all have roles that we gravitate toward—whether it's the caregiver, the leader, the problem-solver, or the peacekeeper. These roles become familiar because they align with the stories we've told ourselves about who we are. But what happens when we try on roles that don't fit neatly into those stories?

For instance, if you've always identified as the peacemaker in your family or group of friends, it might feel foreign to step into a more assertive, confrontational role. You might worry that it will disrupt the harmony you've worked so hard to maintain, or that people won't accept this new version of you. But the truth is, we all have the capacity to embody different roles at different times. Being assertive doesn't negate your ability to bring peace, just as being vulnerable doesn't make you weak.

Stepping into an unfamiliar role is stepping into the unknown, but it's often in these moments that we discover parts of ourselves we didn't know existed. In doing so, we also step into the unknown of our potential. We begin to see that we aren't confined to the roles we've grown

comfortable in. We can expand, adapt, and change, responding to the needs of the moment.

"I've realized how important it is to find the courage to sit in the mud without trying to push it away, because it's not about getting rid of it, but allowing it to just be."

Quinn XCII, a singer-songwriter, shared this insight during his episode on Dualistic Unity. His reflection on anxiety and embracing discomfort mirrors the journey of stepping beyond the fixed layers of identity and sitting with the uncertainty of the unknown. His words remind us that transformation doesn't come from avoiding discomfort but from allowing ourselves to fully experience it.

Something to Reflect On:

Think about a role that feels unfamiliar or uncomfortable to you. What stories have you told yourself about why this role doesn't "fit" you? Now, imagine stepping into that role in a safe, low-pressure environment—perhaps with close friends or in a supportive setting. How does it feel to step into this new identity? What do you discover about yourself when you expand beyond the roles you've grown comfortable in?

One of the most powerful ways to experiment with the unknown is through play. Play isn't just for children—it's a deeply human way of exploring new aspects of ourselves in a safe, non-judgmental environment. When we allow ourselves to play, we suspend the need to be consistent or to uphold the rigid boundaries of our identity. We can be silly, adventurous, daring, and curious without worrying about how we'll be perceived.

In adult life, we often engage in playful identity fluidity without even realizing it. For example, in sales jobs or call centers, role-playing is frequently used as a training technique. Salespeople might practice switching between different tones, personas, or approaches to see how they affect potential clients. This role-play helps them adapt to various social dynamics, learning how to connect with different personalities while remaining fluid in how they present themselves.

Similarly, in therapy, clinicians often use role-playing exercises to help clients explore different sides of themselves or work through emotional challenges. These therapeutic role-plays allow individuals to step outside their usual identity narratives and experiment with new ways of being. Whether it's rehearsing difficult conversations or adopting a different perspective, role-playing creates a safe space to explore parts of ourselves we may otherwise suppress.

Both of these examples highlight how fluidity in identity can be an essential tool for personal growth and adaptability. By allowing ourselves to play with different versions of who we are, we create room for greater self-awareness, creativity, and connection.

In many ways, play is the ultimate expression of fluid potential. Think of how children naturally shift from one role to another while playing—one moment they're pretending to be a superhero, the next they're a chef or an astronaut. They don't question whether these roles align with their "true" identity; they simply embrace the opportunity to explore different ways of being. As adults, we often forget this sense of freedom, becoming more attached to the roles we've defined for ourselves. But the ability to play is still within us, and it's one of the most effective ways to tap into the fluid nature of identity.

Exercise: The Playful Experiment

Set aside some time to engage in a playful activity—whether it's a game, a creative project, or simply an imaginative exercise. The goal isn't to achieve anything specific but to allow yourself to explore without the pressure of "being" a certain way. As you play, notice how you feel when you step outside your usual identity. What aspects of yourself emerge when you let go of the need to be consistent or serious?

As we discussed earlier, authenticity isn't about adhering to a fixed idea of who we are or should be. It's about aligning with the truth of the present moment. Authenticity is not static; it evolves as we do, adapting to the circumstances and experiences we encounter. The idea that we must always be consistent in our identity or behavior is limiting. Authenticity, rather than being a rigid standard, is the freedom to change, grow, and respond to life as it unfolds.

The challenge, then, is how to remain authentic while allowing yourself the space to explore new roles and perspectives. Instead of seeing authenticity as an anchor that ties you to one fixed version of yourself, consider it a dynamic process—something that flows and adapts as you do.

Something to Reflect On:

Think about a time when you felt pressured to maintain consistency in your identity in the name of being "authentic." How did that pressure limit you? Now, consider a broader definition of authenticity—one that embraces fluidity, change, and growth from moment to moment. How does this expanded understanding shift the way you see yourself and your interactions with others?

In this final section, we'll explore the profound sense of liberation that arises when we stop identifying with the stories we've been telling ourselves. This freedom goes beyond the personal; it opens the door to a deeper connection with the world around us and allows us to engage with life from a place of openness and curiosity, rather than fear and self-protection.

Imagine, for example, that you've always identified as an introvert. This label has shaped how you navigate social situations, how you manage your energy, and how you see yourself in relation to others. But what happens if you start to let go of that label? Does that mean you suddenly become an extrovert? No—but it does mean you stop using the label as a boundary that defines your interactions with the world. You open yourself up to the possibility that you can enjoy socializing without feeling drained, or that you can engage in activities that might not fit your preconceived idea of what an introvert "should" do.

Letting go of labels doesn't mean losing your sense of self. It means gaining the freedom to move beyond those labels when they no longer serve you. It's about recognizing that you are more than the roles and labels you've adopted—you are a dynamic, evolving being with limitless potential.

Something to Reflect On:

Think of a label or role that you have strongly identified with—one that feels central to how you see yourself. Now, imagine what it would be like to release that label for an extended period. How might your actions, choices, or even relationships shift without the need to uphold that role? What would it feel like to live without defining yourself by any label at all, allowing yourself to flow from one identity to another as circumstances change?

One of the biggest challenges in letting go of a fixed identity is the discomfort that comes with uncertainty. We've spent our entire lives constructing a sense of self, and the idea of stepping into the unknown—without the familiar markers of identity—can feel unsettling. But remember the lessons from earlier: fear and discomfort are not enemies but invitations to grow. Just as we learned to see fear and failure as allies in our personal growth, we can now approach the unknown in the same way.

What if this uncertainty wasn't something to resist, but something to lean into with curiosity? What if stepping away from the safety of a fixed identity is the key to true freedom? By embracing the discomfort, you open yourself up to new dimensions of yourself— free from the constraints of who you've been told to be.

In doing so, something remarkable happens: we begin to live without boundaries. The lines we've drawn between "who I am" and "who I am not" start to blur. We stop seeing ourselves as separate from the world around us, and we begin to experience a deeper connection with life itself.

This doesn't mean that we lose our individuality. On the contrary, it means that we stop limiting our individuality with rigid definitions and carefully written scripts. We become more attuned to the present moment and more open to the infinite ways we can express ourselves. We stop clinging to the idea of who we are supposed to be and start embracing the freedom to be whoever we are in each moment.

This shift in perspective allows us to engage with life from a place of openness and curiosity. Instead of fearing change or uncertainty, we begin to welcome it. We no longer need to defend our sense of self because we realize that our true self is not something that can be threatened. It is vast, boundless, and beyond definition.

Something to Reflect On:

Consider an area of your life where you've set boundaries for yourself—whether in your relationships, career, or personal growth. How have these boundaries been shaped by your sense of identity or fear of the unknown? Now, imagine what it would feel like to release those boundaries. How might your relationships, career, or personal growth change if you allowed yourself to move beyond the limits you've set for yourself and embrace the fluidity of your evolving self?

Over the next week, choose one situation where you would normally act from a fixed sense of identity—whether at work, with friends, or in a relationship. Consciously allow yourself to break away from the usual role or mask you wear in that situation. Instead of responding in your typical way, experiment with a different approach that embraces the fluidity of your identity. At the end of the week, reflect on how this shift affected your interactions and how you felt about yourself in those moments of change. Did questioning and stepping away from a fixed identity feel liberating, uncomfortable, or both?

As we let go of the constraints of a fixed identity, we begin to experience a deeper connection with the world around us. The boundaries between "self" and "other" that once felt so solid start to dissolve, and we realize that we are not separate from the people, experiences, or environment we engage with. This is where the journey of questioning identity ultimately leads—not to isolation or emptiness, but to a profound and expansive sense of interconnectedness. It is in this space that we find a deeper understanding of ourselves and our place in the larger flow of life.

As we close this chapter, remember that the journey beyond identity is not a destination. It's a process of continual discovery, one that allows you to live with greater authenticity, openness, and curiosity. And in this process, you will find the freedom to become whoever you need to be, in each moment, as you step fully into the unknown.

We've explored the fluid nature of identity, peeled back the layers of stories, roles, and labels that often define us, and taken the bold step of questioning who we think we are. We've begun to see that identity isn't something fixed or permanent; it shifts and adapts much like life itself. And when we let go of the need for certainty about who we are, we find a freedom that opens up new possibilities.

Living without the false certainty of a fixed identity can feel like stepping into uncharted territory, but it's also where some of life's most meaningful experiences unfold. When we're not attached to a particular idea of ourselves, we can meet each moment with curiosity, rather than fear. This doesn't mean losing your sense of self; it means finding a deeper, more authentic connection to life as it unfolds, moment by moment.

Consider this: What is one role or label you can consciously loosen your grip on this week? Whether in a social setting, at work, or in a personal relationship, choose a situation where you typically define yourself by a certain identity and intentionally step away from it. Notice how it feels to engage with others, or with yourself, without reinforcing that role. What new aspects of connection or understanding begin to emerge, both within yourself and in your interactions with others, when you let go of the need to define who you are?

This small experiment is not about abandoning your sense of self, but about creating space for your identity to flow with life's changes. By embracing this fluidity, you not only open the door to discovering new possibilities in each moment for yourself but also invite others to do the same. Your willingness to let go of rigid roles can ripple out, allowing for deeper, more authentic connections with those around you.

In the chapters to come, we will explore these new horizons of interconnectivity, but for now, simply sit with this newfound openness. There's no need to rush into answers or to figure out what comes next. Just be with the questions, and allow yourself to move forward without the need for certainty.

You've begun the process of stepping beyond the boundaries of identity—seeing that the dance of waves is really the dance of a single ocean—let's see where it takes you.

> "To be yourself in a world that is constantly trying to make you something else is the greatest accomplishment."
>
> — Ralph Waldo Emerson

Chapter 7 - The Dance of Separation

We've been walking an epic path—one that has required deep reflection, courage, and a willingness to confront everything we thought we knew about ourselves. Along the way, we've stripped away layers of identity, dismantled the stories we've carried for so long, and faced the uncomfortable truths that were hidden beneath them. It hasn't been easy, but step by step, we've moved closer to a deeper understanding of who we are, and who we are not.

In this journey, we've questioned the narratives we've clung to, recognizing how much of our identity was shaped by the world around us—society, family, past experiences. With each layer we've removed, we've felt the weight lift, and with it, the freedom to see ourselves as more than the roles we've played. We've come to realize that our identity is not the fixed, unchangeable story we once believed it to be, but something far more fluid, capable of being rewritten in every moment.

Through loosening our attachments—whether to control, validation, or certainty—we've begun to recognize how deeply these things have shaped us. The need to control outcomes, to shape the future, to cling to what feels familiar—it all seemed necessary at one point, but as we've let go, we've started to taste the freedom that comes from allowing life to unfold on its own terms. We're no longer as bound by the need to steer the ship. Instead, we're learning to navigate the current.

This path hasn't been without fear. At times, we've had to face the very things we've spent our lives avoiding—fear of failure, of change, of not knowing who we are without our familiar identities. But in confronting the many faces of fear, something powerful has emerged: the realization that fear is not an enemy to be overcome but a guide, showing us where we still hold on too tightly. By leaning into it, we've discovered that failure is not a barrier but a gateway to deeper understanding and growth.

In letting go of control, we've begun to explore the true meaning of authenticity. What does it mean to live without the masks we've worn for so long? As we've allowed those masks to fall, we've come to see that authenticity isn't about adhering to some fixed idea of who we are. It's about being present in the moment, aligning with the truth that is unfolding within us. With each step, we've come closer to living a life that feels genuine, even if it doesn't fit the expectations of others.

And now, having softened the rigid boundaries of identity, we find ourselves at the edge of a profound realization. The very notion of a solid, unchanging self has begun to dissolve. What once felt like a fixed core—the 'I' we've always known—is revealing itself to be far more fluid, far more expansive. With that realization comes a new question, one that shakes the very foundation of our beliefs: If we are not who we thought we were, then what does that mean for the separation we feel from others?

As we release the need to cling to our old identities, we are left with this pressing, liberating question: Are we truly separate from others, or have we only believed we are? Could it be that the boundaries we've lived by—the distinctions between self and other, me and you—are not as real as we once thought? Is it possible that this sense of division is just another illusion, one we've clung to out of habit and fear?

These questions challenge our deepest assumptions. From childhood, we're taught to see the world in divided terms—me and you, this and that, self and other. We build identities to carve out our place in this seemingly divided world. This sense of separateness gives us a false sense of control, like a dancer clumsily trying to impose steps on a rhythm they barely hear. But life is not something to be controlled—it's a dance of connection, and when we let go of our mind's rigid choreography, we find ourselves moving effortlessly with the natural flow.

After all we've uncovered—the fluidity of identity, the release of control, and the deeper truths revealed—it's becoming clearer that this story of separation may be the most pervasive illusion of all, keeping us disconnected from the interconnectedness that has always been there, waiting for us to see it.

Alan Watts often spoke of life as a dance, emphasizing that its meaning isn't found in reaching a final goal, but in fully participating in the moment-to-moment flow. In a dance, the joy comes not from arriving at the end, but from moving with the music as it unfolds. Life, too, reveals its depth when we stop striving to control each step and instead allow ourselves to be carried by the rhythm. Watts reminded us that when we stop seeing life as a series of destinations and start embracing it as a dance, the illusion of separation begins to dissolve. The dance was never about solitary movements—it's always been about moving together, in harmony with the world and those around us. This recognition, Watts believed, is where true freedom lies—not in control, but in effortless participation.

We've already seen how our sense of identity is more fluid than we once assumed. Now, it's time to take that understanding even further, moving beyond the personal to explore how this illusion of separation has shaped our view of the world.

This isn't about jumping to grand conclusions or rushing toward abstract ideas. It's about gently unraveling the threads that hold the assumption of separation together, starting with the everyday experiences that shape our lives. The way we move with others, the way we interact with nature, and even the way science explains the universe all offer subtle glimpses of something more—a deeper interconnectedness that often goes unnoticed.

Exploring this idea requires patience and curiosity. The recognition of unity can seem overwhelming, but it doesn't have to be. You've likely felt it in small, quiet moments—a shared glance, a sense of belonging in nature, or the rhythm of a single action. These moments are invitations to transcend the superficial and recognize that we are all part of something greater.

Let's move through this together. By the end of this chapter, you may find that the lines between 'you' and 'me,' 'this' and 'that,' start to blur—not in a confusing way, but in a liberating one. The question shifts from 'Who am I?' to 'Where do I end and you begin?"'

> That which is the finest essence—this whole world has that as its soul. That is Reality. That is the Self. And thou art that."
>
> — Upanishads

As we unravel this question, the natural world offers clear evidence that interconnectedness is not just a philosophical concept but a reality we can observe in everyday life. Nature shows us that nothing truly exists in isolation. From the smallest particle to the largest ecosystem, life constantly reveals the ways in which everything is connected, whether we recognize it or not. By looking beyond our personal experience and turning to the natural world and science, we see that interconnectedness is not merely an abstract idea—it is a visible and fundamental aspect of reality.

In nature, every plant, animal, and microorganism plays a role in maintaining the balance of its environment. The survival of each species depends on the health of the whole, creating a delicate dance of relationships that constantly shifts and adapts.

Consider a forest: Trees provide shelter and food for countless species, from birds to insects. Their roots create networks underground, allowing them to communicate and share resources with other trees, a phenomenon known as the "Wood Wide Web." Fungi connect the roots of trees through a mycorrhizal network, helping them access nutrients and water, while in return, the trees provide the fungi with sugars produced through photosynthesis. Even the fallen leaves that return to the forest floor complete their role in the dance, nourishing the entire system.

Every element in the forest, whether visible or hidden, contributes to the survival and health of the whole. When one part of this system is removed or disrupted, the entire balance can be thrown off. This is a living example of how interconnectedness is fundamental to life. Just as individual cells cooperate to form tissues and organs, the forest isn't a collection of isolated trees and creatures—it's an ecosystem of cooperation, where each element contributes to the survival of the whole.

This same dance of interconnection extends beyond the forest, into the social and cultural fabric of human life.

> "The whole world is fragile, but unity makes it strong. When harmony is found in nature, the whole universe becomes one."
>
> — Tao Te Ching

And while nature offers us a tangible, everyday example of our connection, science takes us even deeper. Some of the most intriguing insights about the interconnected nature of reality come from quantum physics.

Quantum entanglement describes how two particles can become so deeply connected that the state of one instantly influences the other, regardless of the distance between them. This connection, which occurs faster than light, challenges our perception of even space and time as boundaries.

Albert Einstein famously referred to this as "spooky action at a distance," and for good reason. It challenges our understanding of how the universe works. If two particles can be connected across vast distances, what does that say about the nature of reality itself?

Something to Reflect On:

Reflect on a time when you felt unexpectedly connected to someone far away—emotionally or spiritually. How did that connection affect your sense of distance or separation?

What quantum physics suggests is that separation may be a human construct, not a universal truth. Just like the interconnected forest, we too may be entangled in connections that go far beyond what we can see or understand. Our thoughts, actions, and even our very existence may be tied to a larger, deeper reality.

Bees, for example, rely on flowers for nectar while pollinating them in return. Trees communicate and share resources through underground fungal networks, forming a network of interdependence. When one part of this system is disrupted, the entire balance is thrown off. This illustrates that nature is not a collection of isolated organisms but a single interconnected system, where the well-being of each element depends on the health of the whole.

These realizations invite us to consider how interconnected we are with the world around us, not just in theory, but in practical, biological ways. We are not solitary beings; we are part of a vast network of life, where every action, no matter how small, influences the whole.

Just as the brain is a network of interconnected cells, perhaps our awareness is part of an even larger network, one that connects all life. The mind, in this sense, is not an isolated phenomenon locked inside our heads. It is shaped, influenced, and perhaps even extended by the world around us. The more we understand this, the more we can see that our thoughts and actions are not just individual events but part of a larger, interconnected reality.

At this point, you might be wondering how all of this—forests, quantum particles, bees, and neurons—relates to your everyday life. After all, it's easy to think of interconnectedness as something that happens "out there," in nature or in the lab, but not in our day-to-day routines.

Think about how your mood can influence those around you, or how a single act of kindness might set off a chain reaction of positive events. Just as every tree affects the forest, every choice you make extends beyond yourself, influencing others in ways you may never fully see.

Imagine a moment in a coffee shop where one act of kindness changes everything through a series of 'pay it forward' gestures. It begins with one person paying for a stranger's order, and soon, others are moved to do the same. In this small, everyday moment, a cascade of kindness forms, touching lives beyond what anyone involved could have anticipated. This shows how each of us, through even the smallest actions, can influence the whole of life, often in ways we never directly witness.

When we realize that separation is more illusion than reality, we see that everything we do matters—not just for ourselves, but for the larger dance of life. Our thoughts, words, and actions are all part of this interconnected dance, whether we're aware of it or not.

The natural world, science, and our own bodies all reveal the same fundamental truth: interconnectedness is not an abstract concept— it's a living reality.

As Lao Tzu wrote in the *Tao Te Ching*: "He who knows that enough is enough will always have enough." This insight points to the fact that our sense of separation often arises from a feeling of lack—a belief that something is missing from our lives. But when we recognize that we already have everything we need, the illusion of separateness dissolves, and we see that we are part of a larger whole.

This doesn't mean that life suddenly becomes easy or that our challenges disappear. Instead, it's about shifting our perspective. Recognizing that we already have everything we need means understanding that true fulfillment comes from within, not from external achievements, possessions, or approval. Life will still present difficulties, but when we stop striving to fill an inner sense of lack, we approach these challenges with more clarity and resilience.

This realization doesn't require us to abandon the practicalities of life. Instead, it offers a new lens through which to view the world. We can still pursue goals and solve problems, but without the constant pressure to seek external validation or control. It invites us to see ourselves as part of something much larger, where every action, no matter how small, contributes to the whole. And as we'll explore in the next sections, this shift in perspective has profound implications for how we live, work, and relate to one another.

This week, commit to noticing how your thoughts, words, and actions influence those around you. In a conversation, decision, or interaction, pause and reflect on how your emotional state or choices might affect the people you're with. How does your presence shape the experience for others, and how are you impacted in return? At the end of the week, take a moment to write down your reflections. How has this awareness changed the way you see your role in the interconnected dance of life?

If nature and science reveal unity in the physical world, then culture and relationships show us how deeply this connectivity is woven into the fabric of our everyday lives. As we've explored in previous chapters, whether we realize it or not, our sense of identity, our beliefs, and even our ambitions are shaped by the people around us and the cultures we live in. Just like a forest or an ecosystem, human life is a network of interdependent relationships, constantly influencing and shaping each other in both subtle and profound ways.

Our emotions, like our identities, are influenced by the people around us. Relationships are one of the most immediate and direct ways we experience interconnectedness in our daily lives. Even those who lead solitary lives—like committed hermits—are inextricably linked to others through the broader influences of culture, history, and the natural world. Whether through family, friendships, workplaces, or communities, we are all part of a greater dance of connection, moving in ways that are influenced by others, even when we don't realize it.

Think about how your moods, thoughts, and behaviors shift depending on who you're with. Around certain people, you may feel more confident or open; with others, more reserved or cautious. These shifts are subtle but constant, reflecting the complex connections that make up our social world. We are always responding to one another, often without realizing it.

Psychology refers to this as emotional contagion—the way our emotions and attitudes subtly influence those around us. If you've ever walked into a room filled with stress or anxiety, you've likely felt your own mood shift. Similarly, being around someone calm or joyful can lift your spirits, grounding you in their presence. But this emotional exchange goes deeper than just momentary mood changes; it plays a significant role in shaping how we interact with each other over time.

"The mind is the friend of the conditioned soul, and his enemy as well."

— Bhagavad Gita

Something to Reflect On:

Consider a time when your mood shifted based on the emotions of others around you. How did their energy affect your behavior, and how might your own emotional state influence those around you? What does this reveal about the interconnected nature of our relationships?

In relationships, the emotions we consistently bring into our interactions—whether calm or stress, joy or frustration—shape how we communicate, trust, and connect. Over time, these repeated emotional exchanges create patterns that influence the dynamics of the relationship itself. The way we feel and behave in these relationships gradually forms how we see each other and how we respond to one another.

As we interact with those closest to us, their responses can help us understand more about ourselves. Sometimes, these interactions are supportive and affirming, strengthening our connection and reinforcing our sense of belonging. Other times, they challenge us, bringing out other aspects of ourselves—like insecurities, fears, or judgments—that we might otherwise avoid. These difficult experiences, though uncomfortable, offer opportunities for personal growth and deeper understanding of how we relate to the world. In this way, relationships are not just about our connections with others—they also play a crucial role in shaping our self-awareness. The emotions we share and experience in these relationships continually shape our views of ourselves, influencing both personal growth and how we engage with others.

Beyond personal dynamics, the choices we make and the emotions we carry affect more than just our closest relationships. They extend to our broader communities, workplaces, and social circles. Just as no tree in a forest stands alone, none of us live in isolation from the people and systems that surround us. Every decision we make influences others, whether we are aware of it or not, touching not only our immediate relationships but the wider world as well.

Something to Reflect On:

Think of a time when your small action—whether intentional or unintentional—had a noticeable impact on someone else. How did it affect their mood, decisions, or interactions with others? How does recognizing this influence change how you approach your daily actions?

Consider a simple conversation with a coworker. Maybe it's just a quick exchange about a project, or maybe it's something deeper—a moment of vulnerability, empathy, or support. That interaction, no matter how small, leaves an imprint. It shapes how the other person feels, how they approach their work, and even how they interact with others. Over time, these small moments of connection build into something larger, creating the culture of the workplace itself.

"Awareness is the greatest agent for change."

— Eckhart Tolle

Our actions influence the communities we're part of. If you volunteer your time, donate to a cause, or simply help a neighbor in need, you're contributing to a collective effort, impacting more people than you may ever realize. This isn't about grand gestures or heroic acts; it's about recognizing that everything we do, no matter how small, influences the dance for everyone.

A powerful example of interconnectedness comes from the story of *Rachel Carson*, a marine biologist whose book, "Silent Spring", reshaped the way society views the environment. In 1962, Carson exposed the dangers of pesticides like DDT (Dichloro-Diphenyl-Trichloroethane), showing how they not only harmed insects but also poisoned birds, wildlife, and even human beings. Her research illustrated how no part of nature exists in isolation—how the choices we make ripple out into the ecosystems that sustain life.

Carson faced strong opposition from chemical companies that sought to discredit her work, but her courage sparked a movement that would eventually lead to the ban of DDT in the U.S. and the creation of the Environmental Protection Agency. Her individual action—writing a book—became the catalyst for global environmental awareness, a wave that transformed public policy and shifted the way we think about human responsibility to the planet.

Carson's story is a reminder that the consequences of our actions often extend far beyond what we can immediately see. Each choice, no matter how small, is part of a larger network, influencing the world in ways we may never fully understand. Her legacy demonstrates the power of recognized unity: that one voice, one action, creates waves of change across the world.

Even the way we treat ourselves has an ongoing impact. When we approach life with acceptance and self-awareness, we foster emotional and physical well-being, which naturally improves how we engage with others. On the other hand, resistance and self-judgment create stress and emotional disconnection, weakening our health and making us more prone to irritability, withdrawal, and strained interactions.

All of this—the cultural stories we internalize, the relationships we nurture, and the cascade of our actions—connects us to one another in ways we rarely think about. This connection is always there, whether we're aware of it or not, influencing how we see ourselves, how we treat others, and how we move through the world.

So what does it mean to live in this interconnected reality? In one sense, nothing changes, and yet everything does. It doesn't mean we need to abandon our individuality or lose ourselves in the collective. Rather, it's about expanding our awareness to include both our personal experience and our connection to others. It's about realizing that we are not alone in this world, and that every interaction, no matter how small, has the potential to create connection, understanding, and growth.

As we move through life, the more we see the interconnectivity of culture and relationships, the more we can embrace our role within it. We can begin to approach our interactions with a deeper sense of responsibility and awareness, knowing that we are always contributing to something larger than ourselves. This understanding can transform not only how we see the world but how we show up in it—more connected, more compassionate, and more aware of the ways in which we are all deeply intertwined.

Interconnectedness might seem like a distant idea at first, but you've likely already experienced it in subtle, everyday moments—often without realizing it. These moments appear as quiet epiphanies, where the narrative you've held onto is questioned, offering a glimpse of something bigger. These moments may not be grand or dramatic, but they are powerful in their simplicity. They remind you that you're not navigating life alone—your actions, thoughts, and emotions are constantly extending outward, influencing the world in ways you might not always see.

Think back to a time when you felt an unexpected sense of connection to someone or something. Maybe it was during a meaningful conversation with a friend or stranger. Perhaps it was while watching the sunset, when for a brief moment, you forgot your worries and simply felt at peace with the world. Or maybe it was in a time of crisis, when you saw the kindness of others lift you or someone else in ways that felt deeper than words could express.

These moments may seem fleeting, but they're anything but random. They offer glimpses into a reality where connection is more apparent. When you experience them, you temporarily step out of the divisive narrative and feel the deeper links that exist all around you. And while these moments often arrive unbidden, they have the power to subtly reshape how you see your relationships, your ambitions, and the way you move through life.

Take, for example, the experience of empathy. When someone you care about is going through a difficult time, you may feel their pain as if it were your own. This ability to emotionally connect with others—whether they're family, friends, or even strangers— demonstrates how intertwined our emotional lives are. We are not as separate as we think. In fact, our capacity to feel for one another may be one of the clearest signs of our inherent interconnectedness.

Consider your closest relationships. How much of who you are has been shaped by the people around you? Your friends, family, colleagues, and even casual acquaintances all play a role in shaping your thoughts, behaviors, and decisions, often in ways that are invisible but undeniable. In fact, many of the choices you make every day are influenced by the needs, desires, and expectations of those you care about. This is not a weakness or a lack of independence—it's a reflection of how deeply connected we are to one another.

Imagine a time when you were struggling with a decision, unsure of which path to take. Perhaps it was advice from a loved one or even a quiet moment of connection that helped you move forward. That moment wasn't just about you making a decision—it was an exchange of energy, wisdom, and support between you and the people in your life. Whether you were aware of it or not, the outcome was shaped by your connection to others.

These invisible bonds are what create the fabric of our lives. We are constantly in a network of cooperation with those around us, much like cells working together to sustain the body. This cooperative influence extends far beyond the immediate situation, shaping the fabric of our lives and relationships. When you act with kindness, support, or understanding, the impact of that energy can spread through your relationships, inspiring others to do the same. Conversely, when you act from a place of fear, anger, or isolation, those states can create further disconnection, not just for you but for others as well.

When we're looking for a sense of value, certainty, and control, it's easy to think of our professional life and ambitions as separate from this deeper sense of connection. But they're not. In fact, the workplace is one of the most powerful arenas where our constant relationship with one another plays out, even if we don't always notice it. Think about how much of your day-to-day experience at work depends on relationships—collaborating with colleagues, interacting with clients or customers, and contributing to a larger organizational goal. None of these things happen in isolation.

"I am not a self-made man. I got a lot of help. I had so many people help me along the way. I had a lot of help, and I had to tell that to the world because they always say that I'm a self-made man. I'm not. Everyone needs help, whether it's training partners or teachers or coaches, mentors, or people who inspire you."

— Arnold Schwarzenegger

Have you ever had a moment at work where a small gesture—like a word of encouragement or a collaborative breakthrough—changed the course of your day, or even your career? These moments may feel like personal victories, but they're often the result of a complex series of interactions and relationships. You didn't achieve that success alone, even if it felt like it. The ideas, inspiration, and support from others played a part in shaping that outcome. Recognizing this doesn't diminish your personal achievements—it enriches them by acknowledging the wider context in which they occur.

This recognition can also shape how you approach your ambitions. When you understand that your success is intertwined with the success of others, you begin to see collaboration as a powerful tool rather than a compromise. Your goals become less about individual achievement and more about contributing to something larger. This shift doesn't mean you lose your personal drive—it means you gain a deeper sense of purpose, knowing that your efforts are part of a broader tapestry of influence and connection.

These small, personal moments of connection reflect a larger truth: we are part of a collective experience. Our individual realizations alter the communities we belong to.

Think about how your relationships might change if you approached them with this awareness of your impact. How would your interactions shift if you saw every conversation, every moment of connection, as something that extends far beyond the immediate situation? How might your ambitions and goals evolve if you recognized that your success is deeply linked to the success of those around you?

These are not just theoretical questions—they are opportunities to see the world through a less restrictive lens. By doing so, you open yourself up to a deeper, more meaningful way of living. You start to realize that every action, no matter how small, contributes to a larger whole. And in this realization, you find both empowerment and responsibility. Empowerment because you are not alone in this journey, and responsibility because your choices have a far-reaching impact, touching the lives of others in ways you may never fully understand.

Your choice influences your daily habits, the products you purchase, and the people around you—not because you're part of a movement, but because your own clarity and integrity inspire others to reflect on their own choices. A compelling example of this is the Nestlé boycott that began in 1977. Concerned individuals and grassroots organizations objected to Nestlé's aggressive marketing of infant formula in developing countries, where it contributed to malnutrition and infant mortality. The boycott, which spread through word-of-mouth and community networks rather than marketing or social media, grew steadily over the years and eventually led to international guidelines on infant feeding products. This demonstrates how individual ethical choices can inspire wider action and create meaningful change.

This approach to life is about recognizing your personal power in every choice. The change you create in your own life will have an impact, not through joining collective efforts, but through the influence that comes from living with awareness. When you refuse to participate in divisive ambitions or harmful intentions—you're making a stand for everyone.

Instead of focusing on large-scale action or activism, the emphasis here is on clarity of personal priorities. For example, if your priority is to live sustainably, you might make intentional changes in your lifestyle, such as reducing your use of plastics, supporting companies that offer environmentally friendly alternatives, or finding ways to consume less overall. These are not grand gestures—they are deliberate choices made with awareness of the relationship between your actions and the world around you. And as you change, the world changes around you.

Consider the example of a household reducing its plastic consumption. Without preaching or organizing, the simple act of consistently choosing reusable products over single-use plastics can inspire curiosity among friends or family members. They might ask, "Why do you choose this over that?" This is the natural unfolding of influence, one person's clarity opening the door for others to reflect on their own habits and priorities.

In contrast, telling people what's best for them and the world often threatens their sense of value, certainty, and control, immediately making you the problem rather than the issue you hoped to address. This reaction is rooted in a fundamental truth: beneath almost every problem you want others to solve, there's usually someone else trying to maintain control. When we push too hard, we inadvertently become part of that same dynamic, reinforcing the very resistance we're trying to change.

By making clear, intentional decisions in your own life, you contribute to a larger shift without needing to control or direct that shift. Just as your emotional state influences those around you in subtle ways, your decisions and priorities have an impact, affecting others who are ready to consider new possibilities.

When you operate from a place of personal integrity and clarity, the intention influences how you contribute to the environments you are part of—whether it's in your professional life, your neighborhood, or your interactions with those around you.

At work, you may notice that your personal approach to collaboration, ethics, or problem-solving starts to shape the atmosphere without any conscious effort to influence others. By aligning your actions with awareness, you create a space where others may feel encouraged to do the same. This isn't about leading movements or pushing for collective change—it's about showing up fully in your own clarity and allowing that to resonate outward.

In your community, the same dynamic applies. Choosing to live with awareness and alignment naturally enhances the well-being of the people and places around you. When you prioritize sustainable practices, show empathy, or offer support in ways that align with your personal values, those around you may be quietly impacted by your example. The change spreads, not because you intended it to, but because the authenticity of your actions speaks louder than any organized effort ever could. Much like the delicate flutter of a butterfly that sets off a distant typhoon, this chain reaction unfolds quietly and often imperceptibly, yet its impact is undeniably real.

Living with awareness—whether it's through boycotting plastics, being mindful in your work, or simply treating others with understanding—creates a quiet but profound impact. The more you embody this, the more the fact of unity reveals itself, through the small, consistent choices you make every day.

In this way, the power of change lies in individual transformation, where each person's clarity, priorities, and actions create immeasurable change. Caught up in our roles as parents, workers, or friends, we tend to view our lives as separate. But when we pause and look deeper, we start to notice how much we share, even if our experiences take different forms.

Think of a time when you've struggled with something—a personal challenge, a tough decision, or a moment of uncertainty. Now, consider how many others around you, even strangers, are likely going through something similar, whether or not they speak of it. The specifics of the situation may vary, but the underlying emotions—fear, doubt, hope, or relief—are universal. When we strip away the storylines that make us feel like our struggles are unique, we see that we are all navigating the same emotional landscape. This shared experience is not a matter of perspective; it's an inherent part of being human.

How often have you found yourself in conversation with someone, thinking that they couldn't possibly understand what you're going through, only to discover they've had similar thoughts, worries, or experiences? The connection was always there, waiting to be acknowledged, but sometimes we miss it because we're too focused on our own experience. When the mind's walls begin to soften, these moments of shared understanding become more visible, more natural.

Without our commitment to identity driving us toward constant competition, the need to prove ourselves, or the desire to "win," collaboration begins to flow more freely. In any setting—whether in work, family life, or community projects—the pressure to outperform others or to maintain a certain image creates unnecessary tension. But when those pressures are released, it becomes obvious that we are all working toward the same goals, even if our individual paths look different.

When we recognize that we're all in this life together, the competitive mindset that drives so much of our professional and social lives loses its grip. Instead of focusing on what separates us— who is better, smarter, or more capable—we can begin to see how much stronger we are when we collaborate. This isn't about suppressing individual ambition; it's about realizing that our ambitions don't need to be at odds with the ambitions of others. In fact, they often complement each other.

For example, in a workplace, there are many moving parts— different people with different roles and responsibilities. In a competitive, ego-driven environment, these roles can feel siloed, with each person or team focusing solely on their own tasks and goals. But when we get out of the way and collaboration becomes the focus, those silos dissolve, and the collective goal becomes clearer. Just like cells within an organ, each with its own specialized function, people work together to support the greater system, creating something more robust than any one part could achieve alone. Each person's efforts contribute to the larger success of the project, the team, or the organization. When we recognize that we're all in this together, collaboration happens naturally, without the need for forced teamwork or superficial partnerships.

In family and community life, this same principle applies. We can spend so much time trying to manage our individual roles—being the "responsible one," the "successful one," or the "independent one"—that we forget how interconnected our lives truly are. But when we let go of these labels, even briefly, we start to see how much we rely on one another, not out of weakness but out of shared human experience. This realization fosters deeper cooperation, not because we have to, but because we begin to understand that the well-being of those around us is inextricably linked to our own.

Whether we're facing global crises or personal hardships, the common thread is that we are all navigating uncertainty. This shared vulnerability is often hidden beneath the surface, masked by our desire to appear strong, capable, or unaffected. But when we allow ourselves to see past these defenses, we begin to recognize the shared nature of our challenges.

For example, consider a community experiencing economic hardship. At first glance, each person's struggle might seem individual—one family dealing with job loss, another with healthcare costs, another with housing issues. But at the root, these challenges stem from the same source: a shared dependence on systems that affect us all. As Malcolm Gladwell explains in *The Tipping Point*, small actions can create larger societal change. One example is the transformation of New York City's subway system in the 1990s. By addressing small issues, like cleaning graffiti and fixing broken windows, the city eventually saw a significant reduction in crime. This 'Broken Windows Theory' demonstrates how addressing seemingly small, local problems can strengthen the whole community. Similarly, when one person finds support, it strengthens the entire system. When one family gets back on their feet, it contributes to the community's resilience, creating a ripple effect that benefits everyone.

As we move through life without identity's boundaries, compassion becomes less of a choice and more of an instinctual response. When we see ourselves in others, it becomes natural to offer support, a kind word, or understanding, because we recognize that their experience is not so different from our own. Kindness isn't something we need to cultivate or force—it arises naturally when we realize that we are all participating in the same life, navigating the same struggles, and seeking the same peace.

This kind of empathetic response isn't grand or performative. It shows up in everyday moments: in the way we listen to a friend, in the patience we offer a colleague, or in the small acts of kindness we extend to strangers. Without the egoic need to separate ourselves from others, we stop viewing these moments as acts of charity or favor. Instead, they become simple acknowledgments of our shared humanity.

Compassion, in this sense, is not something we "do" for others—it's a natural consequence of seeing life as it is. The barriers that once made us feel separate soften, and what remains is a genuine connection, not based on effort but on a deep understanding that we are all in this together.

When we remove our barriers, it becomes clear that we are truly all in this together. Each of us brings something unique to the table— our perspectives, talents, and journeys—but these differences don't divide us; they enrich the collective whole. We are not separate entities moving through life on parallel tracks. With this realization, life becomes less about defending our personal boundaries and more about participating fully in the dance of connection that has been there all along.

In the chapters to come, we will continue to explore how this shared experience deepens and transforms as we move toward greater awareness. For now, simply recognizing that we are not separate— and that we never have been—is enough.

"The self is all-pervading, beyond birth, beyond mind, transcending all reality. He who realizes this knows all."

— Upanishads

Chapter 8 - The Paradox of Control

At the core of our struggle lies a deep-seated belief in separation—this illusion that we are fundamentally divided from one another and from life itself. Yet, as this illusion begins to unravel, another rises to the surface: control.

We construct systems and ideologies to maintain order, hoping to create stability. Yet, despite our efforts, the gap between peace, unity, and connection and our reality only seems to widen. The harder we try to bridge this gap through force, the bigger and more insurmountable it becomes. The more we attempt to close it with control, the more distant and unreachable peace and connection seem.

This is the paradox of control: the more we pursue it, the further we drift from the peace we so desperately seek.

We can envision a world built on the foundations of empathy and cooperation, where communities flourish and individuals trust one another. In this vision, our structures of society would serve to enhance human connection and well-being rather than exacerbate the gap of disconnection and competition. It is a world where identity, attachment, and control are not the guiding force—where we recognize the interconnectedness of all life and act from a place of mutual understanding and respect. But this is not the world we live in.

In reality, the world we inhabit is shaped by systems and structures that reflect our deepest insecurities and fears. Governments, corporations, and institutions operate on the premise of control—seeking to manage resources, people, and outcomes in a constant effort to maintain power. We, too, as individuals, live in this mode of control, trying to manage our lives, relationships, and emotions through the lens of separateness and self-interest. The result is a world where division, conflict, and exploitation are the norm, not the exception—something we touched on in Chapter 4 when exploring how our attempts to control outcomes often create the very chaos we seek to avoid.

Consider the collapse of the Soviet Union, a regime that exemplified the dangers of centralized control. Built on the premise of dominance and power, the Soviet Union exerted control over its people, resources, and even its global standing through the Cold War. Yet, this need for control only deepened internal instability, leading to economic collapse and political fragmentation. What began as an attempt to maintain power ultimately led to its downfall, illustrating how control at the societal level often creates the very chaos it seeks to prevent.

The gap between the world we could live in and the world we do live in is staggering.

This paradox is not just an abstract concept; it manifests in our everyday lives. As discussed earlier, our desire for control breeds stress and anxiety. On a larger scale, this same desire fuels wars, environmental destruction, and societal discord. Attempting to manage every outcome only deepens the sense of confusion and instability in our lives.

This chapter is not about providing solutions or inspiring hope for a better future. It is about confronting the reality of where we are—facing the truth that our pursuit of control is the very thing that keeps us from peace. We must acknowledge the weight of this contradiction and the emotional, psychological, and societal cost of living in a world built on the illusion of control. The world we see around us, filled with division and destruction, is not the result of a few isolated problems but the inevitable outcome of a massive collective of individuals rooted in the belief that control is the path to safety and success.

"You never change things by fighting the existing reality. To change something, build a new model that makes the existing model obsolete."

— R. Buckminster Fuller

As we move through this chapter, we will explore the consequences. We will examine how the desire for control shapes our emotional lives, fractures our relationships, and creates the systems of power and exploitation that define the modern world. And as we confront the painful reality of this paradox, we will begin to ask the deeper question: why, despite our best intentions, does the world continue to reflect the very forces we wish to transcend? What are we missing? Why, despite our efforts to untie the knot, does it always seem to get tighter?

At the core of human behavior lies an enduring belief: that if we can dictate the flow of life—if we can manage people, circumstances, and events—we can secure happiness, safety, and peace. This belief drives our decisions, shapes our relationships, and underpins the systems we create, from governments to corporations to personal relationships. But this need for domination, rather than delivering the peace we seek, leads us further into anxiety, conflict, and disconnection. The harder we strive for authority over life, the more it spirals into chaos.

Whether at the individual or societal level, control leads to barriers, locks, and weapons. Societies built on control are as fragile as the personal illusions we cling to, and the same instability emerges on every scale.

Instead of fostering cooperation and empathy, these systems reinforce the mind's belief in separation, leading to needless competition, exploitation, and conflict. The collective fear of losing control drives governments to wage wars, corporations to callously strip the planet of its resources, and individuals to inadvertently see one another as threats rather than partners in a shared existence.

As we've already uncovered, our need for control stems from a deeper fear—the fear that arises from the illusion of separation. When we believe that we are isolated, disconnected from others and from life itself, the desire to exert control becomes an attempt to shield ourselves from the unknown. But this need only perpetuates the cycle of disconnection: the more we try to control life, the more separate we feel, and the more separate we feel, the more we try to control life.

> "When you let go of who you are, you become
> who you might be."
>
> — Rumi

In relationships, this dynamic plays out as a constant struggle for power and influence. Whether in romantic partnerships, family dynamics, or friendships, the drive to control or impose one's perspective leads to conflict, resentment, and emotional distance. Instead of fostering intimacy and understanding, relationships become environments where efforts to maintain control create barriers to genuine connection.

On a broader scale, this same dynamic drives conflicts between nations, political ideologies, and social groups. The desire for control and dominance, rooted in the belief in separateness, leads to wars, economic exploitation, and systemic oppression. The need to assert superiority and maintain dominance manifests as both overt and structural violence.

Striving for control leads to anxiety, stress, and disconnection. Always chasing peace, we end up exhausted, disconnected from the currents of life that could bring fulfillment.

Something to Reflect On:

Reflect on a time when you tried to control an outcome in your life—a relationship, career decision, or personal goal. How did that desire for control impact your emotional state? Did it bring the peace you hoped for, or did it lead to greater anxiety and frustration?

The systems we have built to govern the world—political, economic, and social—are crumbling under the weight of their own contradictions. The more we try to exert dominion over nature, the more we destroy the ecosystems that sustain life. The more we attempt to regulate populations through violence and coercion, the more resistance and unrest we create. The more we commodify human relationships, the more isolated and disconnected people become.

By trying to control life, we deny its fundamental nature: that it is ever-changing, fluid, and beyond the grasp of any one individual or system. This attempt to impose control creates division and conflict, blinding us to the deeper truths of our shared existence.

What makes this paradox so difficult to overcome is that we fiercely resist recognizing that control is an illusion, clinging to it as though it could offer us security. Letting go of control can feel like losing everything—security, identity, even survival. But until we confront this misunderstanding, we will remain trapped in a cycle of control and reaction. The peace we long for cannot be achieved through control, because control itself creates division. The more we chase it, the further we move from the sense of peace that comes from acceptance.

The first step in breaking free from this cycle is to recognize that control is not the solution—it is the very thing fueling the cycle we seek to escape. This recognition is not easy. It requires us to let go of deeply ingrained beliefs about how life should be, and to accept that much of what we strive for is based on a misunderstanding of life's true nature. But until we make this shift in awareness, we will remain caught in this paradox of control, forever chasing peace and stability through methods that only deepen our disconnection from ourselves, each other, and the world.

Something to Reflect On:

In what areas of your life do you feel the strongest need for control? How might your relationships or sense of peace change if you let go of that need?

The allure of control shapes the entire world we live in. The drive to control, when magnified across societies and institutions, results in a world that mirrors our inner turmoil. From broken relationships and dysfunctional communities to governments and corporations driven by greed, fear, and domination, the need for control manifests outwardly in every structure we've created.

This fragmentation is not accidental. It is the inevitable result of building, using, and maintaining systems that reflect the egoic mindset—systems designed to ease our fear, ensure superiority, and secure resources, rather than foster cooperation and mutual well-being. The result is a world marked by division, conflict, and competition—a world where control has not led to peace but to deepening disconnection.

When we try to control others—whether consciously or unconsciously—relationships become battlegrounds of power struggles, manipulation, and unmet expectations. This dynamic is most visible in families, where parents may attempt to control their children out of fear, believing that by managing their behavior, they can protect them from harm or failure. But this control often backfires. Children, feeling suffocated by expectations, either rebel or withdraw, leading to emotional distance and resentment.

Partners who attempt to mold or control one another—driven by fear of vulnerability or loss—end up creating emotional walls rather than closeness. The need to control another person's actions, thoughts, or feelings creates a relationship based on power dynamics, where neither partner feels fully seen or accepted. The more we try to control others, the wider the gap grows between us, turning relationships into arenas of frustration and disconnection, often leading to their breakdown.

In environments where individuals feel the need to compete for dominance or influence, trust erodes. Instead of seeing others as allies, we view them as potential threats or competitors. This creates a culture of mistrust and isolation, where genuine collaboration is replaced by politics and power plays.

In schools, students are taught to compete for grades, achievements, and future success, reinforcing the idea that life is a contest to be won rather than a collaborative journey. This emphasis on control— over outcomes, performance, and others—teaches children from an early age that their value lies in their ability to dominate or outshine their peers. The result is an education system that produces more stress and anxiety than it does curiosity or creativity.

"Education is what remains after one has forgotten what one has learned in school."

— Albert Einstein

In workplaces, the culture of control is equally pervasive. Companies that prioritize profits above people foster environments where employees are valued not for their inherent humanity, but for their productivity. However, some companies, like Patagonia, have thrived by letting go of traditional corporate control. Yvon Chouinard, the founder of Patagonia, built the company on trust and environmental responsibility. Rather than controlling every aspect of the business or maximizing profits at any cost, Patagonia encourages customers to buy less, repair what they own, and take care of the planet. By empowering both employees and customers to make responsible choices, Patagonia has become a leader in sustainable business practices. This approach shows that businesses can succeed by trusting people and supporting collective well-being, rather than trying to control every outcome.

Workers constantly pressured to perform are trapped in a system where management—over time, resources, and results—is the measure of success. Collaboration and mutual support are often sacrificed in the name of efficiency, and individuals feel isolated and disconnected in their pursuit of personal advancement or survival.

An extreme yet telling example of this is the installation of suicide prevention nets at Foxconn factories in China, where workers assemble products for global tech giants like Apple. The relentless drive for efficiency, production, and profit led to such grueling conditions that employees, feeling isolated and dehumanized, resorted to suicide. Rather than addressing the root causes— overwork, lack of autonomy, and disconnection—the solution became a literal net to catch those who tried to escape. This starkly illustrates how the pursuit of control and efficiency in corporations can reduce individuals to mere cogs in a machine, sacrificing human well-being for the sake of output.

Communities, too, are shaped by this drive for control. Neighborhoods are divided by economic class, race, and political ideology, with each group attempting to secure its own interests, often at the expense of others. Instead of fostering spaces for connection and understanding, communities become places of division, where differences are seen as threats rather than opportunities for growth.

The rise of homelessness in many urban areas is a stark reflection of this dynamic. Cities like San Francisco, Los Angeles, and New York have become epicenters of wealth and opportunity, but also of extreme poverty and housing insecurity. As real estate prices skyrocket and gentrification displaces long-term residents, lower-income individuals and families are often left with nowhere to turn. Wealthier neighborhoods, driven by the desire to maintain property values and social order, resist the construction of affordable housing or shelters. This creates a stark divide—those with resources fortify their positions, while those without are pushed further to the margins, resulting in a growing homeless population with no place to call home.

Rather than addressing the root causes of homelessness—such as a lack of affordable housing, mental health care, and income inequality—many cities resort to measures aimed at controlling the problem. Laws criminalizing homelessness, the installation of "hostile architecture" like spikes on benches, and sweeps of encampments serve only to push homeless individuals out of sight. These actions, aimed at maintaining a certain appearance of order, perpetuate the division and deepen the isolation of vulnerable populations. As communities fragment along economic and ideological lines, the homeless crisis grows, highlighting how the drive for control and self-interest undermines collective well-being and compassion.

The result is a world where those in power enforce separation through policies of dominance, exploitation, and division. Governments justify acts of violence, suppression, and coercion in the name of security or order, perpetuating a cycle of fear and conflict. Corporations, driven by profit, exploit both people and the environment, reinforcing the idea that control over resources is more valuable than the well-being of individuals or the planet.

Something to Reflect On:

Consider a current global issue—climate change, inequality, or political conflict—and reflect on how the desire for control, both personally and institutionally, has influenced this issue. How might loosening the grip on control lead to different solutions?

This normalization of control creates a world where power is concentrated in the hands of a few, while the many are left vulnerable, disenfranchised, and disconnected. The systems we've built, far from creating stability, produce inequality, injustice, and oppression. The more these systems try to exert control, the more unstable they become, increasing social unrest, economic inequality, and environmental destruction.

"It's not about rejecting what you've learned—it's about questioning why you hold onto it."

Lisa Ann, public speaker and entrepreneur, shared this insight during her Dualistic Unity episode. Her words remind us that releasing control begins with questioning our attachment to beliefs and systems we've long accepted. By letting go of what no longer serves us, we create space for more peace and understanding.

These systems of power are not separate from the individuals who uphold them. They are reflections of the same ego-driven need for control that exists within each of us. Just as individuals seek control in their personal relationships, governments and corporations seek control on a larger scale. And we allow it, because to do otherwise would mean to let go of what we want, our own campaigns under the banner of control, in order to address it.

This cycle of control and fragmentation feeds on itself. The more individuals, communities, and institutions seek to exert control, the more disconnected and divided they become.

As we've explored in earlier chapters, the illusion of control— whether over our identities, relationships, or the world around us— is deeply rooted in fear. The desire to control stems from our attachment to certainty and the belief that we can shape outcomes to fit our personal expectations. Yet, as we've seen, this attachment only deepens our sense of isolation and frustration, pulling us further from the peace we seek. True change, both personal and societal, often arises not through force or rigid control, but through the willingness to relinquish these attachments and desires for comfort.

Consider the example of Rosa Parks, whose simple yet profound act of resistance—refusing to give up her seat on a bus—ignited the Montgomery Bus Boycott. Rosa's decision wasn't part of a centrally controlled movement but a personal act of courage, rooted in her willingness to face fear, judgment, and potential consequences. What followed was a decentralized, grassroots movement that relied on the collective actions of the community, rather than top-down control. People organized carpools, walked miles to work, and refused to ride segregated buses for over a year. This cooperative effort eventually led to the Supreme Court ruling that desegregated public transportation, proving that true change often begins with an individual's willingness to act despite uncertainty, and unfolds through shared, organic action.

The disconnection we experience within ourselves is mirrored by the division within societies, creating a cycle that deepens and reinforces these fractures. As individuals become more disconnected from themselves and from one another, societies fragment further, threatening to unravel the very fabric of humanity. Nations are at war, communities are fractured by fear and mistrust, and individuals find themselves locked in personal struggles, both internal and external. This widespread disconnection manifests in every corner of our world: environmental degradation as we exploit the natural world for short-term gain, political corruption as leaders grasp for control, and economic inequality that leaves billions struggling while a few amass vast wealth. These are not isolated issues, but interconnected symptoms of the same underlying problem—our collective disconnection and the relentless drive for control that fuels it.

This cycle of disconnection and division is not inevitable. At any moment, we can choose to break free from the roles that keep us isolated and at odds with one another. A powerful example of this occurred during World War I, when soldiers on both sides of the conflict laid down their arms on Christmas Eve in 1914. Stepping outside the roles of enemy combatants, they met in no-man's land to share food, exchange gifts, and even play football. For a brief moment, the madness of war gave way to a shared humanity, reminding us that the structures and divisions that separate us are not fixed. The truce did not last, but it demonstrated that the potential for connection and peace exists—even in the most extreme circumstances—when we choose to recognize our shared humanity and let go of the need for control and dominance.

Something to Reflect On:

Consider the dynamics in a relationship or community you're part of—whether at work, in your family, or among friends. How does the need for control show up in these spaces? What impact does it have on trust, connection, and communication?

Now think about the broader systems you engage with—economies, schools, governments. How does the drive for control and competition manifest in these environments? In what ways might these dynamics shift if cooperation and empathy were prioritized over control?

The need for control doesn't just ripple outward to the systems we live in—it seeps back into our inner world to wreak more havoc. Individually, we carry the emotional weight of this need every day. We live in a gap between what we long for—peace, connection, and fulfillment—and the reality of our lives, which are dominated by fear, anxiety, and conflict. This gap is the emotional price of living in a fragmented world shaped by the need for control. Each attempt to close the gap through control only serves to widen it further. The more we push, the more distant peace becomes, leaving us caught in a cycle of frustration and self-doubt. We begin to question our worth and abilities, unsure of why our efforts to control seem to lead only to deeper dissatisfaction and exhaustion.

The emotional toll of living like this is immense. It manifests as constant striving, relentless anxiety, and a sense of gnawing dissatisfaction with ourselves and the world around us. On one hand, we sense that there is a better way to live—one marked by presence, connection, and ease. On the other hand, we are trapped in patterns of control that perpetuate fear, insecurity, and stress. This tension between the peace we desire and the control we cling to is the source of much of the emotional turmoil that defines modern life.

Our desire for dominion creates perpetual emotional chaos. The need to regulate outcomes, relationships, and even ourselves places us in a constant state of striving. We're always grasping for something—be it success, security, or validation—only to find it perpetually slipping just beyond our reach. This constant striving generates anxiety, because control is, by its very nature, elusive. Life, with all its unpredictability and complexity, cannot be controlled, and yet we continue to think that if we try harder, plan better, or work more, we can achieve it.

We obsess over managing every detail—whether it's our careers, our families, or our future—believing that if we can just get everything in order, we'll find peace. But peace never comes. Instead, we find ourselves caught in futile cycles of stress and frustration, unable to relax, unable to let go. Even when we achieve the things we think will bring us happiness, the satisfaction is fleeting. We quickly move on to the next goal, the next fear, the next need for control.

As Lao Tzu teaches in the *Tao Te Ching*: "He who conquers others is strong; he who conquers himself is mighty." Letting go of the need to dominate life's unpredictability brings real power, as we find that peace lies not in controlling others, but in mastering our own responses to life.

Something to Reflect On:

As you reflect on your life, where do you feel the strongest need for control—whether it's in your relationships, career, or within yourself? How does this need manifest emotionally? Consider how anxiety, frustration, or fear might arise. What might shift in your relationships or sense of peace if you allowed life to unfold more naturally, without trying to manage every outcome?

The fear of losing control doesn't protect us from chaos—it creates chaos. Micromanaging life's details disconnects us from the present and the awareness that comes with accepting uncertainty.

Much like cells return to balance when we trust the body's ability to regulate itself, life too will restore its natural order when we step back and allow it to flow. By letting go of the need for control, we close the gap and allow life's processes—both within us and around us—to recalibrate, just as cellular homeostasis is restored when left to its natural rhythm.

Yet, despite knowing that balance and peace are possible, we often remain trapped in the need for control. Perhaps the most painful aspect of this cycle is the gap between the peace we intuitively sense and the emotional reality we experience. On some level, we know that peace is available to us. We catch glimpses of it in moments of connection, stillness, and presence. We can feel what life might be like if we weren't constantly trying to control it—if we could just let go and trust in the natural flow of events. But these moments are fleeting, quickly overtaken by the pressures and demands of daily life.

This canyon between what could be and what is creates a sense of frustration and despair. We know there is a better way to live, but we cannot seem to access it for more than a few brief moments. We are trapped in a world that reinforces control at every turn—a world where productivity, achievement, and self-discipline are prized above presence, connection, and acceptance. The result is an emotional landscape filled with longing, frustration, and a sense that something essential is always just out of reach.

Many people, unable to cope with the emotional toll of living in this paradigm, turn to suppression. The feelings of anxiety, fear, and inadequacy become too much to bear, so we numb ourselves through distractions, addictions, and busyness. We fill our lives with activities, entertainment, and consumption, hoping that these distractions will ease the discomfort of living in a fragmented state. But this suppression only deepens the disconnection.

By suppressing our emotions, we cut ourselves off from the possibility of healing. The feelings of fear and insecurity remain beneath the surface, unacknowledged and unresolved. Over time, this suppression leads to emotional numbness, where we become disconnected not only from our pain but also from the joy, spontaneity, and presence that are available to us when we let go of control.

The systems of control that we've built—our economies, our governments, our social structures—reinforce this disconnection, creating a world where people are valued for what they can produce or achieve, not for who they are.

And so, we stand on the edge of an emotional abyss. We can see the peace that is possible, but we are unable to cross the chasm that separates us from it. As long as we remain committed to the illusions of control and separation, we will continue to feel emotionally fragmented—anxious, fearful, disconnected, and unsatisfied. The gap between what is and what could be will remain, and the emotional toll of standing on its edge will only grow heavier.

Something to Reflect On:

What emotions arise when you reflect on the gap between the peace you long for and the emotional reality of your life? How does the need for control contribute to your feelings of anxiety, frustration, or disconnection?

Now think of a recent moment of stress or frustration. How much of that experience was driven by your desire to control the situation? How might you have approached it differently if you had trusted in life's natural flow?

It is tempting to think that the systems of control we live under are too large or too entrenched to change—that they exist independently of us, and that we are powerless to influence them. But this is another assumption and if there's anything we've discussed in this book, it's the importance of questioning assumptions. The truth is that these systems are made up of individuals, and they reflect the collective state of human consciousness. When individuals are driven by fear, greed, and the need for control, the systems they create will reflect these qualities. And when individuals begin to live from a place of empathy, compassion, and interconnectedness, the systems they participate in will start to reflect those values as well.

While it's true that many systems—such as governments and economic institutions—are built on control, fear, and competition, deepening the divisions they seek to manage, this is not the only way forward. The more governments attempt to control, the more resistance they create, leading to cycles of conflict and instability. Similarly, economic systems that prioritize profit and competition over well-being perpetuate inequality and exploitation. But even within this landscape, there are examples of a different approach— one that challenges these dominant systems and proves that change is possible.

Another clear example of this shift can be seen in the Mondragon Corporation, which began in the Basque region of Spain. In 1956, a group of workers, led by a visionary priest, José María Arizmendiarrieta, founded the cooperative based on principles of solidarity and shared ownership. What started as a small initiative grew into one of the largest worker-owned cooperatives in the world, demonstrating that when individuals and small groups prioritize empathy and awareness, they can create systems that promote equality, well-being, and sustainability. Mondragon stands as proof that the transformation of systems, from competition to collaboration, begins with a shift in mindset.

The wars we fight, the inequalities we perpetuate, the environmental destruction we cause—all of these are external manifestations of the fear, greed, and disconnection that exist within each of us. The systems of control we have built are not the root cause of our problems; they are the symptoms of a deeper issue: our fear.

But just as the world reflects our fear, it can also reflect our awareness. When individuals begin to see through the illusion of control, the gap between the world as it is and the world as it could be starts to close. The more people awaken to the truth of life's complexity and interconnectedness, the more the world shifts from reflecting our fear and division to reflecting our empathy and unity. We've already seen glimpses of this in companies like Patagonia, which focus on environmental stewardship and employee well-being, and Mondragon, where cooperation and shared ownership are foundational principles. These examples show that when individuals and organizations bridge the gap between control and connection, they create systems that reflect empathy, compassion, and collective well-being, offering a path toward a more unified and sustainable world.

This healing process is slow, much like the body's return to balance through cellular homeostasis—it requires patience and time. The systems of power and division that have been built over centuries will not change overnight. But just as the body gradually restores balance, every shift in individual consciousness, every act of awareness and compassion, contributes to closing the gap and restoring harmony in the broader system. Each of these actions helps to recalibrate the larger societal structure, gradually transforming it from one of division and fear to one of unity and connection.

The systems we have built are fragile, and they can be reshaped. The world can heal, but the healing must begin and continue to unfold in each of us. As we awaken to the truth of our interconnectedness, we plant the seeds of a new world—one built not on control and domination, but on compassion and mutual respect.

Something to Reflect On:

How does your internal sense of control or separation influence the systems you participate in—whether it's your workplace, family, or community? What small changes could you make in your own mindset or behavior to foster greater connection and cooperation in those systems?

Consider a system or institution you're part of (school, work, government). In what ways does your participation reinforce control and separation? What would change if you approached it with an awareness of interconnectedness?

The collective drive for control has set the world on fire—both literally and metaphorically. The systems and structures built on control have brought us to the brink of environmental collapse, social upheaval, and widespread inequality. The systems we have created are unsustainable. Our economies exploit natural resources without regard for the long-term consequences. Our political systems perpetuate division and conflict in the name of security. Our social structures reinforce inequality, keeping billions of people trapped in cycles of poverty and oppression.

The global economy is perhaps the most visible example of our collective obsession with control. Capitalism, with its emphasis on competition, profit, and growth, is built on the belief that the world is a resource to be controlled and exploited for personal gain. In this system, wealth is concentrated in the hands of a few, while the majority struggle to survive. Corporations, driven by the need to control markets and maximize profits, strip the planet of its resources, exploit workers, and commodify every aspect of human life.

One of the most influential moments in shaping our current global economy occurred in 1910 on Jekyll Island, where a secret meeting of powerful bankers and politicians laid the groundwork for what would become the Federal Reserve System. This system gave private bankers control over the U.S. monetary supply, allowing them to regulate interest rates and dictate the flow of money within the economy. The creation of the Federal Reserve institutionalized the idea that nations must borrow money—at interest—from private institutions, thereby embedding the logic of control and debt into the foundation of the modern economy. As former Congressman Ron Paul noted, *"It is absurd to believe that we can borrow ourselves out of debt, especially when we are borrowing from a private banking system that benefits at the expense of the people."* The centralization of economic control through the Federal Reserve has since enabled corporations and financial institutions to dominate markets and further consolidate wealth, intensifying the inequality that defines our world today.

This system of control does not create abundance—it creates scarcity. The relentless pursuit of profit and control over markets and resources leads to environmental degradation, as natural resources are consumed faster than they can be replenished. Forests are cleared, oceans are polluted, and species are driven to extinction, all in the name of economic growth. The more we attempt to control and exploit the natural world for short-term gain, the more we push the planet toward irreversible damage, creating a cycle of destruction that mirrors the broader societal consequences of prioritizing control over sustainability.

A clear example of this unsustainable cycle of control and consumption is the U.S. government's continual raising of the debt ceiling. Since its inception in 1917, the debt ceiling has been raised over 100 times, with the rate of increases accelerating dramatically in recent decades. In the last two decades alone, it has been raised numerous times as the national debt spirals beyond $33 trillion, highlighting the absurdity of trying to maintain economic growth by borrowing more and more from future generations. Each increase allows the government to temporarily avoid financial collapse but deepens the long-term problem of debt and reliance on a system driven by control, profit, and unsustainable consumption.

The consequences of this cycle are profound. Each time the debt ceiling is raised and the government increases borrowing, it leads to inflationary pressures that erode the everyday buying power of individuals. As the value of money decreases, the cost of goods and services rises, making it harder for people to afford basic necessities like housing, food, and healthcare. In fact, as of 2023, U.S. inflation had reached a 40-year high, with prices for essentials like groceries rising over 13% in just a single year, squeezing household budgets even further. Those who are already struggling find themselves in an even more precarious situation, while those who hold significant assets — such as stocks, real estate, and other investments — see their wealth grow, further widening the wealth gap. Shockingly, during the same period, the wealthiest 10% of Americans owned more than 70% of the nation's wealth, a disparity that continues to increase as asset prices soar and wages stagnate.

This growing disparity between the wealthy and the rest of society creates an environment where control is concentrated in the hands of a few, while the majority become increasingly vulnerable to economic shocks and instability. The relentless pursuit of profit, coupled with the unchecked rise in debt, fuels a system that prioritizes short-term financial gains over the long-term well-being of individuals and the planet.

Just as the global economy is driven by control, so too is the political landscape. Governments, motivated by the desire to maintain power and regulate populations, perpetuate division and conflict. Nationalism, xenophobia, and authoritarianism are on the rise, fueled by political leaders who capitalize on fear and insecurity to consolidate their grip. Instead of fostering cooperation and unity, politics has become a battleground where dominance over resources, borders, and ideologies is fought over with increasing intensity.

The political systems in place today are built on the same foundation as the economic system: the belief that control is necessary for security. Governments enact policies of surveillance, militarization, and suppression in the name of protecting their citizens. But these actions only deepen the divisions between people and nations, creating an atmosphere of distrust and hostility. The more governments seek to control their populations, the more unrest they create. The more they attempt to dominate the global stage, the more conflict they provoke.

This dynamic is evident in the alarming rise of global conflict and the erosion of diplomacy in recent years. According to the Global Peace Index, global peace has declined for 13 of the past 15 years, with an increasing number of countries experiencing internal conflict, militarization, and societal instability. The rise of authoritarian regimes, military coups, and suppression of dissenting voices has exacerbated tensions between nations and within borders. Diplomatic efforts have also weakened, as global trust in international organizations like the United Nations has eroded, with member nations more frequently prioritizing national interests over collaborative problem-solving. Reflecting this growing instability, the Doomsday Clock, a symbolic measure maintained by the Bulletin of the Atomic Scientists, was moved to 90 seconds to midnight in 2023, the closest it has ever been to global catastrophe. This ominous indicator reflects not only the increased risk of nuclear conflict but also the accelerating threats posed by climate change, deliberate misinformation, and emerging technologies. The more governments seek to assert control through dominance and militarization, the closer the world inches toward widespread conflict and instability.

Perhaps the most tragic consequence of our historic collective obsession with control is the destruction of the natural world. Humanity has operated for centuries under the assumption that the earth is a resource to be dominated, exploited, and consumed. This mindset, rooted in the belief that nature exists for our benefit, has led to the widespread, multi-generational degradation of ecosystems, the loss of biodiversity, and the acceleration of climate change. The natural world, which once provided the foundation for human life, is now being dismantled in the name of progress and control.

The consequences of this mindset are becoming increasingly dire. According to the World Wildlife Fund, the planet has lost nearly 70% of its wildlife populations in just the past 50 years, a staggering decline that highlights the rapid destruction of ecosystems essential for biodiversity and human survival. The deforestation of critical areas like the Amazon rainforest, often referred to as the "lungs of the Earth," is accelerating, with over 17% of the Amazon already lost due to agriculture, logging, and development. In addition to habitat destruction, industrial agricultural practices, particularly tilling, are contributing to the rapid erosion of topsoil, which takes centuries to regenerate naturally. Tilling disrupts soil structure, depletes nutrients, and releases stored carbon into the atmosphere, exacerbating climate change. Experts warn that if current trends continue, we could lose up to 90% of the world's topsoil by 2050, leading to widespread food insecurity and ecological collapse. These practices, driven by the need for control and short-term gain, are dismantling the very systems that sustain life, pushing the natural world—and humanity—toward an uncertain and perilous future.

If the world we live in today is the inevitable result of our collective focus on control, then the only way to bring about true transformation is to shift that focus. These control-driven systems—rooted in fear and competition—are designed to resist opposition. They thrive on resistance, having been built to withstand force and conflict. Direct confrontation only strengthens their grip, reinforcing their structures in response to external pressure.

A more effective approach is to engage these systems with awareness and adaptability. Rather than seeing them as immovable barriers, recognize how they reflect collective fear and the desire for control. By observing without immediately reacting, you can reduce their influence over your life. Imagine water carving its way through stone—not by force, but through steady, persistent presence. Your awareness, like that steady flow, can gradually reshape even the most rigid structures over time, allowing you to remain grounded and flexible as these systems shift around you.

Consider how social movements throughout history have created profound change, not by waiting for governments or corporations to act, but by individuals deciding to live according to their awareness, empathy, and willingness to grow. The civil rights movement, environmental movements, and more recent social justice movements began with individuals who refused to participate in systems of control, exploitation, and inequality. They chose instead to live in a way that reflected their awareness of interconnectedness and justice. These movements were not top-down reforms—they were bottom-up awakenings that eventually reshaped the systems they sought to change.

At the heart of this shift in consciousness is empathy and compassion. Empathy allows us to see the world through the eyes of others, breaking down the barriers that we create between "us" and "them."

When individuals begin to live from a place of empathy, they naturally create environments where cooperation, trust, and mutual support flourish. These environments—whether in families, workplaces, or communities—become models for larger systemic change. This collective awakening isn't about revolution or overthrowing the systems we currently live under; it's about a fundamental shift in how we relate to one another, to the planet, and to ourselves. As we've learned, letting go of control isn't about surrendering our influence or power, but about recognizing the interconnectedness of all life. It's about seeing that the peace, stability, and justice we seek cannot be achieved through force or control—they emerge when we step into trust, empathy, and openness.

We can see the possibility of a different world—one grounded in empathy, cooperation, and interconnectedness. We know that it exists, not just as an abstract ideal, but as a real and tangible experience we glimpse in moments of presence and connection. Yet despite our best intentions and efforts, this world remains just out of reach. The systems of control we have built, from governments to economies to social institutions, continue to dominate our lives, perpetuating the very suffering we long to transcend.

As we move forward, we must ask: Despite our best intentions and visions for a better world, why do our efforts so often fall short? What are we missing? Why does the gap between the world we long for and the world we live in seem so impossible to cross?

"No problem can be solved from the same
level of consciousness that created it."

– Albert Einstein

Chapter 9 - The Confusion of Concepts

A concept is an idea or mental framework we use to understand and interpret the world. It allows us to categorize, label, and organize our experiences, providing structure to our thoughts and perceptions.

Throughout this journey, we've examined several key concepts. We began by exploring *identity* and challenging the idea that it is fixed or permanent. We have questioned *failure* as something to fear, instead seeing it as a valuable tool for growth. We have also confronted the illusion of *control* and the need for certainty, recognizing that letting go opens the door to freedom. Lastly, we've touched on *authenticity*, encouraging us to live beyond societal expectations and imposed narratives.

Concepts form the foundation of how we make sense of reality. From birth, we inherit these frameworks to help us understand the world around us. They shape how we perceive ourselves, others, and the world. Concepts give names to things, assign labels to people, and provide rules for how we live. While they simplify the chaos of life, this simplification comes with a hidden cost.

What if, in our attempt to make life more comprehensible, we're actually distancing ourselves from reality? By oversimplifying life's infinite complexity into neatly packaged ideas, we risk losing touch with a deeper, more authentic experience. Rather than expanding our awareness, concepts narrow our perception, limiting our sensitivity, empathy, and engagement with the present moment.

In the previous chapter, we explored how the illusion of control distances us from life. Now, we look even deeper into how we exercise control through concepts. Concepts provide the illusion of certainty—a mental map that makes the world seem knowable and predictable. While they offer a sense of security, that security is ultimately an illusion, allowing us to avoid the discomfort of life's inherent uncertainty.

Conceptualization is not inherently bad. In fact, it is built into the very structure of the human brain, particularly in the prefrontal cortex. This part of the brain, which is one of the more recent developments in human evolution, is responsible for ordered thinking, allowing us to form concepts, plan for the future, and organize our thoughts. It helps us categorize experiences, communicate ideas, and navigate the complexity of life. However, the problem arises when we mistake these conceptual tools for reality itself. We begin to live in the blueprint, rather than the building it represents. Concepts, by their very nature, reduce the boundless, ever-changing reality into something static and simplified. While this makes life easier to navigate, it also prevents us from experiencing life as it truly is—alive, dynamic, and unpredictable.

> "He who knows does not speak. He who speaks does not know."
>
> — Tao Te Ching

Beyond personal identities, concepts are deeply embedded in societal and institutional structures. Cultural, educational, and political systems rely on conceptual frameworks to create a sense of order. These frameworks influence how we think, act, and perceive reality on a collective level. They shape how societies function, but they also contribute to the rigidity of thought, often reinforcing divisions and limiting our capacity for open, fluid engagement with the world.

Consider the educational system, where concepts like intelligence are often narrowly defined by standardized testing. This narrow lens determines the opportunities people receive, shaping entire life paths based on a restricted view of ability. Similarly, political systems often rely on binary thinking—left vs. right, us vs. them—creating divisions that simplify the complexities of human societies into polarized narratives.

These systems act like drawn plans, reducing the richness of human experience into simplified, superficial outlines. While they provide structure, they also obscure much of what lies beyond their narrow boundaries. As David Bohm said, 'Thought creates divisions out of itself and then says that they are there naturally.' Concepts, particularly in politics or morality, give us the illusion that these divisions—whether ideological or ethical—are fixed and inherent, when in fact they are mental constructs imposed on a much more complex, interconnected reality.

Something to Reflect On:

Think of a societal concept you encounter regularly—whether it's political labels, cultural norms, or career expectations. How has this concept shaped how you view the world? What might change if you started to question the simplicity of these labels?

A poignant example of the dangers of rigid conceptual frameworks is the story of Ignaz Semmelweis, a Hungarian physician who, in the 19th century, discovered that hand-washing could drastically reduce mortality rates in hospitals. Despite clear evidence supporting his findings, his peers rejected them because they were bound to the established conceptual frameworks of medical practice, which were rooted in tradition and authority. Their attachment to these existing concepts blinded them to the simple yet revolutionary truth in front of them. Rather than reexamining their beliefs in light of new evidence, they dismissed Semmelweis' findings, leading to continued suffering and needless deaths. This tragic story highlights how mistaking conceptual frameworks for reality not only limits progress but also distances us from essential truths that could transform our understanding and experience of the world.

As Lao Tzu wrote in the *Tao Te Ching*: "The Tao that can be told is not the eternal Tao; the name that can be named is not the eternal name." While concepts may help us navigate the world, they are not the world itself. They are merely representations, and no matter how precise they are, they will always fall short of the vast, interconnected complexity of life.

Consider how we use concepts to label and judge. While these labels help us organize and communicate, they can distort our experience. We begin to see people, events, and even ourselves through these conceptual lenses, missing the full complexity of what's truly there. Instead of experiencing life as it unfolds, we interact with a simplified version of it that aligns with our preconceived ideas. In doing so, we lose the ability to engage directly and authentically with the present moment.

Something to Reflect On:

Consider a concept you've encountered in daily life—perhaps an idea like success, intelligence, or even failure. How has this concept shaped your decisions or your perception of yourself? What new possibilities could emerge if you loosened your attachment to this concept?

An excellent example of breaking free from limiting labels is the story of Temple Grandin, an autistic professor of animal science.

Defying societal assumptions about neurodiversity, she used her unique perspective to design humane livestock handling systems, revolutionizing the industry. By rejecting oversimplified concepts about her abilities, Grandin showed that when we release conceptual limitations, we open the door to innovation and a deeper understanding of ourselves.

This idea aligns with Krishnamurti's teaching: "To know oneself is to study oneself in action, which is relationship." His wisdom emphasizes that true understanding—whether of ourselves or others—arises not from concepts, but from direct, moment-to-moment observation. Temple Grandin's success illustrates this perfectly: rather than accepting society's preconceptions about her, she observed and engaged with her reality as it unfolded, allowing her unique insights to emerge. When we define ourselves or others through concepts, we limit the depth of our interactions. Instead of responding to the present moment, we fall back on preconceptions that simplify and distort the truth.

This reliance on concepts often stems from our desire for stability in a chaotic world. Concepts offer a way to summarize and make sense of life's complexities, giving us the illusion of control. However, this control is fleeting—an illusion that distances us from the unpredictability and richness of life. By clinging to ideas, we sacrifice the opportunity to engage with life as it unfolds.

"When you put words to things, you start racing away from truth at light speed. So take everything I say with a grain of salt, because all of this is, in a way, accidental lies."

Sean Webb, author of Mind Hacking Happiness, shared this insight during his episode on Dualistic Unity. His reflection echoes the challenge of mistaking words and concepts for reality. When we rely on words to define truth, we distance ourselves from the actual experience of it.

Morality, for example, is a widely accepted framework that simplifies human behavior into categories of 'good' and 'bad.' While these labels give us a sense of order, they strip away the complexity of human experiences and motivations. A person's actions are often driven by a multitude of factors—emotional, psychological, cultural—that cannot be reduced to a moral binary. By labeling someone or something as 'good' or 'bad,' we disconnect from the nuances of their experience and miss the opportunity to engage with their humanity in a meaningful way.

History is filled with atrocities committed in the name of being 'good' or 'just.' Wars, crusades, and genocides have been justified under the moral guise of righteousness, where the destruction of the 'other' was seen as a necessary sacrifice for the greater 'good.' From the Inquisition to modern-day terrorism, rigid moral frameworks have allowed people to commit heinous acts while feeling morally justified. In these cases, morality becomes a weapon, not a guide for empathy or understanding. The more we cling to these moral concepts, the more we lose the ability to be present, to feel deeply, and to respond with genuine empathy. In doing so, we close ourselves off from the opportunity to understand and connect with others beyond the surface level of judgment.

Yet, recognizing the limitations of concepts doesn't mean we should discard them. The goal is not to stop using concepts but to see them for what they are—tools, not truths. When we realize that concepts are not reality, but representations of reality, we can begin to use them skillfully. We can employ concepts to help us navigate life, but we can also remain open to the fullness of experience that lies beyond those labels and frameworks. The challenge is to avoid becoming trapped in the oversimplifications that concepts impose.

A common manifestation of this can be seen in how we label people based on their professions, social status, or even moral standing. We might define someone as a "successful businessperson," a "struggling artist," or a "good" or "bad" person, depending on our perception of their actions. While these labels provide a quick snapshot, they fail to capture the full complexity of an individual's character and circumstances. For instance, a person labeled as "successful" might be financially secure but emotionally unfulfilled, or a "struggling artist" may be living a deeply meaningful life despite external challenges. Similarly, someone deemed "good" by society might harbor prejudices, while someone seen as "bad" may have acted out of desperation or fear. By relying on these simplified labels, we reduce people to static categories and miss the richness of their dynamic, multifaceted nature, engaging with a concept of the person rather than the person themselves.

We often define both ourselves and others through simplified concepts. Whether labeling ourselves as 'successful' or 'a failure,' or categorizing others as 'smart' or 'difficult,' these labels offer a sense of stability. However, they also trap us in fixed, limited versions of who we are and who others are. Limited versions, with limited opportunities for growth.

Something to Reflect On:

Think of a label you've used to define yourself—whether it's related to your career, personality, or past experiences. How has this label shaped your sense of identity? Has it limited you or opened new possibilities? Reflect on how loosening this label could change your experience of yourself.

Success is frequently reduced to external markers like wealth, career achievements, or social status. However, this oversimplified definition fails to capture the broader spectrum of success. By focusing narrowly on these external measures, we overlook the personal, emotional, and spiritual dimensions that define a meaningful life. This not only limits how we see others, but it also confines how we measure our own self-worth.

Think about how often we categorize people based on their job titles. When someone says they are a "doctor," "teacher," or "artist," we may form a quick impression of who they are. But these labels don't capture the full picture. A doctor may be a passionate musician, a teacher may be an adventurous world traveler, and an artist may also have a deep interest in science. By focusing on these narrow identifiers, we miss the opportunity to understand the richness of a person's experiences beyond their professional role.

Whether we are considering concepts like 'government' and 'justice' or societal labels such as 'nation,' 'race,' or 'religion,' these concepts provide a sense of order and stability, but they also limit our ability to engage with the deeper, more fluid nature of human experience. As a result, we fall into a mindset of 'us versus them,' dividing us and others into groups and reinforcing division, conflict, and exclusion.

Society often assigns specific traits to certain groups—such as the assumption that men should be strong or that certain races are naturally predisposed to certain behaviors. These stereotypes not only fail to account for the individuality within those groups, but they also contribute to bias, discrimination, and division.

Research shows that stereotypes disproportionately harm marginalized groups by reinforcing inequality. For instance, a 2019 study from the National Bureau of Economic Research revealed that Black job applicants with names perceived as "ethnically Black" receive 50% fewer callbacks for job interviews compared to applicants with traditionally "White-sounding" names, despite having identical resumes. Similarly, a 2017 study by the American Association of University Women found that women in the U.S. earn only 82 cents for every dollar earned by men, with the gap widening significantly for women of color.

Something to Reflect On:

Think of a societal label—such as nationality, race, or political affiliation—that you've used or encountered. How has this label shaped your understanding of a group or individual? How might your perspective change if you viewed them as more than the concept assigned to them?

One domain that actively seeks to avoid this trap is science, specifically through the use of the scientific method. Unlike static belief systems or fixed ideas, the scientific method encourages us to remain open to revision, to continuously question our assumptions, and to never mistake any current understanding for the final truth.

The beauty of the scientific approach lies in its recognition of uncertainty. Scientific inquiry begins with observation, but it does not end with conclusions that are never to be questioned again. Instead, science embraces an ongoing process of experimentation, skepticism, and reevaluation. Every hypothesis is subject to revision based on new evidence, and every conclusion is seen as tentative—always open to deeper understanding.

In this way, the scientific method provides a crucial counterpoint to the human tendency to fall into the trap of oversimplification. The process of inquiry never assumes finality; it avoids the inflexibility of assuming we "know" once and for all. Through science, we are reminded that life is far more complex than our conceptual spectrum can capture, and it encourages us to remain open to discovery.

But, of course, the scientific method is not immune to our need for false certainty. While the scientific method encourages open inquiry and revision, scientism transforms science into a rigid belief system. In scientism, current scientific knowledge is treated as absolute and unquestionable, reducing the dynamic, evolving nature of science to a dogma. This shift undermines the very spirit of the scientific method, which thrives on skepticism and continuous exploration. The result is intellectual stagnation, where questioning is discouraged, and the unknown is either ignored or rejected.

A powerful example of scientism gone wrong can be seen in the early 20th-century embrace of eugenics. Grounded in a misapplication of Darwinian evolutionary theory, eugenics became a scientific dogma that justified harmful social policies. Proponents of eugenics, including respected scientists of the time, claimed that selective breeding could "improve" the human race by eliminating undesirable traits. This pseudoscientific belief led to forced sterilizations, discrimination against marginalized groups, and, in its most extreme form, contributed to the atrocities of the Holocaust. The unquestioned acceptance of eugenics as scientific fact shows how scientism—the belief in the infallibility of current scientific knowledge—can lead to devastating consequences when skepticism and ethical considerations are abandoned. It serves as a stark reminder of the dangers of treating science as dogma rather than a tool for continuous inquiry and understanding.

But the cost of believing in superficial labels isn't just intellectual—it's emotional and psychological too. When we define ourselves or others with fixed concepts like "valuable" or "worthless," we trap ourselves in narrow stories that limit growth and healing. For example, someone who defines themselves as "worthless" based on past setbacks may miss opportunities for transformation. On a larger scale, this kind of rigidity has had devastating societal impacts. The eugenics movement, driven by the pseudoscientific label of "genetic superiority," not only justified horrific social policies but also inflicted profound psychological harm on individuals and entire communities deemed "inferior." Entire groups were dehumanized, and the consequences were far-reaching, leaving deep scars on both individuals and society. This illustrates that when we allow concepts to take hold—whether about ourselves or others—we risk creating disconnection, oppression, and suffering on every level.

Perhaps the greatest danger of getting lost in the blueprint is that it leads us to believe that we "know" things that we do not—about the building, about others, about ourselves. Once we believe we know, we stop questioning. We stop being open to new information, new perspectives, or new experiences. Our minds become closed, locked into fixed ideas, and we lose our sense of curiosity and wonder.

Life is far too fluid and unpredictable to be any concept or label. When we cling to the illusion that the description is the described, we close ourselves off to the richness of what is. We trade the mystery and complexity of life for the comfort of false certainty.

Something to Reflect On:

This week, choose one aspect of your life where you typically rely on labels or concepts—whether it's in how you view yourself, others, or the world. Consciously practice letting go of those concepts and approach the situation with curiosity and openness. Notice how this shift changes your perception, your interactions, and your emotional experience. At the end of the week, reflect on how letting go of unquestioned concepts affected your sense of connection and awareness.

We cling to concepts because they offer us a way to organize the chaos of life into neat boxes: good and bad, right and wrong, success and failure. But by doing so, we close ourselves off from the full spectrum of human experience. Concepts provide a false sense of certainty, but this very certainty limits our capacity to grow, connect, and embrace the unknown.

The challenge is to hold concepts lightly, understanding that they are temporary and adaptable rather than fixed. Instead of relying so heavily on superficial labels or static categories, we can remain open to the nuances of life as it unfolds.

You've already been actively working to loosen the grip of restrictive concepts, embracing the idea that you are not bound by the roles and labels imposed on you. Through previous chapters, you've already developed key skills: questioning the beliefs you've held, recognizing the limitations of attachment, facing the fear of uncertainty, and learning to let go of the need for control. You've practiced observing your thoughts and emotions without judgment, allowing them to arise and pass without needing to define who you are.

At this point in your journey, you are no stranger to the discomfort of stepping beyond these familiar boundaries. You've already learned to loosen your attachment to roles, identities, and outcomes, and have begun to trust in the fluidity of life. Now, the challenge is to deepen this practice, to continue letting go—not by force, but by recognizing when you are slipping back into old familiar patterns.

Something to Reflect On:

Think about an area of your life where you rely heavily on labels or concepts—whether it's your self-image, your relationships, or your view of the world. What might happen if you let go of these labels and approached life with more openness and curiosity?

"For him who has conquered the mind, the mind is the best of friends; but for one who has failed to do so, his mind will remain the greatest enemy."

— Bhagavad Gita

By reducing the complexity of life into neat, controllable ideas, we create a sense of safety and predictability, but we also limit our emotional engagement with the world. This becomes a form of emotional control, where concepts shield us from the discomfort of uncertainty, fear, and vulnerability. When used as escape mechanisms, concepts trap us in what we think we know, preventing growth. But when used as tools, they help us navigate life while remaining open to its complexity.

Using concepts as tools means recognizing their limitations while appreciating their utility. Concepts are not inherently bad or harmful—on the contrary, they are necessary for organizing our experience and making sense of the world. The key is to remain aware that concepts are not the final word on reality; they are a way of pointing to something larger and more complex. This awareness helps us avoid becoming trapped in rigid interpretations of life, allowing us to stay open to the unfolding nature of reality and the limitless potential for growth and change.

This flexibility is especially important when it comes to understanding our emotions. Even something as seemingly harmless as the way we define emotions can reinforce concepts. We label certain emotions as "positive" (happiness, excitement) and others as "negative" (sadness, anger, fear). By placing emotions into these categories, we create beliefs about what is acceptable to feel and what should be avoided. As a result, we often suppress so-called "negative" emotions, seeing them as problems to be solved rather than valid experiences to be understood. This conceptualization of emotions narrows our emotional range, making it difficult to fully engage with the richness of human experience.

When we label emotions as "inferior" or "unwanted," we build barriers around our inner experience, disconnecting from what we are genuinely feeling. This rejection of certain emotional states prevents us from understanding their deeper meaning and from fully embracing the present moment. In the same way that concepts limit our intellectual flexibility, emotional labels prevent us from engaging with our emotional life in an open, compassionate way.

Just as science thrives on revision and discovery, living with openness to change is essential in our personal lives—particularly in how we approach relationships and our own identities. When we approach relationships without expectations, we allow them to evolve naturally. Instead of fitting someone into a role, we engage with them as a living, evolving person. This mindset opens the door to deeper connections, greater empathy, and more authentic relationships. The same is true for our relationship with ourselves: when we stop trying to define ourselves through fixed ideas, we give ourselves the freedom to grow, change, and explore new possibilities.

To practice this state of attentive openness, we must first cultivate the ability to question our assumptions and embrace the reality of not knowing. Life does not conform to our mental constructs, and our attempts to simplify it can only take us so far. The deeper we go into any area of exploration—whether it's science, relationships, or self-understanding—the more we realize how much we don't know. Rather than fearing this uncertainty, we can see it as liberating. It frees us from the pressure of having all the answers, inviting us to engage with the mystery of life in a more authentic and open way.

Embracing complexity means being willing to sit with uncertainty, to question our assumptions, and to remain curious about the world. It means recognizing that life is not something to be controlled or fully understood but something to be experienced, explored, and appreciated in all its richness. When we let go of the need to categorize and label everything, we open ourselves up to the possibility of seeing the world—and ourselves—more clearly.

Something to Reflect On:

Consider a time when you labeled someone based on limited interactions. How did that label shape your relationship or your perception of that person? What might change if you let go of that label and approached them with an open mind, allowing them to be more than the concept you created?

This shift in perspective also transforms how we relate to others. Once we've judged or conceptualized someone, it becomes much harder to connect with them on an emotional level. Instead of seeing them as a dynamic, evolving person with a range of experiences, we relate to them through the filter of our concept. This limits our ability to feel with and for others. Empathy requires openness and emotional flexibility, but when we rely on concepts, we close ourselves off from that flexibility. We end up interacting with the label we've assigned to the person rather than with the person themselves.

The emotional cost of this disconnection is significant. When we interact with others through the lens of conceptual categories, we miss out on the possibility of healthy emotional connection. Conceptual relationships remain superficial, based on preconceived ideas rather than authentic engagement. Consider, for instance, how labeling someone based on their political affiliation can create an invisible barrier. Instead of seeing them as a nuanced individual with a wide range of beliefs and experiences, we reduce them to a single, polarized identity. This reduces the chance of meaningful dialogue and prevents us from connecting with them in a meaningful way, fostering division rather than collaborative understanding.

In education, we see similar effects when students are labeled as "gifted" or "slow learners." These labels often define their relationships with teachers and peers, trapping them in narrow expectations. A "gifted" student might feel immense pressure to constantly perform, while a student labeled as a "slow learner" may be underestimated, limiting their opportunity to grow. This labeling stifles emotional engagement, as teachers and students relate more to the label than to the individual's actual needs and potential.

In family dynamics, conceptualization can also create distance. For example, if a parent constantly sees their child through the lens of being "the rebellious one" or "the responsible one," they might fail to see the child's evolving needs and emotions. This can prevent a non-role based connection from forming as both parties remain stuck in a parent-child dynamic that no longer serve them.

In all these cases, we fail to recognize the shared vulnerability and complexity of human experience that binds us together. Instead, we remain isolated in our own conceptual worlds, disconnected from the deeper emotional truths that lie beneath the surface of our interactions.

Think about the language we use to describe those we disagree with or fear. Words like 'enemy,' 'criminal,' 'terrorist,' or 'radical' reduce people to simplistic, one-dimensional labels. These labels strip away the complexity of their experiences, reducing them to a single concept that justifies emotional detachment or even hostility. When we think of someone as an 'enemy,' it becomes impossible to empathize with them, to understand their motivations, or to acknowledge their humanity.

A common example of this emotional insulation can be seen when people hear terms like 'radical left' or 'alt-right.' These labels immediately evoke associations with extreme positions, making it easier to distance ourselves emotionally and avoid engaging with the person behind the label. We start to view them not as individuals with nuanced perspectives, but as the physical embodiment of a threatening ideology. This emotional canyon allows us to justify aggression, discrimination, or indifference toward others. The concepts we use to conceptualize people protects us from the discomfort of engaging with their humanity.

But this sense of false comfort comes at a cost. The certainty we gain from concepts is superficial. It gives us the illusion of control over our emotions, but it also closes us off from the richness of experience. When we cling to concepts for emotional security, we limit our capacity to grow, learn, and connect wholeheartedly with others. We stop questioning, stop being curious, and stop being open to new perspectives or new emotional experiences.

For example, someone who believes in eternal salvation through the resurrected Jesus Christ—who died for our sins and is the only Son of God, along with the Father and the Holy Spirit—may attach their emotional well-being to this concept. If they experience doubt or encounter perspectives that challenge this belief, they may feel panic, anxiety, or guilt regarding their spiritual standing. These emotions are not necessarily the result of their actual spiritual experience but rather of the gap between their current feelings and the unyielding concepts they've adopted. In this way, concepts can trap them in a cycle of emotional highs and lows, determined by how closely their lives align with the expectations built around these ideas. This attachment can also lead them to become pushy or insistent that others believe as they do, seeking validation for their own beliefs by ensuring that those around them adopt the same framework. The need for others to share their belief system becomes a way to reinforce their own emotional security, further deepening the dependence on the concept.

This need for validation and control does not remain confined to personal interactions; it often expands into larger societal movements. Many individuals, driven by fear and a desire for certainty, seek to impose their beliefs on others through political and social systems. According to a 2021 Pew Research Center study, 70%

of white evangelical Protestants believe that religious values should play a more significant role in public life, and 52% of U.S. adults support the idea that the government should uphold Christian values. This entanglement of religion and politics often stems from a deep-seated fear of change or of losing moral superiority. For instance, 81% of white evangelicals supported a presidential candidate in 2016 whose platform strongly reflected their religious values, illustrating how religious belief can become a vehicle for political influence and societal control.

Historically, this drive for religious and moral dominance has manifested in extreme ways under Christian dictators. Leaders like Francisco Franco of Spain and Augusto Pinochet of Chile used religion to justify authoritarian regimes, imposing strict moral codes and suppressing opposition in the name of righteousness. These dictators, much like many religious-political movements today, were driven by the belief that their worldview was the only path to salvation or moral order. In seeking control, they suppressed dissent and undermined the freedom of those who did not conform to their religious ideology.

This pattern continues today, as the attachment to belief systems—rooted in fear and a need for certainty—leads to efforts to impose these beliefs on society at large. The lack of empathy for differing perspectives often blinds such groups to the harm they cause. Whether through historical dictatorships or modern political movements, the desire to control others' beliefs reflects an unwillingness to engage with the complexity of human experience, perpetuating division and conflict in the process.

A contemporary example of this drive for religious and moral control is evident in the recent U.S. Supreme Court rulings on abortion rights. The 2022 decision to overturn Roe v. Wade, which had guaranteed federal protections for abortion access, was heavily influenced by religiously motivated groups who view abortion as morally wrong based on their interpretation of Christian teachings. This ruling has significantly impacted reproductive rights across the country, with 13 states immediately implementing abortion bans through so-called "trigger laws," while others have followed with similar restrictions.

This push to restrict abortion access is deeply tied to religious beliefs about the sanctity of life, which are often framed as universal truths. Those who oppose abortion on these grounds seek to impose their moral framework on all women, regardless of differing religious views, personal circumstances, or health considerations. However, the personal and collective consequences of banning abortion are significant and well-documented.

For example, research highlighted in the book Freakonomics suggests that the legalization of abortion in the 1970s contributed to a dramatic decrease in crime rates in the U.S. during the 1990s. This theory posits that by giving women the option to terminate unwanted pregnancies, there were fewer children born into situations of poverty, instability, or neglect—factors that often correlate with higher crime rates later in life. When abortion access is restricted, these socio-economic conditions may lead to more individuals being born into environments that foster long-term societal issues like poverty and crime.

On a personal level, studies show that women who are denied abortions are more likely to experience economic hardship and lower educational attainment. A 2017 study from the University of California, San Francisco, known as the Turnaway Study, found that women denied an abortion were four times more likely to live below the federal poverty line than those who were able to access the procedure. Additionally, restricting abortion has serious public health implications, as women may resort to unsafe, illegal abortions, putting their lives at risk.

These personal and societal consequences are rarely considered by those pushing for abortion bans, whose fear-baseed religious beliefs prioritize moral absolutes over the complexities of real-world situations.

The belief in a concept like eternal salvation can bring profound emotional highs—comfort, joy, and a sense of righteousness—especially when the believer feels they are living in alignment with their moral code. However, the fear of falling short of salvation can lead to shattering emotional lows, particularly in moments of extreme doubt or failure. The fear of eternal punishment or separation from God after death can create ongoing anxiety, especially when one's actions are perceived as sinful or unworthy. This judgment is not only directed inward but can also be projected outward, leading to a sense of self-righteousness. Those who do not share the same beliefs may be viewed as lost or condemned, further reinforcing emotional detachment and a judgmental attitude toward others.

This constant vacillation between emotional highs—when one feels assured of salvation—and emotional lows—when doubt, fear, or judgment arises—limits the ability to engage with others compassionately and without bias. The belief in salvation as the ultimate goal creates an emotional reliance on a narrow framework of judgment and worthiness, making it difficult to fully experience or empathize with the complexity of life and the diverse perspectives of others. In this way, such concepts, while offering comfort, also imprison the believer in a cycle of spiritual and emotional turbulence.

Ironically, the fervent belief in a conceptual God often creates more division than unity. Instead of fostering compassion and connection, it leads to judgment, exclusion, and a sense of superiority over those who do not share the same beliefs. If there were a devil, one could argue that his most cunning creation would be the idea of God—a concept that traps people in belief systems, dividing them from others and from the true essence of their own humanity. The very thing meant to offer salvation instead becomes a tool of separation, turning spirituality into a battleground for righteousness rather than a path toward unity and understanding.

This is the emotional toll of false certainty. It forces us into a limited emotional range, tied to whether we meet the standards of the concepts we use to define ourselves and others. We experience emotional distress when life doesn't conform to the ideas we've created, and we miss the opportunity to engage with our emotions in a more authentic, dynamic way.

Fear of the unknown, fear of uncertainty, fear of change—these emotions push us to seek stability and predictability. Concepts offer a way to create those illusions. By categorizing the world into known, understandable pieces, we create a buffer against the emotional discomfort that comes with uncertainty. In this way, religious faith, when reduced to rigid beliefs and absolute certainties, isn't truly faith at all—it becomes a means of control.

True faith, by its very nature, requires embracing the unknown. It involves trust in something beyond the need for clear definitions or guarantees. When faith becomes tied to specific doctrines or the promise of eternal salvation as a reward for 'correct' beliefs, it becomes an intellectual exercise in false certainty rather than actual surrender to life's inherent mystery. Rather than inviting us to sit with uncertainty, it can become a way to avoid it, providing a false sense of security by dividing the world into black-and-white terms of saved and unsaved, right and wrong, deserving and undeserving. In doing so, we lose the openness, humility, and wonder that true faith encourages.

When we rely on categories to make sense of the world, we become more anxious when those conceptual borders are challenged. Our emotional security becomes fragile because it is tied to a concept that doesn't account for the fluid, ever-changing nature of life.

When we encounter people or ideas that don't fit within our established categories, we often experience discomfort or fear. Rather than confronting that discomfort, we retreat into concepts that make the unfamiliar feel safer. We label others based on stereotypes or assumptions, reducing them to something that will validate our already-existing view, and in doing so, we avoid the emotional challenge of engaging with the full complexity of their humanity.

The concepts we use to manage fear ultimately trap us in a smaller emotional world, where the unknown is avoided or ignored, and the richness of human experience is left unexplored.

The emotional cost of relying on concepts is significant, but it's not inevitable. We can begin to free ourselves from the emotional confinement that concepts create by becoming aware of how they shape our emotional lives. This involves questioning the labels we use, both for ourselves and for others, and recognizing that these labels are not the truth—they are simplifications.

We fear questioning because it destabilizes the conceptual world we've built in our minds. It forces us to confront the possibility that we don't have all the answers, and this triggers feelings of vulnerability and insecurity. If the concepts we've relied on aren't as solid as we thought, what does that mean for our identity, our relationships, or the choices we've made? If we admit that our understanding is limited, we might have to face uncomfortable truths about ourselves and the world around us.

This fear of questioning extends beyond intellectual discomfort; it touches on our very sense of self. Many of the concepts we cling to are deeply tied to our identity. We define ourselves by our beliefs, our values, and the roles we play in the world. To question those beliefs or roles feels like a threat to the self. It's not just that we fear losing certainty about the world—we fear losing certainty about who we are. The refusal to question concepts is not just a matter of intellectual stubbornness—it's a form of psychological defense. By clinging to concepts, we protect ourselves from the existential anxiety that comes with confronting the unknown.

This psychological defense is similar to what happens in psychosis, where individuals cling to a rigid and narrow view of reality because the broader, more complex reality is too overwhelming to process. Psychosis can be seen as a spectrum, and while most of us don't experience its extreme forms, we still engage in subtler versions of the same defense mechanism. We create unbending frameworks for understanding ourselves and the world because it feels safer than living in a state of uncertainty. Even the fear of imagined judgments from others, which we often interpret as real, reflects this same need for control—constructing a version of reality that shields us from the discomfort of the unknown.

In everyday life, this can manifest as an unwillingness to challenge our own beliefs, even in the face of new evidence. We resist questioning the concepts we've relied on because they have become part of our identity, and letting go of them would feel like losing a part of ourselves. This is why it can be so difficult to have open, honest conversations about deeply held beliefs—whether they relate to politics, religion, or personal identity. We cling to these beliefs not because they are always rational or correct but because we hope they will provide us with lasting psychological security and comfort.

But the more we resist questioning our concepts, the more disconnected we become from reality. Life is dynamic, and when we refuse to question our fixed ideas, we create a gap between our conceptual understanding and the ever-evolving nature of reality. This gap leads to frustration, anxiety, conflict, and emotional disconnection because the world refuses to conform to our ideas of how it should be.

In personal relationships, this refusal to question manifests as inflexibility and disconnection. When we hold on to ideas about who someone is—whether it's a friend, a partner, or a family member—we limit the relationship's potential for growth. People are constantly changing, but if we insist on seeing them through the lens of a concept, we fail to connect with who they are in the present moment. Over time, this creates emotional distance and can even lead to conflict, as our expectations clash with the reality of the other person's evolving identity.

On a societal level, the refusal to question concepts leads to polarization and division. When we cling to ideologies, we create an "us versus them" mentality. We stop listening to people who hold different views because we are so certain that our conceptual framework is the right one. This lack of openness fuels conflict, as each side becomes more entrenched in its own rigid beliefs. The inability to question leads to a breakdown in communication, making it nearly impossible to find common ground or to engage in constructive dialogue.

The alternative to clinging to concepts is to embrace uncertainty and to remain open to questioning. This is not easy, and it requires a shift in how we approach life. Embracing uncertainty is not about giving up on concepts altogether. Concepts are useful tools, but we need to recognize their unavoidable limitations and remain open to continuously revising them as we gain new experiences and insights. When we stop clinging to concepts as fixed truths, we free ourselves from the fear of questioning and open ourselves up to a deeper, more dynamic relationship with life.

In personal relationships, embracing uncertainty allows us to connect with others in a more authentic way. Instead of trying to fit people into predefined concepts, we can meet them where they are, recognizing that they are constantly evolving. This creates space for deeper empathy, understanding, and emotional intimacy. We are no longer trying to control or predict the relationship but are instead allowing it to unfold naturally, with all its complexity and unpredictability.

On a broader scale, embracing uncertainty can lead to more constructive dialogue and collaboration. When we are open to questioning our own beliefs, we become more willing to listen to others and to engage in meaningful conversations. We are no longer threatened by differing viewpoints because we no longer feel the need to defend limited concepts. This openness creates the possibility for growth, both personally and collectively, as we learn from one another and expand our understanding of the world.

But living in a state of uncertainty requires courage. It means questioning the concepts we've relied on for security and being open to the possibility that life is far more complex than we've allowed ourselves to see.

When we refuse to question conceptual frameworks or oversimplified narratives, the consequences can be profound. A stark example of this is the 1986 Challenger space shuttle disaster. Despite engineers raising serious concerns about the potential failure of the O-rings in cold weather, NASA—confident in its past successes—chose to ignore these warnings. This unyielding adherence to an assumed safety record blinded them to the present reality, resulting in a fatal outcome. The Challenger tragedy serves as a sobering reminder of how clinging to concepts without questioning them, especially at institutional levels, can lead to catastrophic failures when we overlook the complexities and uncertainties of real life.

By embracing uncertainty, and living in awareness, we not only become more open to the complexity of the world but also more open to the complexity within ourselves.

Something to Reflect On:

Take a moment to reflect on a belief or concept that you've held tightly to—whether it's about yourself, someone else, or the world around you. What emotions arise when you imagine questioning this belief? How does clinging to this concept offer you a sense of security, and what might it feel like to let go of that certainty, even for a moment? Consider how remaining open to questioning this belief could create space for growth, connection, and a deeper understanding of yourself and others. Write down your reflections and explore how embracing uncertainty might allow you to experience life more fully and authentically.

Experiencing life directly, rather than through the filter of preconceived notions, labels, or ideas, is the essence of awareness. It involves being fully present with the complexity of each moment, without the immediate impulse to categorize or judge what we encounter. This requires a shift from thinking to observing, from defining to noticing. In this state of presence, we engage with life directly, without the need to fit it into familiar conceptual boxes.

At its core, this way of living is about presence—meeting each moment with an open mind and heart, allowing ourselves to see, feel, and experience without the interference of mental constructs. Remember, this doesn't mean abandoning concepts entirely. Rather, it's about recognizing when we're using concepts to make sense of the world and when we're relying on them too heavily. It's about holding concepts lightly, remaining open to the possibility that reality is far more complex than any concept can capture.

Awareness is fluid and invites us to embrace the unknown, to remain curious, and to accept that we don't always have to "know" or "understand" in order to engage with life. In this way, practicing awareness is an exercise in humility. It requires acknowledging the limits of our knowledge and surrendering the need for certainty. Instead of trying to control or predict life, we simply allow ourselves to be with it, as it unfolds.

A practical example of this mentality in action can be seen in the story of Captain Chesley "Sully" Sullenberger, who successfully landed US Airways Flight 1549 on the Hudson River in 2009 after both engines failed. Rather than relying on rigid protocols or panicking due to the unpredictable nature of the emergency, Sullenberger demonstrated fluid awareness and presence in the moment. Faced with a situation no manual could fully prepare him for, he remained calm and open to the unfolding reality, adapting as the crisis evolved. Instead of trying to force a controlled solution, he let go of preconceived expectations and worked with the reality at hand. This ability to engage with the situation as it was, without being paralyzed by the need for certainty or perfect understanding, saved the lives of everyone on board. Sullenberger's story illustrates how practicing awareness—remaining present, open, and adaptable—can make all the difference when facing life's most complex and unpredictable challenges.

The Benefits of Living with Greater Awareness

Cultivating awareness brings us closer to the truth of life's complexity. Rather than relying on oversimplified concepts, we begin to see and experience things as they are—dynamic, interconnected, and constantly changing. This shift opens the door to deeper empathy, greater emotional sensitivity, and more authentic relationships with ourselves and others.

Greater Emotional Depth

When we practice awareness, we no longer need to label our emotions as "good" or "bad." Instead, we allow ourselves to feel our emotions fully, without judgment. This openness creates space for emotional depth and understanding. We stop resisting emotions that don't fit into our conceptual framework and start recognizing all emotions as valid parts of the human experience. In doing so, we move beyond the narrow emotional range that conceptual thinking imposes and become more attuned to the richness of our inner lives.

This greater emotional depth is not just about feeling more—it's about feeling more fully. Instead of compartmentalizing our emotions or avoiding discomfort, we learn to sit with our feelings and explore what they have to teach us. Awareness doesn't make life easier or erase difficult emotions; rather, it helps us stop resisting them and engage with them in a way that fosters growth, healing, and self-understanding.

Authentic Connection with Others

Letting go of rigid concepts also creates conditions for more authentic relationships. By remaining present and aware, we stop trying to fit people into categories and instead meet them as they are, in each moment. This openness fosters genuine connection because we are no longer interacting with an idea of who someone is, but with the living, changing reality of who they are right now.

In relationships, this leads to greater empathy and emotional attunement. We stop projecting expectations or labels onto others and instead become curious about their experiences, perspectives, and feelings. This kind of open, nonjudgmental awareness allows us to build deeper trust and intimacy by removing conceptual barriers that block authentic connection.

This flexibility also helps us adapt within relationships. Instead of holding on to fixed ideas about who people should be or how they should behave, we remain open to the natural changes and evolution that occur over time. This responsiveness fosters greater sensitivity and compassion, recognizing that relationships are dynamic processes rather than static structures.

Freedom from the Need for Control

One of the most significant benefits of living with awareness is the release from the incessant need for control. Concepts give us the illusion that we can control or predict life, but this control is always partial and temporary. Life is inherently unpredictable, and no amount of conceptualization can change that. By embracing awareness, we begin to accept the uncertainty of life and, in doing so, free ourselves from the anxiety that comes with trying to control the uncontrollable.

This freedom from control doesn't mean passivity or disengagement. On the contrary, it allows us to engage with life more fully and courageously. When we stop trying to control every outcome or predict every experience, we become more present, open to life's surprises, and willing to take risks. We no longer need to have everything figured out in advance. Instead, we trust that we can respond to whatever arises with flexibility, curiosity, and awareness.

The Practice of Awareness

Awareness is not a one-time decision but an ongoing practice that requires mindfulness, attention, and a willingness to return to the present moment repeatedly—especially when we slip into old patterns of conceptual thinking. This practice involves cultivating openness and non-judgment, observing our thoughts, emotions, and experiences without the impulse to immediately categorize or label them.

One way to strengthen awareness is through mindfulness meditation. This practice teaches us to observe our thoughts without attachment, notice when we get caught in conceptual thinking, and gently return to the present moment. Over time, it helps us remain more fully in the here and now, rather than becoming lost in the abstractions of the mind.

However, as Alan Watts often emphasized, it's important to remember that meditation isn't about achieving a particular outcome. If we meditate with the expectation of reaching a certain state—whether it's relaxation, enlightenment, or personal improvement—we are still engaging with the same mindset of striving and control. True meditation is about letting go of goals and simply being present with whatever arises. It's the practice of awareness for its own sake, not a means to an end. When we stop seeking a specific result in meditation, we open ourselves to the profound experience of awareness itself, free from the pressures of expectation or success.

Another key element of awareness is curiosity. Approaching life with curiosity keeps us open to new experiences, perspectives, and understandings. Instead of assuming we already know how things will unfold or what someone is like, curiosity allows us to stay engaged with the unknown. It prevents us from falling into the trap of rigid, conceptual thinking.

It cannot be emphasized enough that this practice requires self-honesty and humility. It means acknowledging that we cannot know everything, that life is far more complex than our concepts can capture. By letting go of the need for certainty, we embrace the mystery of existence and remain present with what is, rather than clinging to what we think we should know.

Living in awareness can be challenging. It takes courage to face life's uncertainty, to release the safety of fixed, comforting concepts, and to engage with the world as it is—complex, unpredictable, and often uncomfortable. But this courage is essential for growth, connection, and authenticity. True faith is not about clinging to beliefs or seeking comfort in absolutes; it is the willingness to face the unknown with openness and trust. It invites us to let go of the need for guarantees and instead embrace uncertainty, trusting in the process rather than demanding specific outcomes. In this way, faith becomes an act of surrender, grounded in presence rather than dogma.

The more we cultivate this mindset, the more we free ourselves from the limitations of conceptual thinking. We become more attuned to our emotions, more connected to others, and more present in our daily lives. Instead of reducing life to something predictable, we embrace its fluid, ever-changing nature. This openness is key to living a more authentic, meaningful, and connected life.

Just as cells must constantly respond to the signals around them, we too must remain open to the signals life is sending us in the present moment. If cells clung to outdated signals, the body would fall into dysfunction. Similarly, when we hold too tightly to concepts rooted in the past, we fail to adapt to life's evolving nature. To live in awareness is to trust that life's signals—if we listen carefully—will guide us, allowing us to respond fluidly and authentically. By letting go of concepts, we function like healthy cells, responding to each moment with clarity and alignment, free from the distortions of past beliefs.

We have spent this chapter exploring how concepts, while useful as tools, often limit our engagement with reality by reducing its complexity to simplistic, rigid frameworks. We rely on concepts to create a sense of certainty, predictability, and control, but in doing so, we cut ourselves off from the fluid, ever-changing nature of life. The emotional, psychological, and relational costs of this reliance on conceptual thinking are profound, affecting our ability to connect with ourselves, others, and the present moment. The alternative we've explored — living in awareness — requires us to step into the unknown, to let go of our dependence on certainty, and to embrace the uncertainty of life.

As we draw this chapter to a close, it's important to acknowledge the difficulty of this shift. Moving beyond concepts and embracing uncertainty is not something that happens overnight. It's not an easy task, and it's not without its challenges. For many of us, it took a lifetime to construct the concepts that define our identity, our relationships, and our understanding of the world. These mental frameworks have shaped our lives, provided us with a sense of stability, and helped us navigate a complex reality. Letting go of these frameworks — or at least loosening our grip on them — can feel destabilizing, disorienting, and even frightening.

Living without the comfort of false certainty isn't easy. We have spent years, perhaps decades, constructing our understanding of life based on oversimplified concepts. These ideas have given us a sense of control over our identities, our relationships, and our place in the world. Yet as we've seen, this control is an illusion. The more we cling to these concepts, the more we distance ourselves from the richness of reality and from the opportunity for growth. To step into a new way of living — one based on awareness rather than conceptual thinking — is to invite uncertainty, but it is also to invite freedom, curiosity, and deeper connection.

> "You have the right to work, but never to the fruit of work. You should never engage in action for the sake of reward, nor should you long for inaction."

— Bhagavad Gita

The journey from living in the security of concepts to embracing uncertainty and awareness is not a single step but an ongoing process. As we move through life, we are continually faced with opportunities to question our beliefs, challenge our assumptions, and grow beyond the limits we've set for ourselves. This process of growth can be understood through the lens of Loevinger's Stages of Ego Development, which outlines the psychological development of the self as we move from self-centered views of the world toward more integrated, empathetic, and flexible ways of being.

Loevinger's model describes how, in the early stages of life, our sense of self is defined by simple, black-and-white thinking. At these stages, we rely heavily on concepts to understand ourselves and the world around us. We are driven by a desire for certainty and control, and we tend to see the world in terms of fixed ideas. But as we grow, if we are willing to question and challenge these early frameworks, we begin to develop a more nuanced understanding of ourselves and others. We become able to embrace complexity, ambiguity, and paradox. Our awareness expands, and we start to recognize that the world is far more intricate than our early concepts allowed us to see.

Each stage of development comes with its own set of challenges, and moving from one stage to the next requires us to let go of old ways of thinking and being. This process can be uncomfortable, as it often involves confronting uncertainty, questioning long-held beliefs, and embracing new perspectives. We call them growing pains and not growing comforts for a reason. But it is through this pain that we grow. As we progress through these stages, we become more capable of seeing ourselves and others with empathy and compassion. We begin to live in a state of awareness, where we are no longer confined by ideas but are open to the complexity and fluidity of life.

One of the key elements of this journey is developing Faith. It's about trusting that life, in all its complexity and unpredictability, is something we can engage with fully, even if we don't always understand or predict what will happen next.

Faith allows us to let go of the need for conceptual safety and embrace a more flexible, responsive way of living. It gives us the courage to question our assumptions, to open ourselves to new experiences, and to engage with the present moment without trying to force it into a pre-existing framework. Living with faith means accepting that we cannot control or fully understand everything, and we never have, but that we can still navigate life with curiosity, empathy, and awareness.

This faith in uncertainty is not passive; it is active and dynamic. It involves being fully present, fully engaged with life as it unfolds. It means being willing to adapt, to change, and to grow. It requires us to trust not in fixed concepts, but in our ability to respond to whatever arises. Faith, in this sense, is an ongoing practice of openness—a commitment to living in awareness rather than clinging to the false security of beliefs.

The journey from rigid conceptual thinking to living in awareness is a lifelong process. It requires us to question the frameworks that have shaped our understanding of ourselves and the world, to challenge the fear of uncertainty, and to embrace the unknown with curiosity and compassion. As we move beyond the limits of concepts, we become more present, more empathetic, and more open to the richness of life in all its complexity.

In the next chapter, we will explore the challenges that arise when we choose to ground ourselves in uncertainty, live in awareness, and practice faith. We will examine the difficulties of maintaining presence in the face of unpredictability, the practice of honing our awareness, and how we can navigate reality without relying on the false comfort of control or certainty. But for now, let us rest in the understanding that the path forward is one of openness, curiosity, and trust in the unfolding of life. By letting go of concepts and embracing this approach, we step into the fullness of life, where each moment is an opportunity for growth, connection, and discovery.

Something to Reflect On:

Take a moment to reflect on an area of your life where you feel the need for certainty — whether it's in your beliefs about yourself, your relationships, or how the world works. How might this desire for certainty be limiting your ability to fully experience the present moment or connect more deeply with others? What emotions arise when you consider loosening your grip on this certainty and embracing the unknown? Write down your reflections and explore how living with greater awareness and openness, even in the face of uncertainty, could invite new opportunities for growth, connection, and self-discovery.

"The description is not the described; I can describe the mountain, but the description is not the mountain, and if you are caught up in the description, as most people are, then you will never see the mountain."

– Jiddu Krishnamurti

Chapter 10 - The Calm Amidst the Chaos

Congratulations. You've made it to Chapter 10, and that's something worth celebrating. This journey you've been on—of questioning, reflecting, and venturing further into awareness—has likely been a lot to take in. If you're feeling a bit overwhelmed right now, know that it's completely normal. Anyone who begins to pull back the layers of their conditioning, to see the illusions we live in, will at some point feel a sense of disorientation. You're not alone in that.

There's no rush to get everything right, or to fully grasp every insight that's been discussed so far. The way you're understanding this book today is not the way you'll understand it tomorrow, next month, or next year—and that's okay. Your clarity will continue to deepen, not because you're trying harder, but simply because you're staying present and open to growth. The process of change is already happening, often subtly, just by virtue of recognizing what you've learned.

Take a moment to breathe and ground yourself in the progress you've already made. Just like cells initiate repair after stress or injury, you've activated your own renewing resilience throughout this journey. Even if the changes feel small or barely noticeable, healing is happening at a core level, and your capacity to restore balance grows with each insight.

And when things do feel chaotic, when the weight of these insights feels heavy, remember that it's okay to revisit earlier chapters. Sometimes, returning to what you've already read can offer new clarity as your understanding evolves. Often, something that seemed abstract or confusing the first time through will make more sense on a second or third look.

This chapter is designed to help you stay grounded as the shifts you've experienced continue to ripple through your awareness. There's no rush to figure it all out. Your job isn't to master uncertainty or control the outcomes—it's to navigate these waters with an openness to whatever may come, knowing that the more you let go, the more clearly you'll see. You are here, right now, exactly where you need to be.

As we move forward, we'll explore the challenges that come with living in uncertainty and how to maintain mental and emotional balance in a world that often seems chaotic and disconnected. But before we dive into that, take a moment to honor yourself for the work you've already done.

You've come this far, and you're doing just fine.

Something to Reflect On:

What concepts have shifted in your understanding since you began this book? What did you find overwhelming at first that now feels more familiar? How might revisiting earlier chapters help you ground your understanding even further?

At times, control feels like a necessary shield—the belief that we can steer life's events and protect ourselves from discomfort. But as you've come to realize, control is fleeting. Life unfolds unpredictably, despite our best efforts to hold on. This isn't a flaw; it's the essence of existence.

Letting go of control can feel disorienting, even overwhelming. Vulnerability in the face of uncertainty can stir up primal emotions, but it's within that uncertainty that you've found moments of grounding. Not by directing the storm, but by anchoring yourself in the present.

Think of it as standing in the eye of a storm. While chaos swirls around you, there is a stillness at the center—not from an absence of fear, but from accepting it. You've learned that letting go isn't about surrendering to chaos; it's about finding your balance within it. This journey isn't about mastering uncertainty, but learning to navigate it with openness, trusting that clarity will arise when needed.

"I've always been the best version of myself after a performance or after I write a song. It's the most natural drug."

Ben Stewart, frontman of the band Slowly Slowly, reflected on how his creative process allows him to find calm and clarity in moments of uncertainty. His words remind us that letting go of control can lead to moments of pure flow and presence, allowing us to navigate the chaos with a sense of grounded creativity.

As Lao Tzu wrote in the Tao Te Ching: 'Be still like a mountain and flow like a great river.' True peace doesn't come from controlling everything around you but from finding stillness within yourself while adapting to life's inevitable changes. It's in this space—where you can feel both grounded and fluid—that the intensity of uncertainty begins to soften.

Consider the story of Desmond Doss, a conscientious objector during World War II, who made the extraordinary decision to enter the battlefield without a weapon. For Doss, his principles of non-violence were non-negotiable, even in the face of overwhelming pressure from both sides. Imagine the intensity of that decision—stepping into war, surrounded by the constant threat of death, without a means to defend yourself, and enduring the judgment and scorn from fellow soldiers who saw his refusal to bear arms as cowardice or naivety, viewing him with suspicion, and in some cases, outright hostility. They couldn't understand why someone would willingly forgo the safety of a weapon in a warzone. Yet Doss's strength came not from controlling the narrative others had of him, nor from ensuring his own physical safety through force, but from his deep conviction and inner resolve. He became his center amidst the chaos, trusting that by staying grounded in his principles, he could navigate the storm.

In a world where control and safety are often equated with power and force, Doss chose another path. Despite the chaos and danger, he remained unwavering in his values, grounding himself in his personal truth. He focused on what he could do in each moment—saving lives as a medic, navigating the battlefield with nothing but his commitment to his integrity and his trust in his ability to act in the present.

Doss's story illustrates the kind of calm and clarity that can arise not from controlling the external world but from standing firm in who you are, even when everything around you is in turmoil. He didn't achieve peace by trying to direct the course of the battle or shielding himself from danger. Instead, he found peace in each action he took, recognizing that the reward lay in the process, not the result—focusing on the lives he could save and the impact he could make in the present moment.

Like Doss, we face our own battles—not necessarily on a physical battlefield, but in the internal wars we wage against uncertainty, fear, and the desire to control outcomes. His story reminds us that true courage isn't about being invulnerable or having all the answers. It's about embracing vulnerability, trusting that we can become our calm center even when life feels chaotic. We find peace not by trying to control the storm, but by staying present within it, grounded in who we are and open to whatever may come.

"We cannot choose our external circumstances, but we can always choose how we respond to them."

— Epictetus

Another profound example of remaining grounded in the face of overwhelming adversity is Sophie Scholl, a key member of the White Rose resistance movement in Nazi Germany. Sophie, along with her brother, distributed anti-Nazi leaflets, fully aware of the risks. Despite the looming threat of arrest and execution, Sophie remained composed, centered in her integrity, and unwavering in her commitment to justice. Her calm defiance amidst the fear and chaos illustrates the strength that comes from grounding ourselves in our inner truth, showing us that even in the darkest moments, we can find clarity by staying anchored in who we are. In the face of fear and uncertainty, Sophie's quiet strength reminds us that true courage lies not in the absence of fear, but in the ability to stay present and maintain awareness, even when the world around us is unraveling.

Attempting to control everything is like standing in the middle of a storm and trying to hold back the wind with your bare hands. Life, with all its unpredictability, swirls around us—people, events, and circumstances too vast to manage. Yet we often live as though more control will somehow shield us from the chaos. We make plans, set goals, and micromanage our relationships, careers, and even our emotions, believing that control will bring us security and happiness.

But the storm never follows our plans—not really. Even in those rare moments when it seems to, life inevitably shifts in ways we can't predict. Whether it's a career path we've meticulously mapped out or a relationship that doesn't unfold as we imagined, the winds change, and we can feel lost, anxious, or even angry. Why? Because we've anchored our sense of security to something inherently fragile: the illusion that we can and should control our lives. The truth is, trying to hold back the storm only leaves us exhausted and vulnerable.

Instead of struggling against the storm, imagine standing in its eye. There, in the center, is where you find stillness. The winds may continue to rage around you, but in the eye of the storm, you can let go of the need to control every gust and swirl. You come to understand that chaos is not something to be conquered, but something to navigate with presence and openness. The more we release our grip, the more clearly we can see the path forward, even if it's not the one we expected.

When a plan falls apart, or when life takes an unexpected turn, we're reminded that uncertainty is the only constant. The sooner we embrace this, the more adaptable and peaceful we become, trusting that we can weather whatever comes our way.

By now, you've learned how deeply the need for control is ingrained in daily life. You've begun to recognize how this desire to control the storm often manifests in small, habitual ways—like constantly checking your phone or emails to feel on top of things, or refreshing social media for updates in a bid to stay connected and in control of your environment. You've likely noticed the urge to plan every moment of your day or rehearse conversations, trying to predict and manage outcomes before they even unfold.

Perhaps you've caught yourself curating a perfect image on social media, carefully managing how others see you, or feeling uneasy when plans remain uncertain, always needing to know the who, what, and how long. In relationships, it might appear as a tendency to anticipate others' needs and emotions to avoid conflict or seeking constant reassurance for a sense of security.

In health and wellness, you may have seen how closely monitoring food, calories, or workouts gives a false sense of control over outcomes. Or perhaps you've noticed it in your work life, where the need to micromanage or avoid delegation stems from the belief that only you can guarantee things will go smoothly.

Routines can also become a form of control—clinging to them for stability and predictability, or avoiding new experiences out of fear that you can't control the outcome. These habits, which once seemed necessary, are now clearer to you as extensions of the illusion that we can manage life's uncertainties. But as you've already learned, this need for control often only adds unnecessary stress and anxiety.

So, what if, instead of trying to control every detail, you allowed yourself to embrace the unexpected? What if you trusted that life has its own flow and that you have the strength and adaptability to navigate whatever comes, even when you don't see it coming?

This isn't a new realization for you, but it's a reminder of a lesson that deepens with each experience. You've already seen how stepping back can reveal a clearer, more natural path forward. The journey is about continuing to practice this—releasing your tension, allowing life to settle, and trusting the process as it unfolds.

Life is not something to be controlled or forced into order. It's meant to be experienced—fully, in all its unpredictability and beauty.

Grounding yourself in uncertainty is like cellular repair. After injury or stress, your cells activate their own repair mechanisms to restore balance, often without your conscious awareness. In the same way, when you step back and allow life to unfold naturally, you activate your own resilience. Just as your body knows how to heal itself, you have the capacity to find calm and restore clarity amidst chaos, without needing to control every outcome.

There's a deep relaxation that comes when you realize you don't have to manage everything. Life, like the body, has an innate wisdom. When you stop pushing and allow natural processes—both within yourself and in the world around you—to take their course, peace and clarity emerge on their own, just as cells repair themselves after disruption.

"You have power over your mind—not outside events. Realize this, and you will find strength."

— Marcus Aurelius

Letting go of control is a lifelong practice, not something you can, should, or even want to flip a switch on overnight. It's a gradual process of loosening your grip, trusting the unknown, and embracing life's natural unpredictability. The temptation to rush this journey—especially through external means like psychedelics—can be alluring, but it often leads to greater confusion and distortion rather than true clarity.

While psychedelics can offer profound experiences and temporarily dissolve our sense of boundaries, there is a danger in believing that these experiences provide permanent enlightenment or true 'awakening.' It's easy to mistake a temporary shift in perspective for a permanent change in awareness. The habitual patterns of thought we associate with the ego can subtly re-emerge, now cloaked in spiritual language, bragging at length about an 'experienced ego death' that contradicts the statement in itself. Ironically, this is the same process of identity attachment reasserting itself—changing shape rather than dissolving.

True transformation doesn't happen in a single psychedelic journey or a moment of peak experience. These moments can offer glimpses into profound truths, but without continued practice, reflection, and integration, they risk becoming just another layer of egoic identity. The real work lies in the daily practice of staying present, being vulnerable, and engaging with life as it unfolds—something no substance or peak experience can offer permanently.

There are consequences to trying to bypass this gradual process. The rush to 'wake up' overnight or achieve a permanent state of ego death often leads to spiritual bypassing—where real emotional work, healing, and integration are avoided in favor of chasing transcendent experiences. As we will discuss later in this chapter, forcing this process can create even more layers of illusion, leaving you further from the clarity and peace you seek.

Developing awareness is about gradually loosening our habitual identification with thoughts and concepts—not eliminating them, but learning to notice them with awareness. Clarity and peace come through small, consistent moments of openness and trust, rather than through a single grand experience.

Here are a few ways to start integrating this practice into your daily life:

Start Small: Choose one area of your life where you often feel the need to control the outcome. It could be something small, like how a conversation will go or what people think of you. Instead of trying to manage every detail, allow yourself to let things unfold naturally. Notice how this feels. Does the world fall apart without your control? Or do things flow in unexpected ways?

Embrace Uncertainty: When you catch yourself trying to predict or manage the future, pause. Take a deep breath and remind yourself that uncertainty isn't something to be feared; it's an integral part of life. Rather than fearing what you don't know, see it as an opportunity for new possibilities to emerge. By leaning into uncertainty, you open yourself up to new experiences and growth.

Shift from Control to Curiosity: Instead of thinking about life as something to be controlled, approach it with curiosity. Wonder what might happen next rather than trying to dictate it. Curiosity opens the door to flexibility and spontaneity, while control locks us into rigid expectations. Ask yourself, "What might happen if I just let things be?" and see what unfolds.

Practice Presence: One of the easiest ways to let go of control is to focus on the present moment. So much of our need for control comes from future anxieties. When you bring your attention back to the here and now, those anxieties lose their power. Try practicing mindfulness—whether through meditation, mindful walking, or simply noticing your breath. The more grounded you are in the present, the easier it becomes to release your grip on future outcomes.

Trust Yourself: Letting go of control requires trust—not just in life, but in yourself. Trust that no matter what happens, you'll be able to handle it. You've made it through challenges and uncertainties before, and you'll continue to do so. Remind yourself that you don't need to know exactly what's coming next in order to be okay.

I remember a trip I was on where everything seemed to go wrong, yet in acceptance, everything also went right. What made the experience so transformative wasn't just the release of control, but the realization that in abandoning my expectations and perceived needs, I found a deeper sense of joy and freedom. When I stopped clinging to the idea of how things should go, I became more open to what was actually happening.

Flights were delayed, my hotel was overbooked, and to top it off, I lost my phone. At first, frustration was my constant companion as I tried to hold onto some semblance of control. But as I sat in the midst of the chaos, something shifted. I stopped fighting it. I let go of my plans and expectations and began to flow with what was unfolding.

While waiting for that delayed flight, I struck up a conversation with a stranger, who later became a good friend. The overbooked hotel situation led me to a small, family-run bed-and-breakfast that I never would have considered, which turned out to be one of the highlights of the trip. And losing my phone? It forced me to disconnect and be present in a way I hadn't been in years, allowing me to engage fully with the world around me.

What this taught me is that when we stop trying to force life into a box, we open ourselves up to the serendipity that life naturally offers. Surrendering doesn't mean losing control—it means gaining access to the flow of possibilities that are always present, just beyond our rigid expectations. It's about shifting your perspective and recognizing that control was never yours to begin with. It's about lightening your grip, trusting in the flow of life, and knowing that whatever happens, you're capable of moving through it.

Something to Reflect On:

 Where in your life are you still holding tightly to control? How might letting go, even in small ways, create more freedom, joy, and flow?

It's one thing to experience your own internal growth—to recognize the freedom that comes from developing sensitivity, releasing attachment to outcomes, and embracing uncertainty. But stepping out into a world that still clings to fear and conditioned, divisive identities can be challenging. Staying grounded amidst the chaos around you can feel difficult when everything external seems at odds with the internal peace you've begun to cultivate.

This section is about integrating what you've learned into a world that often operates from a place of insecurity and illusion. It's about remaining grounded, compassionate, and open when faced with people and systems that are deeply entrenched in fear and control. As you navigate these situations, it's important to remember that just because you've begun to let go of the need for control doesn't mean everyone else has. And that's okay.

The world around us can often feel chaotic—social media, work environments, the global political landscape—all of it can seem overwhelming at times. The noise of it all can drown out your own sense of calm and make you question whether you've really made any progress at all. But the key to navigating this chaos is not in trying to change it or escape from it, but in learning how to remain grounded within it.

It's about learning to stand firm in the eye of the storm, knowing that you don't have to react to everything happening around you, the storm is change in motion. You can choose how to engage, and more importantly, how *not* to engage.

Krishnamurti once said, "It is no measure of health to be well-adjusted to a profoundly sick society." This doesn't mean that you should disconnect from the world or ignore what's happening, but rather that you should understand that much of the chaos around you is simply rooted in fear. Trying to fit into that chaos is not the solution. Instead, the goal is to remain a stabilizing presence within it.

As you grow in awareness, you'll find yourself surrounded by people who are still deeply attached to their identities, their fears, and their need for control. They might engage in competitive, outcome-based discussions, trying to win arguments or establish dominance. You'll encounter people stuck in their own stories, repeating patterns of fear and insecurity without even realizing it. These behaviors didn't spring up out of nowhere—you just couldn't notice them when you were caught in the same patterns yourself.

The key to interacting with people in this mentality is accepting that you do the same in your own way, without judgment of doing so. Empathy means meeting people where they are, understanding that they're doing the best they can with the level of awareness they currently have, exactly as we have been doing. It means recognizing that our fear-based behaviors come from pain, not from malice. But empathy doesn't mean taking on their energy or trying to 'save' them from their own journey. You don't need saving, and neither do they.

This is where non-attachment comes in. Just because you understand where someone's fear or ego-driven behavior is coming from doesn't mean you have to engage with it or let it affect you. You can remain compassionate without being pulled into their story. You can offer a light touch, a subtle reminder of presence, without needing to force them to see what you see.

One of the challenges of growing in awareness is the temptation to want to "save" others from their illusions. When you start to see the bigger picture—that we're all dealing with fear and identity—it's natural to want to help others "break free". But this desire, while well-intentioned, is a form of attachment itself. This is what's often referred to as the messiah complex—the idea that it's your job to wake others up or pull them out of their conditioned ways of thinking. It's another concept to attach to and if you're attaching to a concept, what do you truly have to teach anyone that you aren't contradicting yourself?

If you try to force people to see an insight before they're ready, they may react with defensiveness or even anger. This isn't because they don't want to grow, but because they're not yet in a place where they feel safe enough to grow in the way you think they should.

That's why a light touch is so important—or better yet, no intentional 'touch' at all. Rather than trying to save people from their own illusions, you can meet them with authenticity, subtlety, compassion, and patience. Sometimes, the most powerful thing you can do is simply hold space for someone—allowing them to be where they are, without judgment or pressure to change. Not only does this respect their journey, but it also acknowledges that someone who feels like they're drowning may unintentionally pull you down in their struggle to stay afloat.

History offers a clear illustration of how people who cling fervently to their concepts in the face of life's storm of uncertainty can become incredibly dangerous. Take Galileo Galilei, for example. His discoveries about the cosmos—that the Earth was not the center of the universe—challenged the rigid beliefs of his time. The church fiercely opposed this new perspective, and for daring to contradict their worldview, Galileo spent the remainder of his life under house arrest. Why did they react so harshly? Because acknowledging Galileo's discoveries would have meant admitting they were wrong, which threatened the authority and image they had built. Their belief in a certain view of the universe wasn't just about understanding the cosmos—it was about maintaining a sense of control, stability, and power in a world that felt chaotic and uncertain.

What's particularly striking, and even a bit ironic, is that it took 359 years for the church to officially pardon Galileo. It wasn't about whether they still believed they were right—it was about the challenge of admitting fault, of letting go of the image they wanted the world to hold of them. Even after the truth was undeniable, the need to protect their perceived infallibility delayed the acknowledgment of error for centuries.

And the pardon? It wasn't really for Galileo—he had long since passed. The church wasn't seeking to make amends with him; rather, the pardon served to reconcile their own position. After all, it was the church that had imprisoned him for challenging their view, not because he was wrong, but because they couldn't face admitting they were. In truth, it seems that it was the church that needed pardon, not Galileo. And perhaps, if he were alive today, he might offer it willingly.

This story highlights how people—whether individually or in groups—can become so attached to their beliefs and identities that they'll go to great lengths to preserve them, creating a potential danger to anyone they deem a threat to the false certainty that drives them.

When you start to speak honestly—especially in a world that still clings to outdated beliefs—you may encounter resistance, much like

Galileo did. People might react with judgment, avoidance, or even outright rejection. But their reaction isn't really about you. It's about their attachment to the beliefs that make them feel safe. Just as the church needed to cling to the idea of Earth's centrality for its own sense of value and certainty, people today cling to their own self-soothing ideas to maintain their sense of stability.

This doesn't mean you should back down from what you've discovered. But it does mean that self-reflection and empathy are as important as expression. Are you trying to convince someone of something? Aren't you the one who should truly know it? The truth has its own weight, and it doesn't need promotion. Galileo didn't need to be pardoned for his discoveries to be real—they were real long before anyone was ready to accept them.

As we've explored in previous chapters, we still live in a world full of systems built on similar foundations of fear and control—whether it's the political system, the education system, or societal expectations around success and identity. These systems are designed to keep people in line, often through reinforcing external achievements and narrow definitions of self-worth. They function by offering a sense of order and certainty, much like the concepts we once relied on to protect ourselves from the chaos of life. These systems give us frameworks that appear stable, but in reality, they limit our ability to see beyond the surface, trapping us in roles and expectations that don't necessarily align with our authentic selves.

As you begin to recognize the absurdity of these systems—how they attempt to impose control and certainty in a world that is inherently unpredictable—it can be tempting to reject them outright. But rejecting these systems aggressively or trying to tear them down is not always the most effective approach. Instead, consider how a storm gradually erodes cliffs over time. The systems we navigate are like these cliffs—seemingly solid and immovable, but in reality, vulnerable to the forces of life's inherent uncertainty and fluidity.

Awareness, like the storm, slowly wears down the resistance of these systems. Rather than fighting against them, you can remain grounded in your own understanding, allowing the natural flow of awareness and life to erode the limitations these systems impose. It's not about force or resistance; it's about trusting that life, with all its uncertainty, will naturally break down what is rigid and outdated. You don't need to tear these systems apart—just as the storm doesn't need to destroy the cliffs in a single moment, but gradually reshapes them over time.

Navigating these systems with awareness means engaging with the world as it is, while still holding your own sense of freedom. These systems may reflect collective fears and a desire for control, but they don't need to dictate your experience. Like cliffs facing a storm, these structures will change over time as you continue to stand grounded in the midst of life's inevitable flow.

I remember a conversation I had with a close friend who was deeply entrenched in a competitive, outcome-driven mindset. Every time we talked, it felt like she was trying to "win" the conversation—proving her point or establishing her superiority. At first, this frustrated me. I wanted to show her that there was no need to compete, that life was not a race, and that we could simply share without the need for judgment or comparison.

But when I tried to explain this to her directly, she resisted. She became defensive, even more attached to her point of view. That's when I realized I wasn't meeting her where she was. I was trying to pull her out of her mindset without considering that she wasn't ready for that yet.

So I shifted my approach. Instead of trying to "fix" her or change her mind, I simply listened. I stayed grounded in my own awareness, but I didn't push. I let the conversation flow naturally, offering subtle reminders of presence when the moment felt right, but without forcing anything.

Over time, something shifted. She began to relax, to open up. And eventually, she started asking questions about why I didn't seem as stressed or competitive as I used to be. That was the opening—a chance for a more genuine conversation about growth and self-acceptance. But it only happened because I stopped trying to save her and started meeting her with empathy and subtlety.

To stay centered in a world that often feels chaotic, here are a few practices you can incorporate into your daily life:

Mindful Listening: When engaging with others, practice being fully present in the conversation. Don't focus on what you're going to say next or how you can "win" the discussion. Simply listen. Allow the other person to express themselves without judgment, and notice how this shifts the energy of the interaction. Mindful listening creates space for empathy and a calmer, more grounded exchange, regardless of the other person's mindset.

Breathwork for Centering: When you feel overwhelmed by external chaos, take a moment to focus on your breath. Slow, deep breaths help bring you back to the present moment and center your attention. Try taking slow deep breaths, inhaling gently, holding briefly, and exhaling patiently. This simple practice can ground you in moments of stress and reestablish your connection to the present.

Set Boundaries: Being empathetic doesn't mean allowing others to pull you into their fears or struggles. Set healthy boundaries in relationships, especially with those who are still operating from fear or control. Boundaries allow you to engage compassionately while maintaining your own sense of balance. Grounding yourself in clear boundaries protects your emotional and mental well-being, helping you navigate interactions without becoming overwhelmed by the dynamics of others.

Grounding Meditation: A grounding meditation can help you reconnect with your sense of inner stability. Visualize yourself as a tree, with roots extending deep into the earth.

As the chaos of the world swirls around you, your roots keep you steady and connected to the ground. This visualization can help reinforce your sense of stability, even in the midst of uncertainty. Taking time to ground yourself from time to time can make all the difference in staying calm and centered in an unpredictable world.

Something to Reflect On:

Think of a recent interaction where someone's fear-based perspective or competitive nature frustrated you. How might a more empathetic, grounded response have shifted the dynamic? What would it look like to engage with subtlety rather than confrontation?

The mind, in its attempt to cope with uncertainty, constructs narratives and assumptions—concepts about who we are, what the world is like, and how we should interact with it. When held too tightly, however, these concepts become limiting beliefs that disconnect us from reality, trapping us in cycles of fear, anxiety, and dissatisfaction. Disorders such as anxiety, depression, obsessive-compulsive disorder (OCD), and dissociative conditions often arise from a prolonged over-reliance on control, certainty, and an attachment to self-concepts, all in an effort to ease the very panic these attachments themselves create. Healing is not about gaining more control over these concepts, but about unraveling our belief in them, questioning them, and embracing the fluidity of the self through mindfulness and compassion.

At the root of most mental health disorders is the mind's attempt to control an unpredictable world. Anxiety, depression, OCD, and dissociation are all efforts to impose control over something that cannot be controlled: the uncertainty of life. The mind clings to assumptions and superficial definitions of ourselves, others, and reality in an attempt to create certainty and soothe fear. But when life inevitably deviates from these concepts, further suffering occurs.

Take anxiety, for example. Anxiety is the fear of the unknown, a chronic hypervigilance that comes from the need to predict and control the future. The anxious mind holds tightly to concepts as a way to feel secure: "If I prepare for every possible outcome, I can avoid failure or disappointment." However, these concepts are not based in reality—they are hypothetical constructs, and the attempt to live according to them deepens the anxiety rather than resolves it. As we know, the more one tries to control, the more elusive certainty becomes, leading to heightened stress, panic, and a constant sense of threat.

Similarly, OCD, often referred to as the "doubter's disease", is rooted in the concept of control. The person creates rituals and repetitive thought patterns in an attempt to manage uncertainty. The mind develops concepts like, "If I perform this ritual perfectly, I will prevent harm," but these rituals are based on imagined fears, not reality. The ritual becomes a conceptual structure that provides a temporary sense of safety, but it also perpetuates the cycle of fear and reinforces the idea that control is possible in an uncontrollable world.

Depression, too, is shaped by concepts. People struggling with depression often hold onto deeply ingrained beliefs about themselves—concepts like, "I am unworthy," or "I am incapable of change." These self-concepts are narratives that have solidified over time, trapping the individual in a cycle of hopelessness. The belief that "I am broken" or "I am not good enough" becomes a rigid identity, reinforcing feelings of despair and disconnection from the world.

At the core of these disorders is the fictitious self we've come to know so well throughout this book—the collection of concepts and assumptions that we mistake for who we truly are. This conceptual self doesn't feel fictitious at all when we believe in it; it feels real because we give it reality. In identifying with this thought-based self, anything that invalidates the idea is felt as though it were an actual physical threat. As we cling to this false identity—and the world we've constructed to support it—we experience conflict with a world that will never be as simple or predictable as the thoughts we hold onto for comfort. This disconnect creates unavoidable suffering, disappointment, frustration, and insecurity. The more we suffer, the farther we feel from the peace we seek. And as the gap between how we think we should feel and how we actually feel grows, we panic. In that panic, we unknowingly widen the gap further by returning to the endless maintenance of a fictitious self and world that can never truly exist, reinforcing the cycle of suffering. This reflexive, habitual response lies at the core of these disorders.

At the root of this false identity lies a deeper pattern: the mind's reliance on assumptions. These assumptions, narratives, or oversimplified concepts, are mental constructs we create to make sense of our experiences. When we encounter painful or challenging events, the mind quickly forms a 'best guess' of reality in an attempt to protect us. However, these assumptions are never based on the full picture, and if left unexamined, they harden into destructive beliefs and behaviors. Over time, they become part of the fictitious self—the narratives we cling to in our effort to define and control ourselves and the world around us.

For example, a child who experiences repeated criticism may develop the assumption, "I am not good enough." This concept becomes a protective mechanism, helping the child navigate rejection and pain. However, as this assumption solidifies, it becomes a core part of their identity. They grow up believing that they are fundamentally flawed, and this concept colors every relationship, every challenge, and every opportunity. It limits their ability to grow, take risks, or see themselves as capable.

Dr. Gabor Maté, a trauma expert, discusses how the "ego" — the tendency to identify — arises from unresolved trauma. The assumptions we develop after traumatic experiences, such as "I must always be strong" or "I am unworthy of love," are protective mechanisms that served us at one point in our lives. However, over time, these initially protective concepts become barriers to living freely in the present moment. They trap us in a cycle of fear and avoidance, disconnecting us from our true selves.

Maté's work emphasizes that healing does not come from gaining more control over these self-concepts or from suppressing them. Instead, healing comes from surrender — releasing the grip on these old concepts and allowing ourselves to experience the full range of our emotions. By abandoning our belief that these assumptions define us, we create space for a more authentic, fluid self to emerge.

While letting go of control is essential for healing, it's important to recognize that this process isn't simply about releasing control over day-to-day decisions. It involves questioning the very concepts we once held sacred — ideas like what is 'normal,' 'real,' or 'sane.' As we begin to let go of these assumptions, the mind can feel unmoored, as if the foundations it relied on are suddenly disappearing. Questioning these deeply ingrained beliefs can be disorienting, especially when they have shaped our understanding of ourselves and the world for so long.

There is a risk that, in the process of surrendering our conceptual safety net, the mind may retreat too far into imagination, hallucination, or dissociation. When confronted with the fragility of concepts we once thought were solid, or overwhelmed by the rigidity of these constructs, the mind may seek an escape. Dissociation becomes a survival mechanism, allowing the mind to disconnect from reality in an attempt to avoid overwhelming emotions or experiences that arise when these beliefs are questioned.

Dissociation often occurs in response to trauma, but it can also arise when the mind is confronted with what it perceives as overwhelming uncertainty. As we begin to question our assumptions and let go of unquestioned concepts, we may experience moments of clarity that feel disorienting or overwhelming. These moments of clarity are, in fact, moments of uncertainty—when we accept that we can't know everything, that control is an illusion, that identity is fluid and not fixed, that our attachments are impermanent, and that life will never conform to our expectations. Recognizing the fluidity of life and the self can be destabilizing, and in these moments, the mind may retreat into dissociative tendencies as a form of self-protection. Dissociation can range from mild, such as zoning out or daydreaming, to more severe forms like Dissociative Identity Disorder (DID).

It's important to remember that uncertainty, as it deepens or as these moments of clarity arise, can feel overwhelming. When the protective layers of our assumptions, narratives, and identities start to dissolve, the mind may panic. The sudden realization that there is no control, and that much of life is unknowable, can be profoundly unsettling. Clarity, at first, can be disorienting before it brings freedom, and the mind may retreat into dissociation to avoid the discomfort of confronting this new awareness.

When the uncertainty becomes overwhelming—when the thoughts and assumptions you've unraveled seem to leave you unmoored—it's important to come back to the present moment. The mind may want to dwell on incomplete thoughts, seeking to find answers or control what feels uncontrollable. But in those moments, your practice is to let go of the need to know, to resist the pull of dwelling on superficial, temporary constructs.

Uncertainty, like a storm, can be intense and unsettling, but the path forward lies not in avoiding it, but in moving through it. As you question your need for certainty, your need to control, you will find yourself reaching the eye of the storm. In this calm center, the uncertainty and fears still exist, but they no longer knock you off balance. They lose their power to pull you from your feet.

This is a crucial moment in your process: staying grounded when the old assumptions dissolve, trusting that you don't need all the answers to find peace. Continue questioning the need to dwell on incomplete thoughts, and instead, practice coming back to the present. In that space, the uncertainty becomes something you can navigate—not something you have to control.

Changing our response to long-held concepts requires self-compassion. It's common to feel frustrated when these old beliefs or assumptions resurface, especially when you've been working to change them. You might ask yourself, "Why am I still stuck in this pattern?" or "Why can't I just move past this?" However, healing doesn't come from judging yourself—it comes from meeting these slowly loosening thoughts with kindness and patience.

Dr. Kristin Neff, a leading researcher in self-compassion, explains that self-compassion allows us to hold space for ourselves in moments of struggle. Instead of getting frustrated or critical when old concepts arise, we can respond with understanding: "It's okay that this thought is here. It makes sense that I would feel this way, given my experiences." By offering yourself this compassion, you create the emotional safety needed to begin transforming these old assumptions.

Recognizing that these concepts were once protective mechanisms can help you approach them with compassion. They served a purpose in the past—whether it was to shield you from pain, protect you from rejection, or help you cope with uncertainty. But just because these assumptions once served you doesn't mean they have to define you now. By acknowledging their origins and offering yourself compassion, you create space to release these concepts and move toward greater emotional freedom.

Let's say, during a mindfulness practice, you notice the thought, "I'm not good enough." Instead of reacting to this thought, mindfulness invites you to sit with it, to observe it without judgment. You can recognize that this thought is just that—a thought. It doesn't need to shape your actions, your self-image, or your emotional state. However, through self-honesty, it can still teach you something about your inner landscape. This practice of mindful non-attachment creates space between the thought and your sense of self, allowing you to see that you are more than your thoughts. At the same time, by observing the thought with honesty, you can start to understand where it comes from—what fear, assumption, or belief might be driving it.

Rather than simply dismissing the thought, self-honest awareness invites you to explore its deeper origins. What does this thought reveal about the expectations you've placed on yourself? Does it reflect an old belief you've outgrown or a fear of the unknown? Often, the thoughts we hold today are rooted in deep, underlying currents—primal influences that stem from our earliest experiences. These thoughts might echo childhood fears of isolation, inadequacy, confusion, or rejection—patterns we learned long before we were aware of their lasting influence.

By bringing mindful, non-judgmental self-honesty to these thoughts, you begin to see how these fears still influence your perceptions and behaviors—and why they no longer have to. With regular practice, you'll notice these thoughts arise less frequently or with less intensity. Even when they do surface, they will no longer feel as powerful or defining. Instead, they can deepen your empathy, helping you relate to others with greater understanding. Over time, you may experience yourself as something beyond these concepts—an evolving self, grounded in the present moment, capable of connecting with others in a more authentic and compassionate way.

Dr. Jon Kabat-Zinn, the founder of Mindfulness-Based Stress Reduction (MBSR), has helped millions of people use mindfulness to manage stress, anxiety, and chronic pain. His approach focuses on cultivating awareness of the present moment and surrendering of attachment to thoughts, emotions, and assumptions.

Kabat-Zinn's work is particularly relevant to individuals dealing with anxiety and depression, where concepts and self-judgments are often at play. By learning to observe their thoughts through mindfulness, people can begin to unravel the deeply ingrained assumptions that contribute to their suffering. Kabat-Zinn teaches that rather than trying to control or fix these thoughts, the key is to meet them with awareness and acceptance.

For example, a person with anxiety might constantly worry about the future, holding onto the assumption that "something bad will happen." Through mindfulness, they can observe this thought as it arises without buying into it. By bringing awareness to the thought without reacting, they begin to loosen its hold and gradually change their response. This practice doesn't eliminate the thought, but it changes the individual's relationship with it, fostering emotional resilience and clarity.

One of the most transformative aspects of this process is your ability to create a new response to the intensity of uncertainty and moments of clarity. As you continue to question the assumptions and concepts that once shaped your identity, you may experience waves of uncertainty that feel overwhelming. But with growing awareness, you can meet these moments not with panic or a need to retreat into old patterns, but with presence, mindfulness, and self-compassion.

When clarity reveals just how fluid and uncertain life truly is, the instinct may be to resist or try to control it. Instead, you now have the capacity to respond differently—to stay grounded in the present, allowing the intensity of uncertainty to pass through without letting it define you. This shift is about meeting uncertainty with openness, trusting that you can handle it, and creating space for new possibilities to emerge without needing to grasp for certainty.

For example, let's revisit the feeling of uncertainty that can arise when confronting deep truths, like the realization that life is far less predictable than we might have believed. Once you recognize this uncertainty as part of the natural flow of life, rather than something to fear, you can begin to change your response to it. You might start by acknowledging that certainty is not necessary for peace — discomfort can coexist with openness. You can practice staying present with the discomfort of not knowing, observing how your body and mind react, and learning to trust that you can navigate through uncertainty without needing to grasp for control.

As you practice responding to these moments with awareness, you'll begin to loosen the mind's reflex to panic or retreat. The narrative of 'I need to know' transforms into 'I can be at peace without knowing everything.' This shift allows for greater emotional flexibility and personal growth, helping you move through the world with more resilience, openness, and trust in the process of life.

Another relevant approach is Tara Brach's practice of Radical Acceptance, which emphasizes the importance of meeting difficult emotions and uncertainty with awareness and compassion, rather than trying to control or avoid them. Brach teaches that much of our suffering arises not from the uncertainty or discomfort itself, but from our resistance to it. When we resist feeling vulnerable or avoid facing the unpredictable nature of life, we reinforce the very patterns of fear and control that keep us stuck.

Through Radical Acceptance, Brach encourages us to stop fighting the uncertainty and instead meet it with kindness. For example, when confronted with the fear that arises in moments of clarity or when old certainties dissolve, instead of trying to push the fear away or fix it, Brach's approach invites us to acknowledge it: 'I see this fear, I recognize that it's painful, and I offer myself compassion.' This act of meeting uncertainty with loving attention creates the space for transformation. It allows us to soften our grip on control and trust the process of moving through the storm with greater self-compassion and ease.

Dr. James Gordon, founder of The Center for Mind-Body Medicine, is another influential figure who uses mindfulness and body-based practices to help individuals heal from trauma, anxiety, and the effects of trying to control uncertainty. Gordon's approach emphasizes the mind-body connection, encouraging individuals to tune into their bodies and recognize how moments of uncertainty, fear, and unprocessed emotions are stored physically.

Gordon teaches that when we resist uncertainty or attempt to control our emotions, these unresolved feelings often manifest as physical tension or chronic stress. By practicing mindfulness, meditation, mindful movement, or expressive writing, individuals can become more attuned to how their bodies hold onto this tension. This awareness helps release not only the physical discomfort but also the mental constructs that contribute to suffering.

As we become more aware of how our bodies react to uncertainty—whether through tension, discomfort, or unease—we can begin to let go of the need for control, allowing ourselves to reconnect with our emotions and move through the discomfort with more ease. These practices help us remain present in the face of uncertainty and create new narratives that support healing and resilience.

Something to Reflect On:

As you reflect on how your body responds to uncertainty, consider how these personal reactions mirror the larger systems of control we live under. Just as unresolved tension manifests physically, outdated societal structures manifest as instability and disconnection. How might letting go of control in your personal life help you better navigate the uncertainty and change occurring in the world around you? How can cultivating awareness and flexibility in your own responses prepare you for the shifts happening on a global scale?

As individuals and societies evolve, we are witnessing the gradual crumbling of many outdated systems. This doesn't necessarily mean the collapse of society, but rather the natural breakdown of structures that no longer serve us. Rather than "the end of the world", think of it more as "the end of the world we know". These systems, which were once seen as stable and necessary, are now showing signs of weakness and instability.

In the financial sector, for example, the global economy has become increasingly volatile. Crashes, recessions, and financial crises have revealed the fragility of a system based on endless growth and consumption. The gap between the wealthy and the poor continues to widen, and many people are beginning to question the fairness and sustainability of the current economic model.

In politics, we are seeing increasing polarization, with governments around the world struggling to maintain unity and stability. The rise of populist movements, civil unrest, and challenges to traditional political structures reflect a growing dissatisfaction with the way power is distributed and exercised. People are demanding more transparency, fairness, and freedom from systems that prioritize control over compassion.

In religion, we see a similar shift. Traditional religious institutions are losing influence as more people seek personal spiritual experiences outside of organized religion. The dogmas of the past are giving way to more inclusive, flexible approaches to spirituality. In the U.S., for instance, the percentage of adults identifying as religiously unaffiliated has risen sharply—from 16% in 2007 to around 29% by 2021, according to Pew Research Center. Additionally, 27% of Americans now describe themselves as 'spiritual but not religious,' reflecting a growing desire for personal spiritual exploration outside of established frameworks. Globally, similar trends are emerging, with many in Western Europe identifying as non-religious, yet still seeking meaning through alternative spiritual practices. People are increasingly questioning the authority of religious leaders and exploring alternative paths to meaning and connection.

As these systems begin to crumble, it's easy to feel disoriented, anxious, or even afraid. Just like our personal concepts, the structures we once relied on for stability and security no longer seem as dependable as they once did.

The key to navigating these changes is to recognize the absurdity of control. Just as we've seen in our own lives, control is an illusion. The more we try to control the external world, the more we realize that life is inherently unpredictable. But rather than being disheartened by this, we can approach it with a sense of humor, curiosity, and a willingness to adapt. It's not about self-confidence—an often rigid belief in our abilities—but about self-faith, the trust in our capacity to meet whatever comes our way with presence and resilience. When we recognize the absurdity of trying to control life, we become more adaptable, flexible, and better able to see and influence new possibilities that emerge when we let go.

As the world around us shifts, we have the opportunity to cultivate greater awareness, both within ourselves and in our communities. We can practice staying present in the face of uncertainty, letting go of the need for control, and embracing the natural ebb and flow of life. This is the key to navigating a crumbling world with grace, humor, and resilience.

Practical Tools for Navigating a Changing World

Mindful Awareness: When you feel overwhelmed by the instability of the world around you, take a moment to pause and reconnect with the present moment. Practice mindful breathing, and remind yourself that uncertainty is a natural part of life. By staying grounded in the present, you can navigate external changes with greater ease.

Set Boundaries with Compassion: As societal systems break down, it's important to set personal boundaries that protect your well-being. This might mean disengaging from toxic media or limiting your involvement in fear-driven conversations. Setting boundaries with compassion helps you maintain your energy while staying present and aware of the world around you.

Focus on What You Can Influence: While we can't control the larger systems of society, we can focus on the areas of our lives where we do have influence. This might mean creating small, positive changes in your community, supporting organizations that align with your values, or nurturing relationships that bring meaning and connection into your life.

Engage with Systems with Awareness: Just because systems are crumbling doesn't mean we should completely disengage from them. We can participate in these systems with awareness, understanding that they are imperfect and in transition. Engage in political, financial, and social systems from a place of mindfulness, knowing that they are evolving and that your actions contribute to that evolution.

Laugh at the Absurdity: One of the most powerful tools we have is our sense of humor. The more we see the absurdity of trying to control life, the more we can laugh at the systems that attempt to impose control. Humor lightens the burden of uncertainty and reminds us not to take life too seriously. It allows us to engage with the world from a place of playfulness rather than fear.

Something to Reflect On:

What systems in your life feel like they are crumbling or outdated? How might surrendering your attachment to these systems, or to the concepts that hold them up, open up space for growth and change?

We've journeyed from understanding the illusion of control within ourselves to recognizing it in the systems that surround us. As we continue this exploration, a crucial question emerges: how do we live with uncertainty, especially when both our internal and external worlds feel unstable? How do we stay grounded when everything around us—our beliefs, our structures, our sense of identity—is shifting?

Living with uncertainty is not about finding a way to escape or solve the chaos. It's about learning how to remain centered within it, letting it constantly inform you. It's about embracing the unpredictability of life and realizing that the search for certainty, control, and fixed answers is getting in the way of awareness, influence, and sensitivity.

And that's where Dualistic Unity's Holy Trinity comes in—no, not a literal sacred doctrine, but a set of three playful and practical tools to help you stay grounded when life feels like it's spinning out of control. **Relax, Pay Attention, and Be Yourself** are deceptively simple yet profoundly effective ways to cut through the narratives that cause fear, confusion, and anxiety.

Relax: Letting Go of Tension and Control

The first tool in the Holy Trinity—Relax—is about releasing the tension and fear that arise from trying to control everything. When uncertainty hits, we often tense up, both mentally and physically, in an attempt to brace for the unknown. But this tightening doesn't help—it adds stress to an already chaotic situation.

Relaxing doesn't mean ignoring what's happening; it means releasing the need to control outcomes that are beyond your control. When you remind yourself to relax, you're allowing your body and mind to let go of the pressure to have all the answers. In moments of uncertainty, ask yourself: "Am I tense? Am I trying too hard to control this?" If so, take a breath, drop your shoulders, and let go of the mental weight you're carrying. Often, we hold tension without realizing it, and by relaxing, we create the space needed to see things clearly and respond with greater ease.

Pay Attention: Grounding Yourself in the Present Moment

The second tool—Pay Attention—helps you reconnect with the here and now. Uncertainty causes the mind to wander—to the past, to the future, to worst-case scenarios. But by grounding yourself in the present, you stop this mental spiraling and return to what's real.

Ask yourself: "What's happening right now? Am I stuck in my head, or am I fully here?" Whether you're in a conversation, working on a task, or simply sitting with your thoughts, paying attention pulls you back from the noise of hypothetical worries. Engaging fully with what's in front of you helps quiet the distractions of past and future concerns, allowing you to respond with clarity and presence.

Be Yourself: Dropping the Act

The third tool—Be Yourself—is about surrendering the need to perform or be something you're not. Uncertainty often makes us feel like we need to play a role, impress others, or pretend we have everything figured out. But trying to live up to external expectations only adds pressure and creates disconnection from who you truly are.

Ask yourself: "Am I being true to myself right now, or am I performing for others?" The more you let go of managing how others perceive you, the more you return to your authentic self. Being yourself isn't about projecting an identity; it's about letting go of the effort to be anything other than what you are. This creates more grounded, real connections with the people around you.

Applying the Holy Trinity in Moments of Uncertainty

In moments of overwhelm, Relax, Pay Attention, and Be Yourself can serve as powerful reminders to come back to the present and let go of the need for control.

> **Relax**: Notice the tension in your body. Drop your shoulders, unclench your jaw, and take a deep breath. Let go of the pressure to have all the answers in this moment. Relaxing resets both the body and mind, allowing clarity to emerge naturally.

> **Pay Attention**: Bring your focus back to the present. What's happening right now? Guide your attention away from hypothetical worries and back to the task, conversation, or moment in front of you. Paying attention helps you respond with more awareness and less anxiety.

> **Be Yourself**: Let go of the need to perform or live up to others' expectations. Ask yourself, "Am I being authentic, or

am I managing perceptions?" When you drop the need to control how you're seen, you free yourself to engage more genuinely with life.

Real-World Examples of Applying the Holy Trinity

At their core, the three aspects of the Holy Trinity—Relax, Pay Attention, and Be Yourself—ultimately point to the same essential truth: **just be**. In moments of uncertainty, stress, or confusion, the act of simply being—free from the pressure to control, predict, or perform—is the most powerful grounding tool we have. Let's look at how this principle shows up in real-world scenarios and how the Holy Trinity can be applied in practical, everyday situations

At Work: Letting Go of Unrealistic Expectations

Work can be a major source of anxiety, especially when we feel the pressure to meet deadlines, live up to expectations, or deliver results. In these moments, it's easy to become tense, distracted, or caught up in trying to perform a version of ourselves that we think others want to see. This is where the Holy Trinity steps in as a guide to help you come back to the simple act of being.

> **Relax**: When you're preparing for a big presentation or about to tackle a major project, take a moment to relax. Instead of letting anxiety build up, release the tension in your shoulders, unclench your jaw, and take a few deep breaths. Relaxation allows you to create space for clarity, and from this relaxed state, you can approach the task at hand with a sense of ease and focus.

> **Pay Attention**: During high-stress moments, it's easy to spiral into thoughts of self-doubt or worry about how others perceive you. Practice bringing your attention back to the present moment. What are you doing right now? Focus on completing the immediate task in front of you, whether it's

preparing the final details of the presentation or having a meaningful conversation with a colleague. By staying present, you quiet the noise of self-doubt and stay grounded in what truly matters.

Be Yourself: When you feel the need to perform or put on a façade to impress others, stop and remind yourself to be authentic. You don't need to win a popularity contest, nor do you need to live up to others' expectations. When you allow yourself to be genuine, your work will reflect your true voice and intentions, freeing you from the pressure of perfectionism and enabling you to perform with confidence.

In Relationships: Navigating Conflict and Emotional Tension

Relationships, whether romantic, familial, or friendships, can stir up emotions and uncertainties. When conflict arises or tension builds, we often react out of habit—either by trying to control the situation or withdrawing to avoid discomfort. The Holy Trinity offers a way to stay grounded, respond authentically, and navigate challenging dynamics with presence.

> **Relax**: In moments of tension or conflict, the instinct might be to defend yourself or try to control the outcome of the conversation. Instead, take a step back and relax. Release the tension in your body, breathe deeply, and remind yourself that you don't need to win the argument or force a resolution. Relaxation helps soften the emotional charge, allowing for clearer communication and a sincere connection.

> **Pay Attention**: Conflict can often make us hyper-focused on our own defenses rather than being fully present for the other person. By paying attention, you can actively and mindfully listen to the other person's words, body language, and emotions. Rather than getting lost in future-thinking or

defensive narratives, staying engaged in the moment transforms the conflict into an opportunity for connection and understanding.

Be Yourself: In moments of emotional tension, it's tempting to people-please or pretend to be someone you're not. Practice being yourself, even when it feels uncomfortable. Be honest about your feelings, boundaries, and needs. Drop the act of trying to manage how the other person perceives you, and focus on showing up authentically. True resolution comes when both parties are genuine and open.

Personal Growth: Facing Self-Doubt and Fear of Failure

We all encounter moments of self-doubt, especially when we're stepping out of our comfort zones or pursuing personal growth. Whether it's starting a new project, making a big life change, or even exploring new aspects of yourself, fear and uncertainty often arise. Applying the Holy Trinity in these moments helps you stay present, grounded, and aligned with your true self.

Relax: When fear of failure arises, we often overthink or attempt to force the successful outcome. Instead, relax into the experience and let go of the need for certainty. By relaxing, you give yourself permission to explore without the burden of getting it all right. Growth often comes through trial and refinement, and relaxing allows you to approach new challenges with curiosity and flexibility.

Pay Attention: It's easy to get lost in negative self-talk or compare yourself to others. Instead of getting trapped in past failures or future fears, bring your attention to what's happening right now. Are you making assumptions based on past experiences, or are you present with the new opportunity? By focusing on the present moment, you can break free from limiting thoughts and fully engage with the process of personal growth.

Be Yourself: Growth requires a willingness to step into who you are, not who you think you should be. In moments of self-doubt, remind yourself that being yourself is enough. Stop molding yourself to fit external expectations, and embrace the uncertainty of self-discovery. Being authentic means trusting that who you are in this moment is more than enough, even as you continue to evolve.

Public Speaking or Social Anxiety: Embracing the Spotlight

Many people experience anxiety in social situations or public speaking. The pressure to perform, impress, or meet social expectations can be overwhelming. The Holy Trinity offers a way to navigate these moments with more ease and authenticity, helping you let go of the need for external validation and focus on being present.

Relax: Before stepping on stage to give a presentation or walking into a social event, notice the physical tension that comes with social anxiety. Your heart might race, your palms sweat, or your breath becomes shallow. Relax. Take a moment to release that tension. Ground yourself by connecting with your body and your breath. Remind yourself that you don't need to control how others see you — you only need to show up.

Pay Attention: Social anxiety often pulls you out of the moment, filling your mind with thoughts like, "What do they think of me?" or "Am I saying the right thing?" Pay attention to what is happening in the here and now. Focus on the people around you, the sound of the room, or the conversation at hand. The more present you are, the less power those distracting thoughts have. You're able to engage fully and naturally.

Be Yourself: Whether in a public speaking situation or a social gathering, the desire to put on a façade can be overwhelming. You might feel like you need to impress others or hide your nervousness. But by practicing being yourself, you can drop the act. You don't need to be flawless or fit an image of what you think others want to see. Being yourself in these situations not only eases your anxiety but also allows you to connect with others in a more meaningful and authentic way.

It should be said again that **Relax, Pay Attention, and Be Yourself** all point to the same core truth: **just be**. These three tools are not separate practices but expressions of the same essential act of being. When you relax, you allow yourself to simply be without the need to control. When you pay attention, you are fully present with life as it unfolds. When you are yourself, you drop the act of trying to be something else and embrace your true nature.

In each of these real-world examples, the Holy Trinity is a reminder that you don't need to have all the answers. You don't need to perform, control, or overthink. You simply need to be—relaxed in your body, present in the moment, and authentic in your expression. This approach to life not only helps you navigate uncertainty but also brings a deeper sense of peace, clarity, and connection to the world around you.

By embracing the simplicity of **being**, you release the burdens of self-doubt, anxiety, and fear. You trust that being here, as you are, is enough.

Reflection: Navigating Life's Uncertainty with the Holy Trinity

In moments of doubt or when you're overwhelmed by life's unpredictability, it's helpful to ask yourself three simple questions:

1. **Am I tense?**
2. **Am I distracted?**
3. **Am I trying to be something I'm not?**

These questions act as "reality checks", helping you stay grounded in awareness instead of getting stuck in fear or overthinking. By using these prompts to **Relax**, **Pay Attention**, and **Be Yourself**, you can reconnect with the flow of life, freeing yourself from the constraints of over-analysis and self-doubt.

Uncertainty doesn't disappear, but by embracing these simple tools, you can face it with more confidence, presence, and grace. The more you practice this, the more you'll find that the unknown becomes less intimidating, and more of an opportunity to explore life's unfolding possibilities without needing answers or plans.

Practical Ways to Cultivate Trust and Presence

In addition to the Holy Trinity, here are other practical ways to stay grounded and cultivate trust when faced with uncertainty:

> **Breathe into Uncertainty**: When you notice yourself becoming anxious or overwhelmed by the unknown, take deep, mindful breaths. Each inhale is an opportunity to acknowledge your fear, and each exhale is a chance to release that tension. Breathing through uncertainty helps you stay connected to the present moment and reduces the urge to seek control.

Set Small, Flexible Goals: Instead of trying to plan every detail of your future, focus on setting small, adaptable goals. These goals provide direction but remain flexible enough to evolve as life changes. Flexibility allows you to move with life, rather than fighting against it. When you embrace flexible goals, you're less likely to feel overwhelmed by uncertainty because you've allowed room for change and adaptation.

Practice Non-Attachment: One of the greatest sources of suffering in uncertain times is our attachment to specific outcomes. We tend to fixate on how things "should" be and get anxious when they don't align with our expectations. Practicing non-attachment means allowing life to unfold without being tied to how things should turn out. This doesn't mean you stop caring, but rather that you remain open to possibilities outside of your initial expectations. Non-attachment frees you from the pressure of needing things to go a certain way and helps you remain adaptable.

Cultivate a Beginner's Mindset: Approach life with curiosity and openness, like a beginner who doesn't expect to know everything or have all the answers. A **beginner's mindset** invites you to see life as a continuous learning experience rather than a series of problems to be solved. It's about releasing the pressure to be an expert and embracing the uncertainty that comes with discovery. When you adopt this mindset, uncertainty becomes less of a threat and more of an opportunity for growth.

Reach Out for Connection: In times of uncertainty, it's easy to feel isolated, as if you're the only one struggling with the unknown. However, uncertainty is a universal experience. Reaching out to friends, family, or supportive communities can remind you that you're not alone in navigating life's unpredictability. But connection doesn't just have to come from the familiar. Stepping outside your routine—by volunteering, visiting new places, or meeting new people—can open the door to unexpected moments of connection.

Volunteering, in particular, can be a powerful way to not only contribute to others but also gain perspective and connect with people who are facing their own uncertainties. Whether it's a local charity, community event, or an online support group, these experiences help you engage with the world beyond your immediate circle, reminding you that uncertainty is shared by everyone. Sometimes, that moment of connection might come from a stranger, someone you wouldn't have met otherwise, and perhaps they could benefit from the connection just as much as you.

By reaching out to new people and environments, you may discover insights, inspiration, or simply comfort in the shared experience of uncertainty. Whether through a conversation with someone new, a shared laugh, or a moment of mutual understanding, these connections offer grounding when you need it most, allowing you to feel less isolated, more supported, and more supportive.

As we explored earlier, living with uncertainty requires **trust**—not a blind trust in specific outcomes, but a deeper trust in life's process. In Chapter 9, we discussed how faith allows us to engage with life fully, without needing to predict or control it. Now, we expand on this idea: Trusting life means recognizing that while we cannot foresee the future, we can trust in our ability to adapt, respond, and grow. It's a shift in perspective, from needing life to go a certain way to knowing that, whatever happens, we have the resilience to meet it.

This trust isn't grounded in external certainty but in faith—faith in our capacity to navigate challenges and the understanding that we don't need to control every detail to live fully. Trusting the process of life invites us to release our grip on outcomes, soften our fear of the unknown, and embrace the flow of existence with all its unpredictability.

Chögyam Trungpa, a renowned Buddhist teacher, once said, 'The bad news is you're falling through the air, nothing to hang on to, no parachute. The good news is there's no ground.' His words point to the heart of surrender—when we accept that there's nothing solid to grasp, we also discover the freedom of living without fear of falling.

When we trust life, we stop waiting for everything to fall into place before we allow ourselves to be at peace. Instead, we cultivate peace within, knowing that we are capable of meeting life as it unfolds, even in its most uncertain moments.

Something to Reflect On:

What would it feel like to trust life's process more deeply? How might you cultivate this trust in your daily experience, especially during times of uncertainty?

By grounding yourself in the present, practicing tools like the "Holy Trinity", and cultivating trust in the process of life, you can move through uncertainty with a sense of ease and curiosity. You don't need to have all the answers to live a meaningful life. In fact, the beauty of life often comes from the unexpected—the paths we didn't plan for, the surprises we couldn't have anticipated.

One surprising way to practice this openness to life's unpredictability is through an activity as simple as karaoke. Research has shown that singing, particularly in a communal setting, can lower stress levels, boost confidence, and create feelings of connection and joy. Karaoke invites us to let go of the need for perfection, step out of our comfort zones, and embrace vulnerability. In doing so, it mirrors the very process of trusting life's unfolding—

being present, accepting the moment as it is, and allowing ourselves to be seen in all our imperfection. It's a playful reminder that we don't need to control everything to find fulfillment; sometimes, letting go and embracing the spontaneity of the moment is where we discover the most joy. And in this process, our presence can support others on similar journeys, offering encouragement and inspiration simply by being an example of openness and authenticity.

Let go of the need for control, embrace life's unpredictability, and ground yourself in the present moment. Life, with all its uncertainties, offers an invitation to grow, to learn, and to experience its richness with an open heart and a flexible mind.

> "Let go of anger, let go of pride. When you are bound by nothing, you go beyond sorrow."
>
> — Dhammapada

Throughout this chapter, we've explored tools and insights for navigating the uncertainty that touches every aspect of life. And while uncertainty may seem intimidating, it also carries the potential for transformation, growth, and self-realization.

At its core, this is the larger message: uncertainty isn't a threat—it's an invitation to truly live. In those moments when we let go of the need for certainty and open ourselves to life's unpredictability, we discover our deepest strength and resilience. This journey is not about conquering uncertainty; it's about learning to move with it, to flow with the storm's natural rhythm rather than resisting it. The more we surrender to this flow, the more we realize that uncertainty itself is the space in which growth occurs.

Take a moment to reflect on how far you've come. The process of letting go and stepping into the unknown is no small feat. You've shown yourself that peace doesn't come from having control but from releasing the pressure to have everything figured out. This is the beginning of a lifelong journey—one where growth never truly ends but continues to evolve as you do.

Yet, as you know by now, the journey doesn't stop here. It continues, not just through the pages of this book but through the unfolding of your life. Growth is ongoing—there will always be new challenges, new uncertainties, and new opportunities for deeper self-awareness. But with every step forward, you are becoming more equipped to navigate life's unpredictability with grace, resilience, and trust.

In the next chapter, we'll dive even deeper. Everything we've built toward will come into sharper focus as we live up to the promise of this book's title.

There's still so much more to discover, so many layers to peel back. But for now, rest in the knowledge that you've already made incredible progress. The journey will continue, and while the unknown remains, so does your capacity to meet it with openness, curiosity, and trust. The adventure is ongoing. The unknown is not something to fear but something to embrace.

Trust yourself, trust the process, and know that the journey is just beginning.

> "On the other side of a storm is the strength
> that comes from having navigated through it.
> Raise your sail and begin."
>
> — Gregory S. Williams

Chapter 11 - Existence

The Echo of Separation: A Story

Once, there was a single cell, nestled in the vast and harmonious landscape of the body. For as long as it could remember, it moved in effortless synchrony with the rhythm of life, an essential part of something far greater than itself. The cell shared nutrients, communicated freely with the others around it, and fulfilled its role without question. There was no "I" or "you." Each cell reflected the intelligence of the whole in acceptance, without resistance to its existence or the experience it was part of. In this state of acceptance, the cells did not exacerbate conflict with one another, nor did they struggle against the flow of life. Their lack of temptation to resist allowed them to move harmoniously within the larger whole, naturally contributing to the body's well-being.

But one day, something shifted. For the first time, a thought crept into the cell's awareness: I am. It was subtle but profound, a ripple breaking the seamless connection it had always known. Until that moment, the cell had simply existed—one with the body, flowing without any sense of individuality. But now, that whisper of 'I am' echoed louder, transforming into something more unsettling: I am separate.

Suddenly, the cell saw itself as distinct from the other cells around it. Where it had once flowed in unison with the body, it now felt isolated. The cells that had once seemed like partners—extensions of the same whole—now appeared as others. And with this sense of separation came an unfamiliar and unsettling feeling: fear. Fear of the unknown, of no longer being held within the body's supportive embrace. The sense of connection was replaced with suspicion.

Fear of the unknown slowly crept into the cell's awareness, distorting its perception of reality. What if the body stopped providing? What if the other cells consumed more than their share?

What if its resources ran out? What began as a ripple of fear soon became a wave, pushing the cell to act out of scarcity rather than abundance. Where it had once shared freely, it now began to hoard. Scarcity, once an alien concept, became its new reality, and the cell guarded its resources as though they were its last.

As fear deepened, the cell withdrew, building walls to separate itself from the other cells. No longer feeling connected to the whole, it now saw itself as an isolated entity in an unpredictable, competitive world. Over time, this led to increasingly complex beliefs. The body, once a trusted source of life, now seemed vast, unknowable, and unreliable. The cell's sense of interconnectedness dissolved into a belief in separation, where external forces became threats. In its confusion, the cell imagined a higher power—a force beyond its understanding that controlled the body's fate. It believed that by acting in specific ways, it could gain favor with this imagined power and secure its survival.

The cell didn't keep these ideas to itself. It began spreading its newfound beliefs to the surrounding cells, preaching the importance of survival, scarcity, and self-preservation. It urged them to protect themselves, prioritize their own interests, and distrust the body's ability to provide. At first, some cells resisted, continuing to move in harmony with the body's flow. But gradually, many gave in to the voice of fear, and together they started to see themselves as separate from the body—and from each other.

The cells that embraced the illusion of separation began to cluster together. They formed isolated groups, driven by the need for self-preservation. Building defenses, hoarding resources, and creating complex rules to manage limited interactions, they gradually forgot their connection to the whole. To them, the body had become the enemy—a force not to be trusted. And so, they lived in fear and isolation, unaware that the separation itself was the source of their suffering.

The tumor, fed by the illusion of separateness, grew larger, and yet the body remained whole. Its interconnectedness, though strained under the weight of the tumor's demands, remained unbroken. The tumor cells, however, could not see this. Trapped in their belief of isolation, they were convinced that survival required independence from the body, blind to the truth that they were never separate at all.

Yet, throughout all of this, there were still cells within the body that never forgot the truth. These cells continued to move in the flow of life, contributing to the body's overall well-being. They, too, observed the tumor cells and felt the strain of their actions. But these cells did not respond with fear or judgment. They continued to interact with the tumor cells, providing nutrients, communicating, but with one key difference: they did not listen to the voice of self-concept. The connected cells moved in acceptance, reflecting the body's wisdom and harmony, while the tumor cells remained blinded by the illusion of separateness. While the tumor cells viewed everything through the lens of fear and isolation, the connected cells did not. They acted not out of fear but out of trust in the larger whole.

However, this empathetic response wasn't always perceived positively by any of the cells involved. The tumor cells, steeped in their fear and distrust, often viewed the actions of the connected cells with resentment, irritation, and suspicion. The connected cells, on the other hand, didn't act with the expectation that their actions would be understood or appreciated. Their interactions were part of the flow of the whole intelligence, regardless of how they were perceived by the individual parts. This understanding freed them from needing validation or recognition from the tumor cells. They simply moved in alignment with the body's wisdom, knowing that the system as a whole was already balanced—even if individual cells couldn't yet see it.

The connected cells treated the tumor cells as though they were still part of the body—because they were. They recognized that, despite the tumor's behavior, those cells had never truly left the whole. The tumor cells had simply forgotten their place within the system. The connected cells understood that the tumor's behavior stemmed from an illusion—an illusion that could be healed not through force, but through patience and empathy. They knew that the wisdom of the body was still present within every cell, even if those cells could no longer sense it themselves.

Though the connected cells could see the harm the tumor was causing, they did not retreat or withdraw. They continued to interact with the tumor cells, embodying the body's natural state of grace and responding without fear, even when the tumor cells lashed out or hoarded resources in return. The connected cells did not act from a place of resistance or conflict; they embodied the body's natural state of grace, responding without fear. They did this not because they were blind to the problem, but because they knew that the solution lay not in fighting the tumor, but in reminding it of the truth: that it had never been separate to begin with. The body's wisdom was ever-present, patiently waiting for the tumor cells to remember their connection.

At first, the tumor cells resisted these interactions. Their entire sense of reality was rooted in separation, self-preservation, and fear. But the connected cells didn't push or demand. They understood that healing from such deeply ingrained illusions would take time. They trusted the body's intelligence and moved with patience, offering small, consistent gestures of care and connection. The tumor cells, even as they clung to their beliefs of isolation, began to notice these acts. Over time, the constant, empathetic presence of the connected cells began to soften some of the tumor cells.

One by one, certain tumor cells began to question the beliefs that had defined their actions. They wondered, could it be that the cells they had once viewed as enemies were, in fact, allies? They began to recognize the body's signals again—faint, but persistent, always there. Slowly, these cells let down their defenses, releasing the resources they had hoarded and allowing them to flow back into the body's natural system. In reconnecting with the cells around them, they rediscovered the ease and grace they had once forgotten—

remembering what it was to be part of something larger than themselves.

The healing process was slow, but steady. For those tumor cells who began to remember their connection, it was not a moment of dramatic transformation, but a gradual return to their natural state of being. They had not needed to earn their place within the body, nor had the body ever rejected them. Their healing came not from effort, but from letting go of the illusions that had held them captive. They simply remembered, in their own time, that they had always been part of the whole.

This was not a sudden transformation, nor was it complete. Some tumor cells continued to cling to their beliefs in separateness, unable or unwilling to let go of their fear. But for those cells that rejoined the flow, the shift came not through control or intellectual understanding, but through the natural return to cooperation and connection. Their health improved as they remembered what they had once forgotten—that they had never truly been alone, and they had never needed to be separate to survive.

Even those cells that remained in fear were not cast out or punished. As they continued along their isolated path, some simply drifted away, their energy dissolving naturally back into the body. There was no penalty for losing their way, only a gentle return to the whole. Their dissolution wasn't a failure, but part of the body's constant cycle of renewal—another way of coming home. Whether through reconnection or through this quiet dissolution, everything was eventually reintegrated into the greater system, as the body continued to embrace them all. The body had never abandoned them, even when they couldn't see it for themselves.

The cells in unitary awareness had simply continued reflecting the intelligence of the whole, unknowingly providing the opportunity for the others to remember their place. Their presence was a constant reminder that survival didn't depend on control, hoarding, or isolation—it came naturally from being part of the whole.

Whether recognized or not, this truth remained; they only had to relax into the flow and experience what had always been.

The connected cells had never stopped treating the tumor cells as part of the whole, even when those cells couldn't see it themselves. Because the connected cells acted without fear or resistance, they had no need to fight or defend themselves. They simply continued to be what they had always been: part of the body, part of the whole. They didn't need to prove anything to the tumor cells, nor did they seek to change them through argument or force. Instead, they simply lived in harmony with the body, effortlessly providing an example of what it meant to move beyond the illusion of separation—without the need for recognition or validation.

The connected cells didn't seek recognition from the tumor cells because they were never seeking anything at all. Their actions were not the result of trying to heal or change the others—they simply reflected the intelligence of the whole. This was enough. Their state of being, grounded in the whole, was both the source and the solution, and it continued without effort or intent to control.

And while their empathetic actions weren't always perceived as positive by the tumor cells, the connected cells moved as part of the body's intelligence, regardless of how they were perceived by individual parts. For some tumor cells, these interactions stirred feelings of resentment or irritation. But even these negative reactions were part of the process—an opportunity for the cells to reflect on their fear and isolation. The connected cells understood that their actions didn't need to be viewed as 'helpful' to be effective. They simply moved with the larger whole, knowing that in time, the system would return to balance.

It was not through the recognition of their connection that healing began, but through relaxing beyond the thoughts, fears, and doubts that accompanied the perception of separation. As the cells stopped paying attention to the voice of fear, their attention was drawn— often through feelings of irritation or resentment—to the cells that reflected unity. These interactions served as subtle reminders of the peace and harmony the tumor cells had once known, even if they weren't consciously aware of it. Though the connected cells didn't act to make others see the truth, their actions offered a quiet invitation for the separate cells to return to the flow of the whole.

The actions of cells living in unitary awareness provided opportunities for others to reconnect, not through force or recognition, but by being fully engaged in their environment and sensing the intelligence of the whole. True healing came not from eradicating perceived 'otherness,' but from the natural remembrance of being. And as the separate cells relaxed into this realization, the system as a whole began to flourish once more.

Over time, more and more tumor cells began to experience the truth. The body had never abandoned them. It had always been there— supporting, nourishing, and patiently waiting for them to relax back into their place within it. The suffering they had experienced was not caused by the body, but by their belief in isolation. As they stopped clinging to that belief, they didn't find peace through realization or intellectual understanding, but by being drawn back into the flow of the whole. They found peace not as isolated entities, but as natural expressions of the whole system.

The body's intelligence continued to reflect the same lesson: the body suffers with every cell that feels separate, just as every cell suffers when it believes it is alone. True healing arises not from control or even from the realization of its need, but from the natural re-establishment of connection. Healing occurs through patience, empathy, and the ongoing reflection of unity. Healing unfolds through patience and empathy, as the connected cells continued their quiet reflection of unity, offering their presence, their care, and their graceful acceptance of life. They knew that the healing of one is always the healing of all.

The body's wisdom didn't require the cells in harmony to understand or take credit for their role in the healing process. They did not need to recognize the impact of their actions, because their engagement with the body's intelligence was enough. The cells didn't act out of a desire to "fix" the tumor cells or change the system. Instead, their presence was enough—a reflection of the body's natural balance, which was always available to every cell that relaxed back into it. Healing wasn't something they sought to accomplish; it was simply a consequence of their own connection to the whole.

"As the same fire assumes different shapes
when it consumes different objects, so does
the one Self take the shape of every creature
in whom it dwells."

– Upanishads

The observer and the observed are separate, I tell myself, the voice within speaking as if it knows the truth. *I exist within reality,* it insists, assuming I still believe it's me. But do I? Is it truth I'm hearing, or just another story meant to shield me from some discomfort I don't even realize I'm influenced by? Thoughts, ideas, beliefs—I've trusted them for so long, only to find they're not what I assumed. How did I never notice that each thought, each concept, is inherently divisive? And how did I forget there is no such division? Like the cell in the story, I too have been led astray by the idea of "I." And now, just like the cell, I wonder: *Am I truly within reality—or am I reality itself?* The question lingers, pulling at the edges of what I've always assumed to be true.

Just as the cell experienced fear from the emergence of 'I', humanity too suffers from this same confusion. We grapple with the experience of individuality. Like the cell from the story, we construct self-defining ideas, identities, and stories that seem to offer certainty, but in reality, only deepen our sense of separation, as we struggle to reconcile the illusion of independence with the truth of interconnectedness.

As we step into the final chapter, take a moment to acknowledge and appreciate the depth of the road we've been traveling. You've explored identity, loosened the grip of attachments, and questioned long-held beliefs about reality and individuality. By now, the lines between what you thought you were and what you might be have blurred, pulling you into a space where false certainty fades, allowing the potential for something more expansive to unfold. This chapter, more than any other, asks you to hold onto that sense of adventure and courage, for it is here that we finally address the title of this book: *Proof That You're God*. The content you're about to encounter is dense, and it's completely normal to feel overwhelmed. Let this be your cue to breathe, ground yourself, and know that it's perfectly okay to take breaks along the way. Sometimes stepping back allows for clarity to emerge. Approach this chapter at your own pace, and give yourself the space to process and integrate what you're discovering. The journey isn't about finding an answer—it's about engaging with the process of discovery itself.

Think about the concept of 'I.' It feels natural to say 'I am this' or 'I am that,' without hesitation. We've explored how we attach labels— student, parent, artist, successful, failure—often without realizing the extent to which these labels shape our sense of self. But what is this 'I' we're defining? Is it truly who we are, or is it just a construct, a way to categorize ourselves in a world that demands definitions and borders? Just as the cell in the story began to think of itself as separate, we, too, see ourselves as distinct from others. We draw lines between "I" and "you," creating boundaries that, while reassuring in their simplicity, reinforce the illusion of separation. As Alan Watts once said, trying to define the self is like trying to bite your own teeth—it's impossible. The more we chase the concept of 'I,' the more elusive it becomes, because the self we seek to grasp is not separate from the whole in the first place.

The boundaries we create—between 'I' and 'you,' between nations and races—are mirrors that reflect our confusion. They are products of human thought, obscuring the reality of our existence.

Concepts are powerful. Once taken as truth, a concept can shape the way we see and interact with the world. They create narratives that define how we relate to everything; the world, each other, and even ourselves. But these stories are often based on fear: fear of the unknown, fear of not being enough, fear of losing control. And fear of facing all that alone. And like the cell in the story, when we act out of fear, we stop trusting others. We stop sharing. We hoard what we have, convinced that survival depends on control. And we unknowingly isolate ourselves further.

Fear, then, is at the heart of our struggle with individuality. It is fear that leads us to cling to our self-defining concepts, to our stories. Fear of the unknown drives us to seek certainty, to define ourselves and the world around us in rigid terms. But the more we try to control, the more we isolate ourselves. The tighter we grip, the more we cut ourselves off from the flow of life that connects us to everything around us.

We fear the unknown because we make an assumption that it is a threat. But we make that assumption based on assumptions we've made about ourselves. And because the assumptions we make about ourselves revolve around a divisive concept like "I", we immediately create the perception of a "reality" that this "I" exists "within". So, despite the fact that you are not separate from reality, your capacity for self-awareness immediately makes it appear so.

But the truth is, we only fear the unknown because we forget that we *are* the unknown. Every situation, every challenge we face is simply another aspect of ourselves reflected back at us. There is no true division between the observer and what is observed. The line we draw between "me" and "reality" is imaginary, a product of the mind. In every moment, it is reality encountering itself. Once we understand this, the unknown no longer feels threatening—it becomes an invitation to explore a deeper part of ourselves, to experience life in all its mystery and unpredictability.

The cell in the story became cancerous because it forgot its connection to the body as soon as it became lost in individuality. It acted out of fear and a desire for control, and in doing so, it harmed not only itself but the body as a whole. But as the story shows, the body still remains whole, still interconnected. The suffering of the cell is not caused by reality, or the unknown, but by the illusion it created in its mind.

We cling to individuality as if it defines us, but it is this attachment to our perceived separateness that causes us to suffer. We build our sense of identity around stories of who we think we are—our roles, our labels, our achievements—and then defend those identities, fearing that without them, we will lose ourselves. But the "self" we cling to is only a fragment, a reflection of the whole, not the entirety of what we are.

What if we let go of this need to solely define ourselves through the lens of individuality? What if we stopped clinging to the stories we've been told about who we are and embraced that we are part of something far greater than individual thought can comprehend?

When the constructs of identity fall away, when the mind is no longer occupied by the need to define, categorize, and separate, what remains is a profound simplicity. This awareness—*your* awareness—doesn't ask for labels; it simply *is*. In the absence of stories and self-defining concepts, we experience the true essence of existence. You experience yourself not only as an individual separate from reality, but as an expression of the same reality you observe.

The lines between 'self' and 'other,' are constructs, not truths. The more we recognize this, the more we can move beyond fear, beyond control, and into a space of openness, where we can truly connect with one another. Just as cells in the story eventually remembered their place within the body, we too can remember our place within the whole. And in doing so, we heal—not just ourselves, but the entirety of life in which we are all connected.

At the core of human experience lies a profound misunderstanding: the belief that we are separate, isolated individuals moving through a world of "others." This belief, reinforced by the self-defining concepts discussed previously, blinds us to a deeper truth that has been echoed throughout history by spiritual teachers, philosophers, and mystics—the truth of our unitary "I." Beneath the surface of individuality, there is only one awareness, one consciousness, expressing itself through countless forms.

This realization has appeared in various forms across spiritual traditions, sometimes hidden beneath layers of dogma, but always pointing to the same truth: separation is an illusion. One of the most well-known references comes from the Christian tradition. In John 14:6, Jesus says, "I am the way, the truth, and the life." This has often been interpreted as a statement about Jesus himself, but what if we consider that the "I" Jesus is referring to is not the personal "I" of an individual, but the unitary "I" within all of us? This "I" is the awareness that animates all life. It is the way, the truth, and the life because it is life itself—flowing through each of us, inseparable from the whole of existence.

Another biblical passage, John 10:30, offers a similar insight: "I and the Father are one." This statement speaks to the non-dual nature of existence. The "I" that Jesus refers to is not separate from the divine, from the source of life. It is one and the same. And the same is true for all of us. The "I" that you experience within yourself is not separate from the universe, from God, or from anything else. It is simply a particular expression of the same awareness that moves through everything.

"In John 10:38, Jesus says, 'I am in the Father, and the Father is in me.' This Oneness has to do with reciprocal indwelling. Later, in John 17, we see Jesus praying that his followers achieve that very same reciprocal indwelling with him, just as he has it with the Father."

— Dan McLellan

This understanding isn't limited to Christianity. It's echoed in the teachings of Islam and Judaism as well. In the Quran, Surah 50:16 states, "We are closer to him than his jugular vein," a passage often interpreted to mean that God's presence is inherent in every being, suggesting that the divine awareness permeates all of life. In Judaism, the concept of Ein Sof in Kabbalistic mysticism describes God as an infinite, boundless presence that is within and beyond everything, indicating that the divine is inseparable from the world. These teachings, like those in Christianity, point toward the unity of all existence and the illusion of separation.

This perspective is also found in the teachings of Krishnamurti, who famously said, "You are the world, and the world is you." This statement deconstructs the boundary between the observer and the observed, between self and world. It suggests that the division we perceive between ourselves and the world around us is a false one. In reality, there is no distinction—what we see as "the world" is simply another expression of the same awareness that we experience as "I."

Alan Watts, too, articulated this insight beautifully when he said, "You are an aperture through which the universe is looking at and exploring itself." This metaphor captures the essence of the unitary "I." Each of us is a window, an aperture, through which the universe experiences itself. We are not separate from the universe, but one of its many expressions. The "I" that we experience as our individual identity is just a perspective—a lens through which the universe, the one awareness, observes and engages with itself.

To grasp the reality of our unitary 'I,' we need to challenge the experience of having a fixed, separate self within each of us. The self that we commonly identify with—our thoughts, our emotions, our roles, our personalities—are all transient. They change constantly depending on circumstances, experiences, and environments. If the "I" were truly separate, unchanging, and independent, it would remain constant no matter what happened. But as we've all experienced, the self is fluid. Who we are at any given moment is influenced by so many factors beyond our control. This alone should hint at the fact that what we call "I" is not as fixed as we think.

In reality, the "I" that we cling to is not separate at all. It is simply one of the countless ways that awareness, the fundamental essence of life, expresses itself. The person sitting next to you, the tree outside your window, the bird flying through the sky—all of these are expressions of the same awareness. They are not separate entities in any meaningful sense. They are all part of the same whole, each one a different aperture through which the universe is experiencing itself.

Remember the metaphor of the ocean and the wave: the wave rises, moves, and eventually falls back into the ocean. From the wave's perspective, it may feel distinct, unique in its movement and form. But it never truly stops being part of the ocean. In the same way, each of us is a wave—a temporary expression of a far greater whole. We may perceive ourselves as separate, as individual entities moving through the world, but beneath the surface, we are always connected to the vast ocean of awareness. When we recognize this, the fear of isolation begins to dissolve, replaced by a sense of belonging.

Consider the implications for how we relate to others. If the 'I' within you is the same as the 'I' within everyone else, then the division between self and other is an illusion. When we harm another, we are in fact harming ourselves. When we act with compassion toward others, we are extending that compassion to ourselves. This is not just true in a metaphysical sense, but also in our lived experience—self-compassion is what makes genuine compassion for others possible.

This is why spiritual traditions emphasize the importance of love, kindness, and empathy. It's not just about being "good" to "others". It's about recognizing that there is no real separation between you and the rest of the world. To love another is to love yourself because at the deepest level, you are not two—you are one.

There's a philosophical idea called *solipsism*, which suggests that only your own mind is certain to exist. According to solipsism, everything outside of your own consciousness—other people, the external world, even time and space—might only exist as experiences within your mind. It's the belief that you can only be truly sure of your own thoughts and perceptions, while everything else might just be a creation or illusion of your imagination.

The real danger of solipsism comes from the assumption that this mind—this consciousness—is "yours" alone. By identifying your mind as something separate and personal, solipsism can lead to the belief that your experiences are the only ones that truly matter. This can make it easy to overlook or dismiss the experiences and emotions of others because, after all, if it's only *your* mind that exists, then why should you care about others, who may just be figments of your imagination? This mindset erodes empathy, as it encourages an engulfing sense of isolation and detachment from the rest of reality, leading to a narcissistic or ego-driven perspective.

Without empathy, solipsism becomes a trap, reinforcing a delusional sense of separation. You may come to see yourself as fundamentally different or superior, since you're the only "real" one. This can breed indifference or even cruelty, as others' feelings, pain, or joy become irrelevant, merely projections of your own mind.

But what if solipsism were true for everyone? I jokingly refer to this paradox as the reality of *mutual solipsism*. Yes, you are all that is, but so am I. This playful twist flips the entire concept on its head, because if everyone believes they are the only real consciousness, it becomes impossible to maintain that just one person's mind is the center of existence. Instead of isolating us, this paradox reveals a deeper connection—an acknowledgment that while each of us experiences life through our own subjective lens, we're all expressions of the same underlying awareness.

In this light, *mutual solipsism* dissolves the dangers of traditional solipsism. Rather than emphasizing isolation or separateness, it points out the absurdity of thinking that one mind could be more real than another. If everyone's mind feels like the only mind, then clearly the idea of a singular, personal consciousness is just an illusion. This realization invites a sense of shared existence—yes, you are the center of your experience, but so is everyone else, and in that shared awareness, we find unity.

Just like the cell in the body, each of us believes we are separate from the whole, unaware that we are all part of the same unified intelligence. Imagine we are characters in a shared dream, each playing a distinct role, much like the cells in a body. From our limited perspectives, we see ourselves as individuals, interacting with "others" who seem separate. But here's the paradox: just as every cell is part of the same body, each character in the dream is part of the same mind—the dreamer. We are both the dreamer and the dreamed, unknowingly playing all the roles, while the dream continues. The separation only exists because of the limited view each character has.

So while solipsism taken literally can lead to isolation and delusion, *mutual solipsism* humorously shows us that we are all "the one," bound together as the same universal mind. This paradox reveals that, rather than being alone in our experience, we are interconnected, each of us a unique expression of the same consciousness playing out across countless perspectives, our experiences seamlessly woven together to facilitate what we experience as the material universe.

This not only deepens our exploration of self-discovery but also addresses long-standing philosophical questions about the nature of reality. Throughout history, philosophers have offered varying views on how we perceive and interact with reality, yet their ideas often leave unresolved tensions. Mutual solipsism bridges these gaps and offers a more holistic understanding of reality, revealing how interconnected awareness resolves these philosophical issues.

Descartes famously divided mind and matter, suggesting that the mind was distinct from the external world. His skepticism left us wondering how the mind could trust its perceptions. Mutual solipsism dissolves this division by showing that mind and matter are interconnected expressions of the same consciousness. Reality isn't external but co-created by all perceiving minds, erasing the need for the rigid separation Descartes proposed.

Locke, the empiricist, believed that our knowledge of the world comes through sensory experience of an external reality. However, Locke's view still implied a gap between perception and the objective world. Mutual solipsism reveals that what we experience through our senses is not a separate, objective reality, but a reality co-created by collective awareness. The external world is a shared perception rather than something entirely independent of us.

Berkeley went further, proposing that reality exists only as it is perceived, sustained by the constant observation of God. While Berkeley came close to understanding the fluidity of reality, mutual solipsism goes beyond his idea by asserting that we are all God. There is no external divine observer; rather, the continuous perception that maintains reality is a collective one, generated by all beings through their interconnected awareness.

Kant argued that we could never know the world as it truly is (the *noumenal* world), but only as we perceive it (the *phenomenal* world). His sharp distinction between these two realms created a gap between reality and our experience of it. Mutual solipsism bridges this gap by showing that the noumenal world is not separate from perception. The "real" world is simply the shared creation of all perceiving beings, and what we experience through perception is co-created through collective awareness, dissolving the distinction between noumenal and phenomenal.

Hegel introduced the dialectic, a process in which history and thought evolve toward self-awareness. However, his idea of the *Absolute Spirit* often seemed like an external force beyond individuals. Mutual solipsism reframes this by asserting that the Absolute Spirit is not separate but is the evolving awareness of all individuals. History reflects the increasing self-awareness of interconnected consciousness, allowing each individual to recognize their role in shaping the collective.

Schopenhauer, with his dualism between will and representation, saw life as driven by an irrational force that led to suffering. Mutual solipsism resolves this dualism by showing that both will and representation are expressions of the same underlying consciousness. Recognizing our role in creating reality helps us transcend the suffering Schopenhauer described, as the "will" becomes part of our collective creation rather than an uncontrollable force acting upon us.

Nietzsche's concept of the will to power can foster an isolated, conflict-driven worldview, where individuals strive to dominate others. Mutual solipsism reframes this by suggesting that power is expressed through the interconnectedness of all beings. Instead of seeking dominance, individuals realize their shared, collective empowerment within the whole, replacing the conflict of Nietzsche's philosophy with a sense of co-creation and collective self-awareness.

Sartre emphasized radical freedom and the burden of creating meaning in an indifferent universe, often leading to existential dread. Mutual solipsism alleviates this by showing that we are not isolated in our freedom but co-creators within a larger collective consciousness. This interconnectedness reduces the sense of isolation in Sartre's philosophy, bringing unity and purpose to the individual's creation of meaning.

Husserl focused on the intentionality of consciousness, stating that reality is shaped by subjective experience. Mutual solipsism expands Husserl's ideas by showing that consciousness is not just individual, but interconnected. Reality is co-created by the shared intentionality of all beings, allowing Husserl's phenomenology to account for a collective, co-creative process.

Each of these philosophical traditions hints at a simple truth: that reality is ultimately awareness itself—but the inability of philosophers like Descartes, Locke, Kant, Hegel, and Berkeley to recognize the paradox of mutual solipsism was shaped by the personal, religious, and cultural contexts in which they lived. During their time, religious dogma—particularly the dominance of Christianity in Europe—heavily influenced intellectual discourse. Concepts such as the separation between God and humanity, the primacy of individual souls, and the belief in an external, objective reality were deeply embedded in the culture. Philosophical ideas had to align with religious frameworks that reinforced dualistic thinking, making it difficult to conceive of a non-separate, interconnected awareness. Additionally, the intellectual emphasis on individualism, particularly in post-Renaissance and Enlightenment Europe, further solidified the idea of distinct, isolated minds and separate identities. Philosophers like Descartes and Locke, who championed rationality and empirical thought, operated within a society that prized the individual's capacity to observe and reason, limiting their ability or willingness to explore more holistic, non-dual perspectives, which were often relegated to mysticism or marginalized viewpoints. While their philosophies advanced human understanding of perception and consciousness, they were bound by the intellectual currents of their time, focusing on the division between mind and matter, subject and object. However, these ideas were necessary steps in the evolution of thought, ultimately leading to the insights offered by science, which reveals the obviousness of unity these earlier frameworks could not fully embrace.

One of the central questions that all of the above philosophers struggled with is how multiple individuals can perceive the same object or event differently while the object itself appears physically unchanged. Mutual solipsism resolves this tension by recognizing that reality exists as a shared foundation, but individual perception filters the experience based on personal perspectives, histories, and mental states. While the object or event exists as part of the collective creation, the way each individual interacts with it reflects their unique consciousness. In other words, the essence of the object remains the same—but each person's experience of it is colored by their subjective viewpoint.

For example, two people can see the same painting, yet one may feel joy while the other feels sadness. The painting itself does not change, but the meaning, impact, and emotional response are shaped by the internal state of each perceiver. The shared reality remains stable because it is sustained by the interconnected awareness of all beings, yet the subjective experience of that reality can vary greatly from person to person.

Scientific discoveries like the famous double slit experiment provides more compelling evidence for the connection between the observer and the observed. The double slit experiment, one of the most well-known demonstrations in quantum mechanics, reveals just how intertwined observation is with the fabric of reality itself. When particles, such as photons or electrons, are fired through two slits toward a screen, they behave as either particles or waves, depending on whether they are being observed. If no one is watching, they behave like waves, creating an interference pattern as if they passed through both slits simultaneously. But when observed, they behave like particles, passing through only one slit and producing no interference pattern.

The observer and the observed are two sides of the same coin, inseparable and deeply connected. Yet, one simple misperception — or assumption, if you will — makes this reality almost impossible to recognize: the belief that our consciousness, or mind, is located 'in our head' or confined to the brain. This perception creates a sense of division between ourselves and our experiences. In reality, science has yet to determine the true nature or origin of consciousness.

John K. Grandy's work on neurogenetics offers a compelling view of consciousness that goes beyond the brain, suggesting that awareness is not confined to a single organ or even to neural structures. According to Grandy, consciousness emerges in phases, from its genesis to its eventual decline, driven by genetic activity. His model challenges the conventional view of the brain as the sole seat of awareness, expanding it to the cellular level, where genes play a fundamental role in maintaining and shaping consciousness throughout life.

Grandy takes this idea even further by suggesting that DNA itself may exhibit properties of consciousness. If we entertain the possibility that DNA is not just a passive repository of genetic information but a dynamic, evolving system capable of self-regulation and adaptation, it opens the door to a broader understanding of consciousness. The notion that DNA might possess a form of proto-consciousness suggests that consciousness is not produced by the brain, but rather expressed through it and the entire body, manifesting in every cell that contains DNA.

This perspective revolutionizes our understanding of thought and awareness. It suggests that consciousness is an embodied process, not localized strictly within the brain. Every thought, every emotion, every sensation we experience might emerge from the interplay of genetic and cellular networks throughout the body. The entire organism, rather than just the brain, participates in the experience of being aware. This holistic view aligns with modern theories of embodied cognition, which assert that our bodily states influence our thought processes. If DNA itself carries elements of awareness, then consciousness becomes an attribute of the entire body—a system of interconnected processes working together to produce what we call thought, emotion, and perception.

In this light, the distinction between the mind and body begins to dissolve. If consciousness isn't confined to the brain but is expressed throughout the entire body—at the cellular and genetic level—then the boundaries we place around individuality become increasingly blurry. We tend to think of our thoughts, feelings, and awareness as personal, as belonging solely to the individual. But if our entire body is participating in consciousness, and if DNA itself exhibits signs of awareness, then the notion of individuality becomes less about a fixed, separate "self" and more about a complex, interconnected process that extends beyond the limits of the body.

This brings us to a fundamental question: If consciousness is expressed by the entire body, and all bodies are made of the same fundamental building blocks—DNA, cells, and molecules—are all of our bodies expressing the same consciousness? Is the awareness you experience truly "yours," or is it the same universal awareness expressing itself through different forms?

Just as gravity is not a force possessed by any one object but a characteristic that emerges based on its form and relationship to the rest of the cosmos, so too is consciousness not something that belongs to any one individual. It is inherent within the very fabric of what we call the "physical universe."

The belief that each individual's awareness is separate and confined to their personal experience feels true intuitively, yet this assumption starts to break down when we consider that consciousness might be a more expansive, interconnected phenomenon.

Recent studies in quantum biology also challenge the conventional, brain-centric view of consciousness. Theories such as the Orch-OR theory, proposed by Roger Penrose and Stuart Hameroff, suggest that quantum coherence could be central to how consciousness arises—not just in the brain, but possibly at the molecular level. DNA itself, with its helical structure and sensitivity to electromagnetic fields, might act as a receptor of quantum information, connecting us to a larger quantum network.

This means that our consciousness could be influenced by quantum signals both within and beyond our bodies, extending our awareness into a broader, more universal field. If DNA can receive and transmit quantum information, then every cell in our body could be involved in conscious processes. Again, consciousness is not localized in the brain, but distributed throughout the entire body, creating a more holistic experience of awareness. The brain may serve as the primary processor for complex thoughts, but the whole body—with its network of DNA and quantum interactions—participates in shaping what we experience as consciousness.

This idea is further supported by biofield research, which investigates the subtle energy fields generated by living organisms. These biofields may extend beyond the body, acting as conduits for information between the body and its environment, and potentially playing a role in consciousness. In many spiritual traditions, these fields have been referred to as Qi or Prana—life energies that flow through and around us. Modern science is beginning to explore how these fields interact with our cellular processes, and if DNA is sensitive to bioelectromagnetic information, it may be part of a larger, shared field of consciousness.

Both quantum biology and biofield research suggest that consciousness may not be confined to individual brains or bodies but could be part of a more expansive, interconnected field. In this view, the separation between "me" and "the world" is another illusion. Consciousness emerges from the interplay of quantum phenomena, DNA activity, and biofields, extending beyond the physical boundaries we typically associate with individual awareness. The brain may be one node in this network, but consciousness itself could be distributed throughout the body and even beyond, connecting us to a broader, unified experience of reality.

In this sense, what we think of as "individuality" is merely a temporary expression of this underlying awareness. The "I" we experience as personal identity is just one way the universe expresses itself through us. The awareness that animates you is the same awareness animating everyone and everything else; the distinctions we make between "self" and "other" are constructs of the mind, useful for navigating the world, but ultimately illusory.

The belief that each being's consciousness is separate, distinct, and contained within their own mind is a powerful assumption, but it is just that—an assumption. If the brain is not the sole seat of consciousness, and if the body itself contributes to this field of awareness, then what we consider to be "me" may be just one expression of a larger, shared consciousness. Just as gravity acts uniformly across all objects regardless of their form, consciousness might be the same force expressed uniquely through each of us, yet fundamentally unified.

The Global Consciousness Project (GCP) provides another scientific insight into this interconnectedness. The GCP has run experiments for decades using random number generators worldwide to measure shifts in global consciousness. The findings show that during significant global events—whether moments of great joy, collective meditation, or tragedy—there is measurable coherence in what should be random data. For instance, during the events of 9/11, GCP data showed significant deviations from randomness in the hours leading up to and during the attacks. This suggests that human consciousness is not isolated but part of a larger shared field, responsive to collective mental and emotional states. Such anomalies indicate that global consciousness may be interconnected in ways that science is only beginning to understand.

Epiphenomenalism adds a further dimension to this understanding.

While the GCP reflects the collective nature of awareness, epiphenomenalism suggests that our individual thoughts, ideas, and sense of identity are byproducts of the larger consciousness in motion. Rather than being in control of our awareness, we are expressions of the whole, with our thoughts arising after the fact— like echoes of the body's interconnected systems.

For instance, consider the common experience of pushing a button. It feels as though we consciously decide to act at the moment we press the button, but studies show that **brain activity associated with the action occurs milliseconds before we are consciously aware of the decision**. In other words, the body has already initiated the action, and our conscious mind merely catches up, giving us the illusion of control.

This view emphasizes that our fixation on individuality is an illusion, a side effect of the whole acting through us. Just like pressing the button, our sense of decision-making is a post-event experience rather than the cause of the event itself.

In essence, while the GCP shows us how we reflect a larger consciousness, epiphenomenalism explains how our individual sense of control is an illusion created by our individual perspective. We are not separate actors but integrated parts of the whole, moving with it even when we feel we are making independent decisions.

Dualistic Unity is proud to be an active participant in the Global Consciousness Project. Through our contributions, we help explore the hypothesis that our individual consciousness plays a part in shaping this larger collective awareness. The GCP's ongoing research aligns directly with our philosophy: while we experience life through our own unique perspectives, we are all interconnected in ways that transcend physical boundaries. The GCP's findings demonstrate how intricately our consciousness is woven into the fabric of the whole, reinforcing that the boundaries we perceive are just another illusion.

Consider a group meditation experiment conducted in Washington,

D.C., in the summer of 1993. This experiment, organized by researchers from the Maharishi University of Management, was designed to test whether a large group practicing Transcendental Meditation (TM) could lower the city's violent crime rate.

The experiment spanned two months, from June to July 1993, and brought together about 4,000 participants from around the world to practice collective meditation. The researchers hypothesized that through the Maharishi Effect—the idea that a small percentage of the population practicing meditation could positively influence the broader collective consciousness—there would be a measurable reduction in crime rates. This effect, they believed, would manifest as increased societal harmony and cooperation.

According to the final report published by the researchers, the results were impressive. During the peak of the experiment, violent crime rates—including homicides, assaults, and rapes—reportedly dropped by 23.3%. This was in stark contrast to predictions made by a panel of independent criminologists, who had forecasted a rise in crime due to the summer heat and historical crime data trends. Such findings suggest that the meditative effort had some influence on the collective behavior of the city.

However, as with any groundbreaking claim, the results were met with both intrigue and skepticism. Critics argue that the crime reduction could be attributed to other variables, such as changes in policing tactics, weather conditions, or simple statistical anomalies. The temporary nature of the crime reduction, with rates returning to previous levels after the experiment, added fuel to these critiques. Additionally, the study's methodology has been called into question, with some arguing that it failed to adequately control for outside factors.

This experiment is often seen as a practical demonstration of the Maharishi Effect, named after Maharishi Mahesh Yogi, the founder of Transcendental Meditation. According to this theory, when a critical mass of people mediate, it creates a ripple effect through the collective consciousness of society, improving societal conditions and fostering cooperation and peace. Supporters of the Maharishi Effect believe it provides evidence of the interconnectedness of human consciousness, with tangible impacts on society as a whole.

Yet, despite the enthusiasm around such findings, the scientific community remains divided. Critics assert that while the results are interesting, they might not necessarily prove that meditation had a direct effect on the city's crime rates. The broader question of how collective consciousness influences reality is still very much open to debate.

What experiments like this reveal, however, is the tantalizing possibility that consciousness, when recognized as universal, could have far-reaching effects on the world around us. While definitive conclusions may be elusive, these studies continue to provoke meaningful questions about the relationship between the individual mind and the collective human experience. If consciousness is truly shared across all beings, what is the true nature of individuality? Could our personal healing and growth impact others in ways we do not fully understand, just as the experiences of others might ripple out to affect us? If the 'I' within each of us is the same underlying awareness, does this explain why acts of empathy resonate so deeply?

"You are not a drop in the ocean. You are the entire ocean in a drop."

— Rumi

The evidence of our shared awareness extends beyond individuals, cultures, and even species. With so much genetic variation, you might expect that each person or animal would experience unique emotions, or that some would even feel things we could never comprehend. But in reality, we all experience the same spectrum of emotions—joy, sorrow, fear, love. Across the animal kingdom, this shared experience is obvious. Primates like chimpanzees and bonobos show empathy by comforting each other in times of distress, sharing in each other's grief, or expressing joy during playful interactions.

Elephants have been observed grieving for lost herd members, staying by their side and showing visible signs of sadness and loss. Dolphins form close social bonds and are known to help each other when in distress. Even rats, in experiments, have shown empathy by freeing their trapped companions, even when it means sacrificing their own access to food.

While there's currently no observable way for us to distinguish plant emotions, a sizable amount of research shows that they exhibit signs of communication and environmental awareness, reinforcing the idea of a collective intelligence that permeates all life. As we discussed earlier, trees communicate with one another through the Wood Wide Web, an underground fungal network that allows them to share nutrients, send distress signals, and support weaker trees by transferring resources. This collaboration demonstrates that even seemingly isolated trees are part of a larger, interconnected system that operates for the benefit of the whole.

Beyond this underground network, recent research has revealed that plants are keenly aware of their environments in ways we might not expect. For example, trees can perceive color. Research on chloroplasts has shown that plants detect different wavelengths of light and adjust their growth and behavior accordingly, enabling them to adapt to changes in light conditions and seasonal shifts. This capacity to "see" color reveals a form of environmental awareness that is essential for their survival.

Furthermore, plants have been shown to exhibit behaviors suggesting they can "learn" from their surroundings. In a well-known experiment with *Mimosa pudica*—the "sensitive plant"—scientists found that after repeated harmless stimulation, the plants stopped closing their leaves in response to touch, indicating they had learned not to react to non-threatening stimuli. This kind of adaptive response is typically associated with learning in animals, showing that plants, too, can modify their behavior based on experience.

These discoveries about plant awareness and communication suggest that intelligence and responsiveness to the environment are not exclusive to animals, but are part of a broader, more fundamental level of awareness shared across all life. Plants, like animals, participate in this collective awareness, sensing, communicating, and responding to their environments in ways that reflect an underlying interconnectedness.

Your awareness is not separate from those of others; they are different expressions of the same underlying reality. What we perceive as individuality is simply a variation in the way consciousness is experienced, shaped by form, but not divided by it. In truth, the same awareness is present in everyone, just as it is present in every cell of the body.

The "I" that you experience as your existence is the same "I" within everyone and everything else.

It's important to clarify that this does not imply a central, all-powerful consciousness that weaves our lives together with some limitless, omniscient intelligence. This would be akin to the traditional concept of God, where a supreme being oversees and directs reality. Instead, the reality we're pointing to is that the universe, or any universe, is not the product of intelligent design at all but is *intelligence manifest*. There is no external architect shaping our experiences; rather, the intelligence of the universe arises from within the unfolding process itself, expressed through the interconnected awareness of all beings. This intelligence is not separate from the forms it takes—it is the very fabric of existence, constantly in motion, fluid, and dynamic. It's not some overarching, omnipotent mind guiding the flow, but the collective awareness of all life expressing itself, moment by moment, without a predetermined plan or goal. In this way, we are all participants in the unfolding of reality, not as fragments of a divine design, but as expressions of the intelligence inherent in life itself.

Reality is not something 'out there,' independent of us. Instead, it is shaped and sustained by the collective awareness of all living beings across time, allowing for individual variations in how each of us experiences this shared reality. The distinctions between mind and matter, between subjective and objective reality, and between individual and divine perception dissolve in the recognition that we are all participants in the co-creation of reality.

As we question the narrative of being separate individuals, we uncover the shared "I" that runs through all life. The self we thought we knew—the one built from personal achievements, failures, and identities—becomes more fluid, less limited. In the space of our interconnected awareness, self-discovery becomes an exploration of the entirety of life, where each insight into ourselves is an insight into the collective. We find that in knowing ourselves, we come to know the world.

"As above, so below."

— Hermes Trismegistus, *The Emerald Tablet*

This shift in perspective also changes how we see ourselves. When we let go of the belief that we are separate, we stop clinging to our personal narratives so tightly. We no longer define ourselves by our successes or failures, our strengths or weaknesses. These things are still part of our experience, but they no longer define our identity. We come to understand that we are not just the limited "I" that we thought we were. We are the universe itself, expressing itself in this moment, in this form.

And in this recognition, we see that life is a paradox to be embraced with light-hearted curiosity. The search for meaning, for certainty, for truth often blinds us to the most liberating realization—that we are both the question and the answer, the dancer and the dance. The universe plays through us, not with a goal in mind, but with the joy of endless exploration. When we let go of the need for resolution, we find that life was never about solving a puzzle. It was about experiencing the richness of existence in all its forms.

With that realization comes a profound sense of freedom. When you recognize that the "I" within you is the same as the "I" within everyone and everything else, you stop worrying so much about how you measure up. You stop feeling the need to prove yourself, to defend your identity, to control how others see you. You realize that you are already whole, already complete, just as you are. You are not separate from the universe—you are the universe, experiencing itself in this particular moment, through this particular form.

And when we live from this awareness, everything changes. We begin to act not from fear or control, but from a place of openness, compassion, and trust. We recognize that we are not alone—we are never alone—because the "I" that we experience is not our own.

We all live in the center of our own universe, experiencing life from the unique vantage point of our personal awareness. Everything we perceive, every thought and feeling we experience, occurs within our own subjective bubble. No one else can see the world exactly as we do.

But this sense of being "alone" is just one side of the coin. Yes, we each experience life subjectively, but the awareness behind each individual's experience is the same. The "I" that experiences your life is not foundationally different from the "I" that experiences mine. We are like countless windows through which the same awareness gazes, each view different but sourced from the same light.

Astronauts who experience the 'overview effect' from space provide a striking example of this interconnected awareness. Edgar Mitchell, who viewed Earth from space during the Apollo 14 mission, spoke of feeling a profound sense of unity with all life on the planet. From the vast distance of space, borders and divisions seemed insignificant, and Mitchell realized that all human life is deeply interconnected, bound by the same awareness that flows through each of us.

This paradox of being 'alone together' speaks to the strange beauty of life: though isolated in our own subjective experiences, we are inextricably linked by the shared consciousness that animates everything. It's as if consciousness is playing a game of hide-and-seek with itself, inhabiting different forms, each one experiencing the world through its own unique lens, but all part of the same whole.

When we realize that the awareness within us is the same awareness that animates others, we begin to see their experiences as our own. Their joy is our joy. Their suffering is our suffering. We are no longer isolated individuals competing for survival in a hostile world. We are interconnected expressions of the same life force, and our well-being is tied to the well-being of others.

This doesn't mean that we lose our individuality. On the contrary, it allows us to embrace our individuality more fully, knowing that it is part of a greater whole. Each of us is a unique expression of the same awareness, like different notes in a symphony. The note you play is not the same as the note I play, but together, we create something beautiful. Our individuality is what makes life rich and varied, but it is our shared awareness that makes life meaningful.

Indigenous cultures around the world have long embodied these principles, living in harmony with the earth and each other in ways that reflect the truth of our collective existence.

The Kogi people of Colombia, for example, see themselves as the "Elder Brothers" tasked with caring for the Earth. They live in isolated mountains, safeguarding their ecosystem with reverence for nature, which they refer to as "Aluna," or the spiritual force behind all life. The Kogi view every tree, river, and mountain as part of a larger whole, understanding that harm to one part is harm to the entire system. For them, the Earth's well-being is inextricably linked to their own, and they work not to dominate their environment but to maintain its balance. In this sense, they mirror the connected cells in our story, acting in unity with the body of life.

Similarly, the Haudenosaunee Confederacy (also known as the Iroquois) has long practiced what is called the "Seventh Generation Principle," where every decision made is considered for its impact on the next seven generations. This forward-thinking approach, deeply embedded in their governance and lifestyle, ensures that their actions contribute to the overall health of their people and their environment. Like the connected cells, the Haudenosaunee understand that their well-being is bound up with the land and future generations, not separate from it.

In Australia, the indigenous peoples have a worldview known as "Dreamtime," which teaches that all life forms are connected through time, land, and spirit. The Australian Aboriginal culture doesn't see a distinction between humans, animals, and the land— they all share the same spiritual essence. Their stories reflect a profound understanding of the interconnectedness of all things, and their rituals emphasize maintaining harmony with the land, ensuring that resources are used sustainably. They see themselves as custodians, not owners, of the land, recognizing their place within the larger whole, much like the cells in our metaphor that live in alignment with the body.

These indigenous cultures demonstrate a profound understanding of what it means to live as part of a whole. They reflect the truth that when we live in harmony with our environment, we contribute to the health of the entire system—be it the Earth, the ecosystem, or the body of life itself. Their wisdom echoes the message that, just like the connected cells, we thrive not through domination, control, or hoarding but through cooperation, empathy, and an awareness of our place within the larger whole.

The paradox of mutual solipsism also offers a different, timeless perspective on freedom. Often, we think of freedom in terms of independence—being free from the influence or control of others. But mutual solipsism reveals freedom: the freedom that comes from recognizing our interconnectedness. When we see that the 'I' we perceive in ourselves mirrors the 'I' in others, the need to defend identity dissolves, to compete for resources, or to prove our worth. We no longer need to cling to the idea of being separate, because we know that, at our core, we are all the same. This frees us to live with greater openness, trust, and generosity.

Consider how this understanding could transform relationships. When we relate to others from the perspective of separation, relationships often become about control, fear, and protection. We worry about being hurt, misunderstood, or rejected. We may act out of jealousy or possessiveness, fearing that someone else's gain is our loss. But when we recognize ourselves in others, these fears begin to dissolve. We no longer see others as threats, but as fellow travelers on the same journey. We can trust them because we recognize that, at the deepest level, they are us. Their happiness is not separate from our own.

By embracing our shared awareness, we allow ourselves to be vulnerable in the face of connection, recognizing that empathy bridges the gap between our perceived aloneness.

Erin Gruwell, a teacher in Long Beach, California, transformed her classroom of at-risk students by using empathy and storytelling. Through the 'Freedom Writers' project, she encouraged students from diverse backgrounds to share their personal stories, dissolving the barriers created by gangs and racial tension. Gruwell's approach showed how empathy can bridge even the deepest divides, helping individuals recognize that their struggles are not so different from one another.

In this empathy lies the antidote to our suffering—the realization that others' joys and pains are reflections of our own. To offer compassion to another is to heal the shared awareness that connects us. In these moments of genuine connection, the illusion of separateness begins to dissolve, allowing us to engage with each other in ways that transcend fear.

This doesn't mean that relationships will always be easy or that conflict will disappear. But it does mean that we approach relationships from a place of connection rather than separation. We are more willing to be vulnerable, to listen, and to empathize, because we understand that the same awareness that experiences life through us is also experiencing life through the other person. We are alone together, but together nonetheless.

Much of human suffering comes from the belief that we are alone, that we are separate from others and from the world around us. When we feel isolated, our struggles seem insurmountable, and our pain feels endless. But when we realize that we are connected by the same awareness, suffering takes on a different meaning. It is no longer just our personal burden to bear, but something that we share with others. We begin to see that our healing is tied to the healing of those around us, and that we are never truly alone in our pain.

This interconnectedness also brings a sense of responsibility. If the awareness within me is the same as the awareness within you, then my actions affect you just as much as they affect me. The choices I make ripple out into the world, shaping the collective experience of life. However, it's important to remember that this sense of responsibility begins within us—it's a personal insight, not a burden to be placed on others. Just as your own expanding sense of responsibility has led you to these realizations, so too must others come to their own understanding in their own time. We cannot— and should not—rush to take responsibility for others. To do so would deny them the opportunity to discover their own role in this shared existence.

By acting with care and compassion, we create an environment where others are empowered to come to their own realizations, rather than being pressured or controlled. In this way, awareness of life's paradox also enhances our sense of responsibility for the world we create—without infringing on the journey of others. We can offer support, where appropriate, but we must allow each individual the freedom to find their own path.

To live from this awareness is to live with an open heart. It is to recognize that the boundaries we perceive between ourselves and others are illusions, that we are all part of the same ocean of consciousness. And when we live from this place, we begin to move through the world with greater ease, compassion, and trust. We no longer see others as separate, but as fellow expressions of the same life force. We no longer need to protect ourselves from the world, because we realize that we are the world. And in that realization, we find not isolation, but connection. Not fear, but love.

Fear is tied to seeing the unknown as something separate from ourselves. But love isn't about embracing the unknown, because that would mean creating an idea of the unknown (from the known) to love—it's about recognizing that, absent the concept of 'other,' we are the unknown. And loving ourselves has nothing to do with loving who we think we are. There is no greater act of love, for ourselves or others, than acceptance without judgment or precondition.

However, acceptance doesn't mean condoning destructive behavior. It's not about turning a blind eye to harm or neglecting accountability. Rather, true acceptance allows us to see things clearly, without the distortions of fear or ego. From this place of clarity, we can respond to harmful behavior—whether in ourselves or others—not with reactive judgment, but with awareness, compassion, and maturity. Acceptance brings us the wisdom to address challenges without getting lost in blame or self-righteousness, allowing us to deal with them constructively and with greater understanding.

One powerful example can be seen in Norway's progressive prison system. Rather than focusing on punishment, Norway's penal approach emphasizes rehabilitation, reintegration, and treating inmates as individuals who have made mistakes but are capable of change. In this system, acceptance doesn't mean ignoring or excusing harmful behavior—it means addressing that behavior with clarity and a focus on healing.

Take Bastøy Prison, for instance. It's an open prison where inmates live in a community with minimal security, participate in daily responsibilities like farming and forestry, and are given the tools to grow and change. Instead of locking them away in isolation, Norway's system prepares prisoners for life outside by equipping them with skills and addressing the underlying causes of their actions. This approach stems from an understanding that simply punishing someone doesn't foster change—giving them the opportunity to take responsibility for themselves in a constructive way does.

The results speak for themselves. With one of the lowest recidivism rates in the world, Norway's focus on rehabilitation has proven far more effective than punitive systems. While in other countries recidivism rates can exceed 60%, in Norway, only about 20% of inmates reoffend within two years of release. This is a clear example of how acceptance, in the form of humane treatment and a focus on personal growth, leads to a better outcome than judgment and punishment alone.

This doesn't mean excusing harmful actions—it means confronting them with awareness, compassion, and a commitment to healing. Acceptance allows for real change, while judgment often reinforces the cycle of harm.

Imagine for a moment a world where the veil of separation no longer holds sway—a world where the awareness that we are all connected is not just a fleeting insight but a foundational part of our shared discussion. What would that world look like? How would our systems—mental health, relationships, governance, economics, sustainability, and education—transform in the light of this understanding of our interconnectedness? The truth is, once we realize that we are not separate, that the "I" within us is the same as the "I" within everyone else, the very foundations of our society would shift.

The systems we've built—economic, social, political—are all grounded in the illusion of separation, perpetuating competition and scarcity. But when we shift our understanding to one of interconnected awareness, these systems too must evolve. Imagine a world where cooperation, not competition, forms the foundation of our interactions. Resources would not be hoarded but shared, and the success of one would contribute to the success of all.

One example of such an alternative system is often referred to as a *gift economy*. In a gift economy, goods and services are freely given without any expectation of direct repayment. The idea behind this system is to foster community ties, generosity, and trust among participants, creating an environment where people give out of goodwill rather than for personal gain. In theory, this kind of economy can reduce competition and scarcity-driven behaviors by shifting the focus from accumulation to sharing.

In a gift economy, the emphasis is on relationships. When someone gives freely, it creates a sense of connection and belonging, reinforcing the idea that we are all part of the same community. Famous examples include the Burning Man festival, where participants share everything without monetary exchange, or the potlatch ceremonies of Indigenous cultures in the Pacific Northwest, where wealth was redistributed through acts of generosity.

However, while the gift economy works well in smaller, tightly-knit communities, it faces challenges when scaled up. One major issue is the reliance on trust—without it, some people may take more than they give, creating an imbalance that threatens the sustainability of the system. In larger or more diverse groups, where personal relationships are harder to maintain, it becomes more difficult to ensure fairness and reciprocity. Additionally, the lack of formal structure can lead to challenges in organizing resources efficiently, which becomes more complex as the community grows.

Another model, often referred to as a *sharing economy*, operates on the principle of access over ownership. In this system, individuals and organizations share resources like cars, homes, or tools, often mediated by digital platforms. The idea is to maximize the use of underutilized assets, reduce waste, and promote more sustainable consumption. Platforms like Airbnb and Uber allow people to rent out spare rooms or provide rides, turning personal assets into shared resources.

In theory, the sharing economy provides flexibility and economic opportunity by allowing people to access goods or services when they need them without the burden of ownership. It also has environmental benefits by reducing the demand for new products and encouraging more efficient use of existing resources.

However, the sharing economy has also faced significant criticism. Over time, many sharing platforms have become highly commercialized, shifting from community-driven resource sharing to profit-oriented enterprises. In some cases, workers on these platforms, like Uber drivers, face exploitation, earning less than a living wage, while the platform owners reap the benefits. The shift away from community building to monetizing personal assets has led to increased inequality and the erosion of worker rights, making the sharing economy a far cry from its original cooperative vision.

Both the gift economy and the sharing economy highlight alternative ways to structure our interactions, but they require a fundamental shift in how we view others. For these lifestyles to truly work, they rely on recognizing the well-being of others as equal to our own. Without this sense of genuine sense of empathy, both models can quickly fall into imbalance, exploitation, or competition—ironically replicating the very systems they aim to replace.

Our collective systems—mental health, education, governance—are mirrors of our own overcommitment to the assumption of individuality and the fear, isolation, and sense of lack it creates within us.

The modern epidemic of mental health struggles—anxiety, depression, loneliness—often stems from these feelings. Many of us move through life feeling disconnected from others, burdened by the belief that we are separate, that we are not enough, and that our pain is ours alone to bear. But in a world that recognizes our interconnectedness, this sense of isolation would dissolve.

Mental health would no longer be treated as an individual issue, something that must be dealt with in isolation. Instead, healing would become a communal experience. We would understand that when one person suffers, the whole suffers, and when one person heals, they contribute to the healing of the whole. Mental health support would become less about fixing the individual and more about fostering environments of connection, trust, and shared care. Therapy, support groups, and community healing practices would focus not only on individual well-being but also on the well-being of the collective. We would understand that caring for one person means caring for the whole, and that no one heals in isolation.

This shift would also change how we approach emotional vulnerability. In a world without such blind commitment to separation, there would be less stigma around mental health struggles, less fear of being seen as weak or broken. Instead, vulnerability would be embraced as a natural part of the human experience, a shared reality that we all navigate together. We would be more open, more compassionate, more willing to sit with each other in our pain, knowing that by doing so, we are not only helping one person but also contributing to the health of the whole system.

Relationships, too, would undergo a profound transformation. In a world based on separation, relationships often become transactional—built on fear, control, and insecurity. We approach relationships with a sense of scarcity, fearing that if we give too much, we will lose ourselves, or if we are too vulnerable, we will be hurt. But when we recognize that the "I" within us is the same as the "I" within the other, these fears begin to dissolve.

Our relationships would be rooted in authenticity and trust. We would no longer see others as competitors or threats but as fellow expressions of the same awareness. Vulnerability would no longer be something to fear but something to embrace and celebrate. It would be seen as the foundation of meaningful connection, a way of showing up fully and honestly in our relationships.

This shift would also mean that we would approach relationships with less need for control. Jealousy, possessiveness, and fear of abandonment would lose their power because we would understand that true connection comes not from holding on tightly but from allowing others to be fully themselves, just as we allow ourselves to be fully who we are. Relationships would become spaces of mutual support and growth, where both parties are free to explore their individuality within the context of a shared reality.

Our current systems of governance and economics are largely built on competition, control, and the hoarding of resources. Nations compete for power and influence. Corporations compete for profits. Individuals compete for jobs, housing, and status. But what would happen if we shifted from a worldview of competition to one of cooperation? If we recognized that what harms one harms all, how would our systems change?

In a world without the false perception of division, governance would be based on cooperation rather than control. Governments would recognize that their primary responsibility is to care for the well-being of all citizens, not just the most powerful or influential. Policies would be designed to promote fairness, equity, and shared well-being, rather than prioritizing the interests of the few. International relations would shift from rivalry to collaboration, with nations working together to solve global challenges like poverty, climate change, and inequality, understanding that these issues affect all of us.

Economics, too, would transform. As we discussed earlier, the current system, which rewards competition, individualism, and the accumulation of wealth, would give way to an economic model based on mutual benefit and shared resources. The idea of "enough for everyone" would replace the myth of scarcity, and economic systems would be designed to ensure that everyone's basic needs are met—food, shelter, healthcare, education—without the need to compete or hoard. Businesses would focus not only on profits but also on the well-being of their employees, their communities, and the planet. The concept of sustainability would become central, as we would recognize that the resources of the Earth are not infinite and that they must be cared for as part of the whole system.

The belief in isolated individuality doesn't just affect how we relate to each other—it also shapes how we relate to the Earth. For centuries, a large portion of humanity has acted as though we are separate from nature, treating the planet as a resource to be exploited for our own benefit. But when we remember that we are not separate from the Earth, that we are part of the same interconnected web of life, our approach to sustainability shifts dramatically.

We would treat the Earth as we have previously, not as something to conquer or control, but as an extension of ourselves. Just as we care for our bodies, ensuring they are healthy and nourished, we would care for the planet, recognizing that its health is directly tied to our own. This shift in perspective would lead to more sustainable practices in agriculture, energy, and resource management. We would prioritize renewable energy, reduce waste, and protect ecosystems, not just because it's the "right thing to do," but because we understand that the Earth is not separate from us—it is us.

Sustainability, in this sense, becomes less about sacrifice and more about harmony. We would see ourselves as stewards of the planet, responsible for its care and preservation for future generations, knowing that the well-being of the Earth is inextricably linked to our own well-being.

Our current education system is likewise largely built on competition and individual achievement. Students are taught to compete for grades, for recognition, for scholarships, and for success in a world that values individual accomplishment. But what if education were reimagined in the light of interconnectedness? What if, instead of competition, we prioritized empathy, collaboration, and holistic growth?

In a world that recognizes our shared awareness, education would focus not only on intellectual development but also on emotional and spiritual growth. Students would be taught not just to succeed in competitive environments but to thrive as part of a connected whole. Empathy, compassion, and collaboration would be central to the curriculum. Instead of learning in isolation, students would be encouraged to work together, to support one another, and to recognize that each person's success contributes to the success of the whole.

Instead of focusing solely on academic achievement, schools would prioritize the development of the whole person—intellectually, emotionally, physically, and spiritually. Meditation, mindfulness, and emotional intelligence would be taught alongside math, science, and literature. The goal of education would be not just to produce workers or achievers, but to cultivate compassionate, aware, and connected human beings who understand their place within the larger system of life.

Additionally, this reimagined system would ensure that education is accessible and free to all. Learning would no longer be treated as a commodity, reserved for those who can afford it, but as a fundamental right and shared resource. In an interconnected society, the success of each individual enriches the whole, so it would be in everyone's interest to provide equal access to education.

By removing financial barriers, we would create a system where everyone has the opportunity to grow, learn, and contribute to the collective well-being of humanity. This would foster not only academic growth but also a sense of belonging and shared responsibility within the global community.

Healthcare would also take on a more holistic approach. We would no longer see health as just the absence of illness in an individual, but as the health of the whole system—physical, mental, emotional, and social. Medical care would focus not just on treating symptoms but on addressing the root causes of illness, many of which stem from stress, isolation, and disconnection from others and the natural world.

Preventative care would become a priority, with a focus on creating environments that promote well-being—access to nutritious food, safe living conditions, opportunities for physical activity, and community support. Mental health care would be integrated into the overall healthcare system, recognizing that emotional and psychological well-being are just as important as physical health. And the connection between individual health and the health of the planet would be acknowledged, with healthcare systems promoting sustainable living practices as a way to protect both human health and the environment.

We are already seeing these principles surfacing in various healthcare systems, despite the overarching structure's divisive nature.

> **Social Prescribing in the UK**: The National Health Service (NHS) has embraced the idea of "social prescribing," where doctors recommend social activities—like joining clubs, exercising, or engaging in community gardening—rather than solely relying on medication. This approach targets the underlying causes of health issues, such as loneliness and stress, promoting well-being through community engagement and connection. This reflects the growing

recognition that social, emotional, and community health are essential aspects of individual well-being.

Blue Zones and Community Health: In certain regions of the world, known as Blue Zones, people live longer and healthier lives thanks to their lifestyle choices, including strong community bonds, plant-based diets, and daily physical activity. These regions highlight the power of community support, healthy environments, and purpose-driven living in promoting longevity and reducing chronic illnesses. This concept aligns with the idea of creating environments that naturally encourage healthier, more fulfilling lives.

Kaiser Permanente's Integrated Healthcare Model (USA): Kaiser Permanente offers one of the most comprehensive examples of integrated care in the U.S., combining physical and mental health services while emphasizing preventive care. They also engage in community wellness initiatives such as farmers' markets and support sustainable practices, demonstrating that addressing the social determinants of health is a vital component of healthcare.

Cuba's Community-Based Preventative Healthcare: Cuba's healthcare system is widely regarded for its preventative focus, with community-based doctors addressing social determinants like housing, education, and nutrition. Doctors live in the communities they serve, focusing on preventing illness rather than merely treating its symptoms. This model shows the importance of community engagement and holistic care in ensuring long-term health outcomes.

Sustainable Healthcare Initiatives: There's growing awareness of the need to link healthcare to environmental sustainability. Global initiatives like Health Care Without Harm are advocating for sustainable practices within healthcare systems, recognizing the deep connection between the health of individuals and the health of the planet. These efforts show how healthcare can lead in environmental stewardship, furthering the idea that human well-being is inseparable from planetary health.

While these examples highlight positive shifts, holistic healthcare faces significant challenges. For instance, resource allocation remains a barrier—shifting from a reactive, acute-care model to a preventative, holistic one requires long-term investments in infrastructure, education, and policy reform. Systems focused on treating symptoms may struggle to transition to models that address root causes.

Moreover, cultural shifts are needed to redefine how we perceive health. Moving from an individualistic view that treats symptoms to a model that focuses on the collective and interconnected well-being requires foundational changes in mindset. These changes take time, as they challenge long-standing beliefs about healthcare and individuality as a whole.

Nonetheless, these emerging models show that alternatives are possible, and in many places, already underway. They suggest that with the recognition of our interconnectedness, healthcare systems can evolve into something more compassionate, sustainable, and holistic, ultimately benefiting individuals and society as a whole.

All of the systems we've discussed—healthcare, education, economics, and governance—are built on a foundational perception of life and death.

At their core, these systems reflect our current belief that life is finite, isolated, and individual, with birth marking the beginning and death representing the end. This perception shapes not only how we interact with one another, but how we prioritize resources, manage well-being, and organize society.

Let's return to the healthcare system as an example. It often revolves around the goal of prolonging life and avoiding death, as though the purpose of medicine is to stave off the inevitable. Similarly, our education system is designed to prepare individuals for a future that is defined by personal achievement within a limited span of time. Economics, grounded in the belief of scarcity, promotes competition for resources as we race against the clock. And governance focuses on securing individual rights, properties, and legacies—each framed within the boundaries of a finite existence.

But what if our perception of life and death shifted? What if we recognized that life and death are not fixed points but transitions in an ongoing flow of awareness? When we see ourselves as part of an interconnected whole, the systems we've built around competition, isolation, and scarcity begin to unravel. Healthcare becomes more about holistic well-being—physical, mental, and emotional—across all stages of life, not just a struggle to extend it. Education would prioritize collaboration and collective growth over individual competition, fostering an understanding of our shared experience. Economics could evolve into systems of shared abundance, moving away from the mindset of accumulation for individual gain. Governance, instead of focusing on protecting separate entities, would work to ensure the flourishing of the whole.

This recognition of life and death as continuous processes opens up new possibilities for how we engage with each other and the world. It allows us to live with more ease, knowing that birth and death are not beginnings and endings, but simply transitions in the ongoing dance of existence. And when we understand this, the fear and rigidity that underpin our systems begin to dissolve.

In a world where we believe ourselves to be isolated individuals, birth is often seen as the beginning of a new, separate existence, and death is feared as the ultimate end—the moment when we lose everything that makes us who we are. But what if this understanding is incomplete? What if birth and death, far from being the definitive boundaries of existence, are merely transitions in the ongoing flow of awareness?

To live with this awareness is to walk lightly, knowing that the stories we tell about beginnings and endings are just chapters in a much larger narrative. Birth and death are not hard stops, but pauses in the rhythm of life's eternal dance. And just as the wave rises and falls, so too do we. In recognizing this continuity, the heaviness of existence fades, and we are left with a profound sense of peace. We are not confined to the identities we've constructed, nor are we bound by the fear of an end. We are participants in an infinite flow, where each moment is simply a new expression of life's endless creativity.

Death is not the end of who we are. It is not the annihilation of our essence but a transition, a shift in the way awareness expresses itself. Just as a wave rises and falls back into the ocean, so too does each individual expression of consciousness return to the larger whole. The awareness that flows through you right now is the same awareness that will continue long after your physical form fades. It transcends time and space; it simply is.

This shift in perspective doesn't negate the emotions that come with death. The loss of a loved one is still painful, and the uncertainty of our own death can still be unsettling. But when we recognize that death is not an end but a transition, the fear of death begins to dissolve. We come to understand that while our physical bodies and our personal identities may pass away, the awareness behind them does not. It simply moves on, taking on new forms, new expressions, in the ongoing flow of existence. Including your own.

This recognition also invites us to live with a greater sense of peace. When we no longer fear death as the ultimate end, we can be more present in each moment, more fully engaged in life. We no longer need to cling to our identities or our achievements, because we know that what truly matters—our awareness—cannot be lost.

Just as our understanding of death transforms, so too does our view of birth. In a world where we see ourselves as separate individuals, birth is often seen as the beginning of a new, independent life—a blank page, a new consciousness emerging from nothing. But if we recognize that awareness is continuous, then birth is not the creation of something entirely new. Rather, it is the manifestation of a new form, a new perspective through which the same awareness that flows through all of life can express itself.

The child that is born is not a completely separate being, but a new lens through which the universal awareness can experience the world. Each birth is an opportunity for life to see itself anew, to engage with the world through a fresh set of eyes. But the awareness within that child is not different from the awareness within you or me. It is the same awareness, simply taking on a different form.

Recognizing this dissolves the idea that we can disconnect from the consequences of our actions by leaving problems for future generations to deal with. The typical mentality of 'I'll be long gone before the world is truly screwed' no longer makes sense, because the same awareness that exists within us now is the same awareness that will live through the children who inherit the world we leave behind. We are not separate from the future—we are the future. The choices we make today are not just for 'others' but for the same awareness that will continue to experience life long after our individual forms have passed. In this way, we are responsible for the future, not as a distant concern but as a part of ourselves.

This understanding of birth also changes how we relate to new life. We often place enormous pressure on the idea of individuality and personal identity, teaching children to see themselves as distinct, separate beings from the moment they are born. But what if, instead of focusing exclusively on individual perspectives and priorities, we were more hesitant and aware of the consequences of reinforcing the belief in identity and concepts? By teaching children to see themselves solely as distinct, separate individuals, we are reinforcing fear and the illusion of isolation. What if, instead, we nurtured an awareness of interconnectedness alongside individuality? This balance could foster a sense of belonging and connection from the very beginning, helping children grow up with an understanding that they are not alone—that their experiences are part of a shared reality, one that includes and connects them to others at the deepest level. In this way, children could learn to navigate life with both a strong sense of self and a recognition of the unity that underlies all existence.

It's important to clarify that this understanding of awareness is not the same as the concept of reincarnation, which often implies a linear progression of a distinct soul or individual identity moving from one life to the next. In the framework we're discussing, there is no individual soul that carries forward from one life to another. Instead, the awareness we're referring to is universal and impersonal—it doesn't belong to any one person. When a child is born, it's not the rebirth of a specific, personal consciousness but rather a new manifestation of the same universal awareness that animates all life. This awareness is not tied to individual identity; it transcends it. It flows through all beings, constantly taking on new forms, but never belonging to any single form. In this way, the awareness within a newborn is the same awareness that exists within all of us, but it is not a continuation of an individual "self" from a previous life. It's the ongoing, ever-present awareness that permeates all existence, manifesting in countless ways.

This shift in how we view birth and death, from beginnings and endings to transitions in awareness, allows us to live with a greater sense of peace, purpose, and connection. We no longer need to fear the loss of our individual selves because we understand that what we truly are—the awareness behind it all—never dies. It simply changes form, continuing to flow through the endless dance of life.

Although it seems counterintuitive, reducing our fear of death actually has the potential to extend our life and help us heal. When we let go of our fear of death, we naturally reduce the underlying stress and anxiety that often prevent us from living fully in the present moment. This shift in perspective is not just psychological—it can also have real, measurable effects on the body. By releasing the need for control, we can ease the stress that wears down our physical systems, allowing the body to function more naturally and efficiently.

All of this points to a profound realization: healing individually leads to healing collectively. It's not the difficult act of force we once thought—it's something that happens naturally when we allow it. Healing occurs when we release the need for control and simply let the process unfold. But with this understanding, there's also a temptation to believe that we can heal 'others' in the same way, forgetting that in doing so, we're once again slipping into the illusion of separation. The contradiction is that trying to heal others without honoring their own process would pull us out of our own state of being, robbing us of the very clarity that facilitates healing in the first place.

In our interconnectedness, it can be tempting to fall back on old concepts of control and belief in an attempt to facilitate collective healing. Traditionally, belief in healing has been seen as a powerful force. The placebo effect, for example, is widely recognized as an illustration of the mind's ability to impact the body. It is often attributed to the power of belief—the expectation that a treatment will work triggers real physiological changes. This understanding has its roots in extensive research, showing that belief alone can lead to measurable improvements in health outcomes.

However, while belief plays a crucial role, it's not the only factor at work. Numerous studies have shown that stress is a critical variable in the body's healing process, regardless of whether belief is involved. For instance, research into the placebo effect reveals that, in many cases, the reduction of stress and anxiety in patients is one of the primary reasons they experienced relief.

- **Pain Management Studies**: Placebo treatments have been shown to reduce pain, not simply because the patient believes in the treatment, but because their anxiety about the pain diminishes. Reduced stress activates the body's natural ability to manage pain, much like how relaxation therapies (such as deep breathing or meditation) do.

- **Post-Surgery Recovery**: In studies involving recovery from surgery, patients who believe they are receiving effective treatment often show faster recovery times. However, the underlying factor is often the reduction in stress and anxiety about their recovery, which leads to improved immune response and faster healing.
- **Immune Function and Stress**: High stress has been shown to weaken the immune system, increasing inflammation and slowing the body's ability to heal. Conversely, relaxation techniques have been proven to reduce cortisol levels and improve immune function. In both cases—whether healing through relaxation or through the placebo effect—the common factor is that stress is reduced.

This suggests that while belief can help alleviate stress, it is the relaxation and reduction in stress that truly allow the body to heal more effectively. The mind, when at ease, provides the body with the space and resources to recover. Therefore, belief may work, in part, because it triggers relaxation and shifts the body into a healing state, but deliberate relaxation can achieve the same effect without the need for external validation.

However, there is a critical vulnerability in belief-based healing—the constant threat of doubt. Doubt can easily unravel the placebo effect because it introduces uncertainty, disrupting the sense of safety that belief creates. When a person begins to question whether their treatment is working or whether they can trust in their healing, the relaxation that belief induces fades, and stress reenters the picture. This fragility highlights the limitations of belief-based healing—it's only as strong as the belief itself, and belief is always susceptible to challenge.

What if healing didn't require belief in an external source at all?

Practices like mindfulness, meditation, and deep breathing activate the parasympathetic nervous system, reducing stress and promoting recovery. When we surrender—when we consciously let go of tension and fear—we allow the body to enter a state of balance where healing can occur naturally. In this way, attentive relaxation mirrors the placebo effect but without the need for external faith. It offers a direct path to healing by fostering a state of calm, acceptance, and openness to the flow of life.

Of course, this perspective is not meant to discount the established understanding of the placebo effect or the power of belief, but rather to expand it. Belief might be one pathway to healing, but relaxation, whether brought about by belief or by deliberate practice, seems to be the underlying mechanism that allows the body to recover—and it is far more resilient against doubt.

In much the same way that belief-based healing (like the placebo effect) is limited for individuals, religion functions as a large-scale placebo for collective healing. For centuries, religions have offered frameworks of belief that provide comfort, meaning, and healing to society. Religion, much like a placebo, is designed to reduce existential anxiety, offering relief through concepts like divine purpose, salvation, and moral structure. By fostering belief in higher powers and divine order, religions provide psychological and emotional comfort, guiding people through suffering and uncertainty.

However, just as the placebo effect has its limits in individual healing, religion too faces limitations when applied on such a large scale. The belief structures within religions, though initially created to unite people under shared concepts, often lead to division when those beliefs become unquestionable. Just as with the placebo effect, where the healing power is capped when the individual's stress levels rise or the condition is chronic, religion's capacity to heal the collective is limited by the division that conceptual beliefs create.

Throughout history, religious conflicts have erupted because of competing belief systems. The very concepts that were designed to bring peace and connection — such as belief in salvation or divine truth — often breed division when they become exclusive or absolute. When one group's beliefs conflict with another's, it can lead to competition, fear, and conflict, exacerbating the illusion of separation rather than healing it.

In this way, religion's capacity for collective healing is limited in much the same way as the placebo effect's capacity for individual healing — both rely on belief, and both reach their limits when faced with life's unbiased unfolding. Additionally, just as doubt can unravel individual belief-based healing, doubt in religious beliefs can erode collective cohesion. When conflicting beliefs create division, it threatens the very unity religion seeks to foster.

But this principle applies not only to the individual body — it applies to the collective body of humanity. Just as stress and tension hinder individual healing, the fear and separation we carry as a society hinder collective healing. When we, as individuals, learn to relax, to trust, and to surrender to our interconnectedness, we contribute to the healing of the whole. The mentality of fear and competition, much like chronic stress in the body, fragments our ability to work together. But when we relax into the truth of our shared existence — when we release the need for control and embrace our connection to each other — we begin to heal not only ourselves but the world around us.

This is the power of surrender or faith. By deliberately relaxing into what we truly are — expressions of the same awareness — we stop resisting the flow of life. We stop clinging to the illusion of separation, and in doing so, we create the conditions for healing both individually and collectively. Just as the cells in our body function best when they work together in harmony, so too does society flourish when we act from a place of trust and cooperation. When we relax into our true nature, we no longer act from fear or scarcity. Instead, we embrace the whole, knowing that healing flows naturally from our connectedness.

Healing, then, is not something we strive for. It's something we allow. By surrendering to the flow of life, we stop trying to control outcomes and start trusting in the natural intelligence of the body—both our individual body and the collective body of humanity. In this way, our personal well-being and the well-being of the world are inextricably linked. To heal ourselves is to heal the whole, and this healing comes not through force or effort, but through the silent power of relaxation, surrender, and trust.

A powerful illustration of this can be seen in the Rat Wonderland study, often referred to as Rat Park, conducted by psychologist Bruce Alexander in the 1970s. The study challenged the then-prevailing belief that drug addiction was solely a result of chemical hooks by showing how environment and connection played a crucial role in the well-being of the rats. When rats were kept in isolated cages with only access to drugs, they consistently consumed the drugs to the point of addiction. However, when placed in an enriching environment—Rat Park—with ample space, food, and social connection, the rats largely ignored the drugs, choosing to engage with their surroundings and each other instead.

This study highlights how healing and well-being arise from supportive environments and a sense of connection. The rats didn't need to be "fixed" through force or medication; they simply needed a nurturing space where they could thrive naturally. In the same way, when we relax into the flow of life, trust in our natural intelligence, and cultivate environments of connection and support, healing becomes a natural outcome.

The insights from the Rat Park study are echoed in the work of renowned physician and addiction expert Gabor Maté, who advocates for a shift in how we understand and treat addiction. Maté argues that addiction is not a moral failing or a simple consequence of chemical dependency but a response to pain, trauma, and disconnection. Like the rats in isolated cages, individuals struggling with addiction are often deprived of meaningful connection, purpose, and a supportive environment.

Maté emphasizes that healing from addiction is not about changing the individual in isolation, but about addressing the underlying causes—their emotional, social, and environmental conditions. In this light, healing addiction becomes less about controlling the person's behavior and more about nurturing the collective environment that supports their well-being.

Just as an unhealthy environment can perpetuate addiction, divisive concepts can create a toxic atmosphere, limiting our understanding of reality and fostering disconnection. Religion, often referred to as "the opiate of the masses," operates similarly to addiction. It offers comfort, but only within a framework that reinforces separation. The very structures designed to heal our existential pain can amplify the illusion of isolation by positioning a divine figure as something external to be sought, obeyed, or feared. In this paradigm, "God" becomes a distant, unattainable ideal, separate from us, and we are left chasing this external force to find meaning and fulfillment. This quest mirrors the addictive cycle: seeking relief from suffering but reinforcing the very conditions that sustain it.

Religion, as it is often practiced today, tends to reinforce the illusion of separation that it aims to heal. Most organized religions operate within the framework of duality—the believer and the divine, the worshipper and God, the sinner and salvation. In this paradigm, "God" becomes an external figure, a concept that exists outside of us, to be worshipped, obeyed, and feared. This framework builds on the idea that we, as individuals, are separate from this external "God," that we must seek something beyond ourselves to find meaning, purpose, or grace.

But what if the very concept of "God" itself is standing in the way of healing and realization? What if "God" is just a pointer—a limited concept that cannot fully capture the vast, ineffable reality of existence? In a world where the illusion of separation dissolves, religion as we know it would transform. Instead of seeking an external "God," we would realize that the sacred is already within us, inseparable from our awareness, inextricably woven into the fabric of existence. Spirituality would no longer be about seeking an external force but recognizing the reality of who we are—the awareness that experiences life.

Many religious traditions describe God as eternal, omnipresent, and beyond description—an all-encompassing force that unites everything in existence. In Christianity, God is often referred to as "the Alpha and the Omega," the beginning and the end, eternal and unchanging. In Islam, God is described as "Al-Wasi" (The All-Encompassing) and "Al-Hayy" (The Ever-Living), signifying a boundless, ever-present existence that is both infinite and eternal. In Hinduism, Brahman is the ultimate reality, an all-pervasive presence beyond all names and forms, the source from which everything emanates and to which everything returns. Even in Judaism, the concept of Ein Sof refers to an endless, boundless presence that is beyond comprehension.

But if we look closely at these descriptions—eternal, omnipresent, indescribable, and unifying—aren't these the very qualities of awareness itself? The awareness that exists within you, within me, and within all life is also eternal. It is the silent witness that has been present through every experience, unchanged by the passing of time. This awareness is omnipresent—it is here, now, in every moment, everywhere, as the field of consciousness in which all experiences arise. It is indescribable, for no concept or word can fully capture the depth and vastness of pure awareness. And, ultimately, this awareness is unifying, for it is the same awareness that flows through all beings, connecting us in a shared experience of existence.

What this means on a practical level is that the universe you are aware of is, in fact, your awareness. And just as the observer in the double-slit experiment influences the behavior of photons, your awareness influences the world you experience. Your subjective awareness shapes your experience of the world, and the world, in turn, shapes your awareness. It's a feedback loop, a dynamic relationship where the lines between self and world, between inner and outer, are blurred.

This realization can be both liberating and humbling. On the one hand, it means that you have the power to influence your reality—not by forcing external circumstances to change, but by changing the way you perceive and engage with the world. On the other hand, it reminds us that we are not the only ones shaping reality. We are part of a larger web of awareness, where every individual's consciousness is contributing to the collective experience of existence.

Rather than seeking to resolve this paradox by choosing one reality over the other, we are invited to hold space for both subjective and objective awareness. We are individuals with unique perspectives and experiences, yet we are also the greater whole, where our awareness and the world we observe are intimately connected.

In a world where interconnectedness is recognized, the need for externalized worship fades. Traditional religious practices—prayers to a distant God, rituals aimed at appeasing a higher power—become unnecessary. Why? Because the very notion of separation between ourselves and "God" collapses. Every moment, every breath, every action becomes an expression of the sacred, not because we are reaching for something beyond ourselves, but because we are realizing that we are already that which we seek.

Our connection to the sacred becomes immediate, direct, and experiential. When we no longer see "God" as something external, we begin to see the sacred in everything—in ourselves, in each other, in the world around us. The morning sunlight, the laughter of a child, or the sound of the wind through the trees—all these become expressions of the sacred, as soon as we recognize that the reality behind all these experiences is inseparable from what we are.

In this world, spirituality isn't something we perform on specific days or in specific places—it is woven into the very fabric of life. No longer confined to temples, churches, or mosques, the sacred becomes something always present, always accessible. Washing the dishes, walking in the park, or conversing with a friend—every act becomes an opportunity to encounter the sacred directly, with no need for rituals or intermediaries. We would begin to live our lives in a state of reverence, not because of religious obligation, but because we are attuned to the flow of life itself, which is the ultimate expression of reality.

One of the challenges faced by organized religion stems from its reliance on dogma—rules and doctrines that attempt to define reality in fixed terms. But reality is far too vast, far too fluid, to be captured by dogma. Dogma, by its nature, tells us how to think, act, and believe, often without room for individual exploration or direct experience. Yet, in a world where we recognize that reality is beyond concepts, dogma inevitably begins to lose its relevance.

There is no need for external validation or belief systems to tell us how to connect with the sacred because the sacred is the reality of our own existence, beyond all conceptual frameworks. We don't need to follow a set of prescribed beliefs or practices when spirituality becomes something we experience directly— intimately—in every moment.

Without dogma, spirituality becomes a living, evolving experience. It becomes a process of opening ourselves to the mystery of existence, rather than following a checklist of rituals or beliefs. This approach fosters openness and humility, as we recognize that reality—the true nature of what we are—is far too extensive to fit into any single doctrine or system of thought. Instead of clinging to concepts of the divine, we would learn to live with the mystery, to embrace the unknown, and to trust in the direct experience of empathy unfolding.

Few conflicts in the modern world exemplify and mirror the destructive power of conceptual division more clearly than the ongoing struggle between Israelis and Palestinians. At its heart, the Gaza/Palestine conflict is a story of two groups of people, each deeply entrenched in their own historical narratives, both fighting for their right to exist, to belong, and to be recognized. But what has fueled this conflict for so long is the belief in separation—the idea that the interests of one group must inherently be in opposition to the other. The result is a seemingly endless cycle of violence, fear, and suffering, with both sides trapped in their self-defining concepts, unable to see the deeper truth of their shared humanity.

To understand the conflict between Israelis and Palestinians is to understand how self-defining concepts and long-held narratives can create and sustain division. On both sides, generations have grown up with deeply ingrained beliefs about their identity—who they are, where they belong, what they "deserve", and what they must do to protect themselves from the "other." These narratives have been passed down through families, reinforced by religious, cultural, and political institutions, and cemented by decades of violence and loss. The more entrenched these narratives become, the harder it is for either side to see beyond them, to imagine a reality in which they are not separate, not enemies, but part of the same whole.

One of the most challenging aspects of this conflict is that both sides have legitimate grievances, and yet, both sides are also trapped in a cycle of blame and retribution. Israelis, many of whom are descended from those who fled persecution or the horrors of the Holocaust, see their homeland as a place of safety, a refuge where they can live free from fear. But this very homeland is also the place where Palestinians have lived for centuries, and for Palestinians, the establishment of Israel has been experienced as a violent displacement, an occupation of their land and identity.

Both sides have experienced immense suffering. Both sides feel justified in their actions. And both sides have used violence as a means of defending their right to exist. But the tragic irony of this conflict is that by clinging to these narratives of separateness, both sides continue to inflict pain not only on the "other" but on themselves. In their attempts to protect their identities and their lands, they have become blind to the possibility that their fates are intertwined, that the security and peace they seek cannot come at the expense of the other, but only through mutual recognition and cooperation.

The cycle of violence persists because both sides are trapped in the illusion that they are fundamentally separate—that the safety, security, and identity of one group must come at the cost of the other. This zero-sum mentality, born from fear and reinforced by decades of conflict, keeps both Israelis and Palestinians locked in a perpetual struggle for survival. Yet, as long as this illusion persists, true peace will remain elusive.

At the heart of the Gaza/Palestine conflict are deeply rooted narratives that have shaped the identities of both Israelis and Palestinians. For Israelis, the establishment of the State of Israel is seen as a fulfillment of a long-held promise from their idea of "God", a return to the land of their ancestors after centuries of exile and persecution. For Palestinians, the Nakba, or "catastrophe," refers to the mass displacement of Palestinians during the establishment of Israel in 1948, when hundreds of thousands were forced to leave their homes. These narratives are not just stories—they are foundational to how each group understands its place in the world.

The problem with these narratives is not that they are untrue—both sides have legitimate claims to their histories. The problem arises when these narratives become so entrenched, so all-consuming, that they prevent either side from seeing beyond them. Each side becomes locked in a victim mentality, focused on the injustices they have suffered while remaining blind to the suffering of the other. The historic narratives become walls that divide, preventing empathy, understanding, and the possibility of reconciliation.

But what if these narratives, while important, could be seen for what they are: stories, passed down through generations, shaped by trauma, fear, and the desire for survival? What if Israelis and Palestinians could recognize that, while their histories are different, their suffering is shared? What if they could begin to see each other not as enemies, but as fellow human beings who are trapped in the same cycle of fear and separation?

The conflict between Israelis and Palestinians can only be resolved when both sides begin to transcend the illusion of separation. This doesn't mean erasing history or ignoring legitimate grievances. It means recognizing the obvious truth: Israelis and Palestinians are not fundamentally separate. They are both seeing themselves in each other, reflecting the same awareness.

What does this mean in practical terms? It means that both sides must be willing to see themselves in the other, to recognize that the pain and suffering of one side is inseparable from the pain and suffering of the other. It means understanding that true security cannot come from domination or control, but only from cooperation and mutual respect. It means releasing the idea of winners and losers and embracing a future where both sides can thrive, that peace can be achieved not through violence but through dialogue, understanding, and compassion.

This shift in perspective requires a willingness to question long-held beliefs, to let go of the narratives that have defined both sides for generations. It requires Israelis and Palestinians to sit with their pain, to acknowledge the trauma they have endured, and to recognize that they see their own suffering reflected in the suffering of those they've been taught to fear. It requires a willingness to engage with the "other," not as an enemy, but as a fellow human being who, like them, wants safety, security, and a place to call home.

The process of successfully integrating individuality into our interconnected reality is not about forgetting history or ignoring the complexities of the conflict. It is about moving beyond the illusion that one side's gain must come at the other's expense. It is about recognizing that both sides are part of the same whole and that the only way forward is through mutual understanding, empathy, and cooperation.

The path to peace in Gaza and Palestine lies not in more violence, more walls, or more division. It lies in the recognition that Israelis and Palestinians are inextricably linked—that the well-being of one depends on the well-being of the other. True peace can only come when both sides are willing to let go of their conceptual divisions and embrace the reality of their shared existence.

This doesn't mean that the path forward together will be easy. There will be resistance, fear, and pain on both sides. But the alternative— continuing the cycle of violence and division—will only lead to more suffering. The key to breaking this cycle is empathy: the ability to see the world through the eyes of the other, to recognize that their fears, their pain, and their desires are not so different from our own.

Empathy is not just an individual experience; it is a force that ripples through the collective. When we extend kindness to others, we are not simply helping them—we are healing ourselves.

> "If you bring forth what is within you, what you bring forth will save you. If you do not bring forth what is within you, what you do not bring forth will destroy you."
>
> — The Gospel of Thomas

In post-genocide Rwanda, grassroots movements like 'Healing Through Remembering' bring together survivors and perpetrators to foster dialogue and mutual understanding. These initiatives create space for empathy and healing, helping individuals on both sides of the conflict reconnect with their shared humanity. By recognizing their pain and suffering as reflections of one another, these communities demonstrate that collective healing begins when we move beyond conceptual divisions.

Every act of compassion strengthens the whole. By showing empathy, we remind others—and ourselves—that we see ourselves in them, dissolving the boundaries that fear and separation create. The healing of one is the healing of all, and in this recognition, we begin to see that true change comes not from isolation but from a shared commitment to remaining open and empathetic in a state of vulnerable authenticity.

This brings us to a new view of cooperation, but not in the traditional sense of working together toward a common goal. True cooperation is a result of each person taking full accountability—not just for their actions, but for the whole. When individuals recognize their sole responsibility in creating the present reality, they become more empathetic, patient, and willing to compromise, because they no longer see the 'other' as separate or merely 'like' themselves. Instead, they recognize the other as themselves, doing the best they can from within an entirely different context. This shift in perspective opens the door for Israelis and Palestinians not only to end the conflict but to build a future where both can thrive. The real challenges—land, borders, political sovereignty—remain, but they can only be addressed when both sides come to the table not as enemies or adversaries, but as partners, fully accountable for the creation of a shared future.

If that were to happen, both sides would quickly realize that their problem isn't each other. They would see that the only true enemy to lasting peace is the weapons we willingly create, buy, and use. As each person takes full accountability for the whole, it becomes clear that the cycle of conflict is perpetuated not by inherent divisions, but by the tools of violence that we, as a collective, continue to empower. With this realization, the focus shifts away from blaming the 'other' and toward dismantling the systems and weapons that sustain conflict. In doing so, the path to peace becomes one of mutual disarmament and shared responsibility, built on the recognition that true cooperation can only exist when we no longer see ourselves as separate.

Instead of fighting over resources, Israelis and Palestinians can work together to share and protect the land they both call home. Instead of building walls, they can build bridges—literal and metaphorical—that connect their communities, fostering understanding and trust. Instead of perpetuating fear and hatred, they can teach their children the values of empathy, cooperation, and peace.

The Gaza/Palestine conflict is a reflection of the divide that lies at the heart of so much human suffering. But it is also a reminder that this illusion can be transcended. Israelis and Palestinians are not destined to be enemies forever. They are fellow human beings, bound by the same awareness, sharing the same earth, and capable of building a future based on mutual respect and understanding.

The path of peace is not easy, but it is possible. It begins with the recognition that the illusion of separation is just that—an illusion. When both sides can see beyond this illusion and embrace their shared humanity, the door to peace will open. And through empathy, cooperation, and a willingness to heal the wounds of the past, Israelis and Palestinians can create a future in which both sides not only survive, but thrive—together.

Change starts with individuals choosing to see things differently, not with governments changing their politics.

Throughout history, revolutions have been sparked by the desire for freedom, justice, and the goal of overthrowing oppressive systems. Monarchs have been deposed, dictators toppled, and corrupt elites driven from power. The people rise up, the government changes, and for a brief moment, it feels like the world has shifted. Yet, despite the fervor and sacrifice that fuel revolutions, more often than not, the new system eventually falls into the same patterns of corruption, inequality, and control as the one it replaced. Why?

The answer lies not in the structures of power themselves, but in the mentality that underpins them. You can remove a monarch or overthrow a corrupt billionaire, but if the underlying mindset that created those figures—the desire for power, control, dominance—remains unchanged, the same cycle will inevitably repeat. Without addressing the internal forces that influence us, true transformation remains elusive.

At its core, revolution is about disruption. It's the shaking up of a system that is no longer serving the people, a collective demand for something new. Revolutions often arise from a sense of injustice, from the recognition that the existing system is failing to meet the needs of the many in favor of the few. This desire for change is powerful, but revolutions, by their very nature, tend to focus on external structures: governments, leaders, economic systems. The rallying cry is to remove the oppressor, to dismantle the regime, to destroy the old and bring in the new.

And yet, what we often fail to see is that while the faces at the top of the hierarchy may change, the mentality that spawned the hierarchy remains. The systems of power—monarchy, dictatorship, oligarchy—are not isolated phenomena. They are born out of the collective consciousness of a society. They arise from a mentality that values domination, control, and the accumulation of resources and influence. This mentality doesn't disappear when the revolution succeeds. It lingers, finding new ways to express itself, whether through new leaders, new systems, or new ideologies.

The French Revolution, for example, overthrew the monarchy, only to see the rise of Napoleon Bonaparte, a military leader who seized power and crowned himself emperor. The Russian Revolution ousted the Tsar, only to pave the way for decades of authoritarian rule under Stalin and his successors. Time and again, we see the same pattern—revolutionary energy focused only on changing the external system, while the internal mindset of control and power remains intact.

This is why revolutions often fail to deliver the lasting change they promise. They may succeed in tearing down the old system, but without a transformation of the collective mentality that gave rise to that system, the same dynamics reemerge. In fact, the word "revolution" itself hints at this repetition—it comes from the Latin word *revolutio*, meaning "a turn around." Revolutions often end up turning us in a circle, bringing us back to the same place we started, albeit with new faces at the helm.

If real, lasting change is to occur, the mentality that gives rise to oppression and inequality must be transcended in each of us. This means addressing the assumptions that drive us to seek power and control in the first place—the fear of scarcity, the desire for dominance, and the belief that success comes from winning at the expense of others. These mentalities are rooted in the fear of individuality: the belief that we are isolated individuals in competition with one another, that we must protect ourselves from scarcity by accumulating more, that others are threats rather than allies.

As long as this mentality persists, revolutions will continue to fail in their intended purpose. The faces of power may change, but the dynamics of power remain the same. We can topple a corrupt government, but unless we address the mindset that allowed that government to rise in the first place, the same corrupt structures will inevitably re-form. This is why revolutions that focus only on external change—new laws, new leaders, new institutions— eventually fall short. They address the symptoms, but not the root cause.

True revolution, then, must begin from within. It requires a shift in consciousness, a recognition that the old mindset of power and control no longer serves us. It requires a deep understanding of our interconnectedness, an awareness that what harms one of us harms all of us. This is not about rejecting all forms of leadership or governance—it's about reimagining them in a way that reflects our shared humanity, our shared well-being.

At the heart of many oppressive systems is a mentality that elevates certain individuals to positions of extreme power and wealth. Monarchs, billionaires, dictators—these figures are often seen as the ultimate symbols of success, the pinnacle of achievement in a world that values control and accumulation. But what drives this desire to be a monarch or a billionaire in the first place? Why do so many aspire to these positions of power?

To seek extreme wealth or power is to operate from a place of scarcity, from the belief that there isn't enough to go around, and that the only way to ensure your survival and success is to accumulate more than others. It is a mentality rooted in fear—the fear of losing, the fear of being less, the fear of not being enough. This drive for dominance is not an inherent part of human nature, but a symptom of the isolating ego, the belief that we are all fundamentally disconnected and must therefore compete for resources, status, and security.

As long as this mentality persists, there will always be people who aspire to positions of extreme power, just as there will always be systems that allow such people to rise. Removing a monarch or deposing a billionaire will not change this. It is the desire for power itself—the belief that having power over others is the key to safety and success—that must be addressed. Without transcending this mentality, we are doomed to repeat the same cycles of oppression and inequality, regardless of who is in charge.

Real revolution is not about replacing one system of power with another—it's about changing the very foundation on which power is built. It's about shifting from a mindset of separation to one of interconnectedness, from competition to cooperation, from scarcity to abundance. This is not the kind of revolution that can be achieved through violence or force. It is a revolution of consciousness, a collective awakening to the reality that we are all part of the same whole, that what affects one of us affects all of us. In the face of a world telling us to invest in the fear of separation, a simple "no thank you" is the most powerful act of revolution possible.

This kind of revolution cannot be imposed from the top down—it must arise from within each of us. It requires each individual to examine their own relationship to power, control, and scarcity, to question the narratives they've been taught about what it means to be successful, and to embrace a new way of being that is rooted in connection, empathy, and mutual support.

The failure of revolutions lies not in the idea of change itself, but in the narrow focus on external change at the expense of internal transformation. Real revolution requires more than just replacing the people in power—it requires a sense of responsibility for how we engage with the world. Our thoughts, our intentions, and our actions ripple out into the world, influencing not only our experience but the collective experience as well. This doesn't mean we control everything, but it does mean that we are active participants in the unfolding of reality.

Embracing the paradox of existence—the tension between individuality and unity—doesn't need to be heavy or burdened with intellectual strain. Instead, it can be playful, light, and full of wonder. Life itself is paradoxical, but this paradox is not a problem to be solved. It's an invitation to engage with the mystery. To approach life with a sense of play is to recognize that we will never fully know, and that's okay. In fact, it's serendipitous. The beauty of existence lies not in certainty but in the openness to surprise, in the willingness to see the world anew with each moment.

The self-concepts we hold onto—whether shaped by societal expectations or personal beliefs—are like sandcastles built on the shore. With each wave, they begin to crumble, revealing the transient nature of these constructs. Yet, rather than resist this dissolution, we can embrace it. We are not fixed, unchangeable beings; we are fluid, constantly evolving with each experience. When we release the need to define ourselves by these crumbling castles, we free ourselves to explore the vast ocean of potential that lies within and around us.

Life is not a test with a predetermined outcome; it is an improvisation, a spontaneous unfolding of creativity. When we allow ourselves to approach existence with playfulness, we open the door to endless discovery. Each moment becomes an opportunity to engage with the mystery, to laugh at the unpredictability of it all, and to marvel at the beauty that emerges when we stop trying to force life into unchanging structures.

Stepping into this fluidity means letting go of the need for certainty. It means allowing ourselves to evolve, to grow, and to expand without clinging to the idea of who we think we are. It means embracing the unknown, trusting that the flow of life will carry us where we need to go, even if we can't always see the path ahead. This is not a passive surrender—it is an active engagement with life, one that allows us to move with the current rather than fight against it.

Authenticity, like a stone cast into a still pond, sends ripples that move outward, touching everything they encounter. When we live in alignment with our true selves, free from the need to prove or control, our actions have a far-reaching impact. These ripples of authenticity extend beyond the self, affecting others and inviting them to do the same. In this shared space of vulnerability and openness, we create the conditions for collective healing and transformation. To be authentic is not just an individual act—it is a contribution to the whole.

In being, we find freedom. We are no longer bound by the narratives that have defined us—narratives of success or failure, of worthiness or inadequacy. We are free to explore new possibilities, to engage with life in a way that is dynamic, responsive, and open to change.

And in this freedom, we discover a sense of belonging—not to any particular identity or role, but to the flow of life itself.

To engage fully with life is to be present, here and now. It is to meet each moment with openness and curiosity, without clinging to the past or worrying about the future. It is to recognize that while we cannot control everything that happens, we can choose how we respond. We can choose to be fully here, now, engaged with the people, places, and experiences that are right in front of us.

This presence doesn't negate the challenges of life. There will still be pain, loss, uncertainty, and fear. But when we are fully present, we allow ourselves to experience these challenges in their fullness without being overwhelmed by them. We see them as part of the larger flow of life, as moments that are just as important as the joyful ones. And in this presence, we find a sense of peace—not because life is easy or predictable, but because we trust that we are part of something much larger than ourselves.

At this point in the journey, the question naturally arises: *So what now?* After exploring the far-reaching paradoxes of existence, the illusion of separation, the interconnectedness of all life, and the fluid nature of subjective and objective awareness, where does this leave us? What does this understanding mean for our daily lives, our choices, and our future?

The answer is both simple and profound: *live.* There is no ultimate answer outside of yourself because you are not separate from the world you are observing. You are the creator and the created, the question and the answer, the individual and the whole. Your actions, thoughts, and choices shape the very reality in which you live.

You don't have to look for answers outside yourself because the awareness that asks the question is the same awareness that contains the answer.

This realization invites you to stop seeking an external "truth" and instead embrace the fluid, dynamic truth of your own experience. It means recognizing that every moment is a chance to express your awareness, to engage with the world as both the observer and the creator. You are not a passive participant in life—you are life itself, unfolding moment by moment.

What you do matters not just because it affects you personally, but because it affects the entire web of life. When you act with kindness, empathy, and compassion, you create ripples of healing and connection that spread throughout the world. When you act out of fear, anger, or separation, you contribute to the cycles of suffering and division.

This doesn't mean that you need to be any specific type of person or that every decision needs to be calculated. It simply means living with awareness. It means recognizing that even the smallest actions—whether it's a conversation with a stranger, a moment of mindfulness, or a decision to help someone in need—have the power to shape the world in profound ways. Every moment is an opportunity to create, to contribute, and to participate in the unfolding of reality.

But this responsibility is not about controlling outcomes or manipulating reality to fit your desires. It's about engaging with life as a co-creator, understanding that while you influence reality, you are also part of a larger flow that you cannot fully control. It's about balancing the power of creation with the humility to recognize that you are part of something far greater than yourself.

Who are you when you stop telling yourself who you are? You're who you always have been. Reality itself.

And so, as promised, you have proof that *you are God*—not in the sense of an omnipotent ruler, but in the sense that the divine essence, the awareness that animates all of existence, is you. You are not separate from the universe, not separate from other people, not separate from life itself. You are both the individual expression of the divine and the divine itself, experiencing life from your unique perspective.

And if this is true for you, it is true for everyone else as well. We are all expressions of the same awareness, the same life force, the same divine energy. We are all in this together, not just as a collection of individuals, but as one interconnected whole. "We" are you. "I" am you.

So, as we reach the end of this journey together, I want to take a moment to acknowledge *you*. You have faced your doubts, questioned your limitations, and walked through moments of uncertainty, confusion, and perhaps even despair. You've wrestled with the unknown, and though those moments may have felt overwhelming, I want you to know that they weren't in vain. Each step, no matter how difficult, has led to greater clarity and depth in your experience of life. And I notice. Even if it feels like no one else does, I see it—and I'm grateful.

It's easy to feel, at times, that all the work you've done to grow, to expand, to understand yourself and the world around you has gone unnoticed. That the moments where you confronted your deepest fears and allowed yourself to be vulnerable have slipped by without recognition. The truth is, most of us are so caught up in our own journey, carrying our own burdens, that we rarely pause to acknowledge the strength and resilience in those around us. But that doesn't mean your efforts don't matter. They do. Every quiet victory, every doubt faced, every question asked has contributed to the whole.

I celebrate your existence. I celebrate the fact that, despite the moments where you felt lost or unsure, you kept going. You kept questioning, kept learning, kept reaching for something deeper. That takes courage, and though it may go unseen by others, it is deeply felt in the larger web of life we all share.

Your willingness to engage with the hard questions, to sit with the discomfort of not knowing, is what makes this journey meaningful. And even though those moments of clarity and growth may have felt isolated or personal, they are part of something much larger. Your work—your inner work—ripples out in ways you can't always see. It influences the collective in ways you may never fully understand. But I want you to know that it matters.

You are not alone in this experience, though it may sometimes feel that way. Every person you meet is carrying their own questions, their own struggles, their own journey toward understanding. We all have our hands full, trying to make sense of life, trying to find peace within ourselves and the world around us. But that's exactly why what you're doing is so important—because your work, your presence, your willingness to engage with the depths of existence is a gift. A gift to yourself, and a gift to the rest of us.

So I thank you. Thank you for showing up, for doing the hard work of self-reflection, and for daring to question the limits you've been told define you. Thank you for being willing to feel lost, to confront your fears, and to embrace the moments of doubt. It's those very moments that have led you to the insights you carry now. They've shaped you, and in turn, they shape the world.

Now, all I ask is that you pass it on. Share this awareness with others, not by preaching or instructing, but by living it. Let your presence, your empathy, your compassion be a quiet, impactful example of the work you've done. Acknowledge those around you, even if only in your heart, and know that just as I see you, others are on their own path of being seen.

Your existence is a celebration. It's not defined by the highs or the lows, by what you've achieved or by what you still seek. It's defined by the fact that you are here, doing the work, living the questions, and showing up to life with all that you are. And for that, I am profoundly grateful.

Grateful to be you.

In Lak'ech
Namaste
Mitákuye Oyás'iŋ
Ubuntu
Tat Tvam Asi
Sawubona
Sama Sama
Sat Nam
Om Mani Padme Hum
Om Shanti
Ekam Sat
Tawhid
Satchitananda
Wahkon-Tah

Epilogue

Thank you for taking the time to explore the insights and reflections in *Proof That You're God*. The journey doesn't end here—it's only the beginning. We invite you to connect with a growing community of engaged and aware individuals who explore these concepts and more every day.

Stay connected and join the conversation:

- **The Dualistic Unity Podcast**: Dive deeper into the insights discussed in this book with our podcast, available on any podcast platform or on YouTube. With a surplus of episodes, starting with episode 1, *Scratching the Surface*, you can join us as we explore the deepening layers of self-awareness and interconnectedness.
- **Dualistic Unity Life Troubleshooter**: Facing challenges or questions as you navigate your journey? Our free Life Troubleshooter is designed to offer support and guidance. Visit https://dualisticunity.com/troubleshooter/ or search for Dualistic Unity in the Chat GPT Store for more.
- **Discord Community**: Connect with others on a similar path. Share your experiences, ask questions, and explore the nature of reality in a supportive, fun, and open environment. Join us at https://dualisticunity.com/community.

We look forward to meeting you within the ever-expanding space of awareness. Your journey is our journey. See you soon.